REINCARNATION
A STUDY OF FORGOTTEN TRUTH

Discovery Publisher

For the English edition:
2015, Discovery Publisher

Author : E. D. Walker

DISCOVERY PUBLISHER

616 Corporate Way, Suite 2-4933
Valley Cottage, New York, 10989
www.discoverypublisher.com
books@discoverypublisher.com
facebook.com/DiscoveryPublisher
twitter.com/DiscoveryPB

New York • Tokyo • Paris • Hong Kong

OF CONTENTS

REINCARNATION

A STUDY OF FORGOTTEN TRUTH

Preface

"The idea of a transmigration of souls has hitherto remained a dream of the fancy, nor has any one yet succeeded in giving it a higher moral significance for the order of the universe" writes Hermann Lotze, the German philosopher, in his magnificent "Microcosm," expressing the common feeling of Christendom. If this little book achieves its purpose it will show the strength and value of that dreamy idea.

The present perplexity of all Christendom upon the deepest problems of life, the sense of blind fate oppressing mankind, the despairing restlessness of many leading poets, the absence of sublime ideals in art, the prevalence of materialism and agnosticism (if not in philosophy, in the most vital form of practical life), all feed a flood-tide of dissatisfaction which Christianity tries in vain to resist, and indicate that the West deeply needs some new truth. Not only the wavering masses of men, but many of those uncompromising devotees of truth who dare surrender themselves, like St. Christopher, to the mightiest, are yearning after a larger revelation. A portion is contained, we believe, in the doctrine variously termed as Reincarnation, Metempsychosis, Transmigration. By this we do not mean the theories concerning rebirth of men in brute bodies, which are attributed to oriental religions and philosophies because popularly accepted by their followers. These are crude caricatures of the true conception. They represent the reality as absurdly as ordinary life in Europe and America illustrates the teaching of Jesus. But we mean the inner kernel of that husk, which in protean forms has irrepressibly welled up in every great phase of thought, which is an open secret lying-all around us and not simply a foreign importation, and which Christendom cannot afford to lose.

For those who are content with the usual creeds this little work will have no attraction. They may be pleased to regard it as a heathen invasion of Christendom. But for truth-seekers it may prove useful, though it claims only to be an earnest investigation of what seems an indemon-strable proposition. Its doctrine was first met as the declaration of the profoundest students of the mysteries enveloping humanity — coming with authority but no proof of weight to most western thinkers. Its vio-lent antagonism to current ideas compelled the writer to dispose of it by independent methods. If true, there must be some confirmation of it such as will impress any candid mind. If false, nothing can force it to live. This led to a careful study of the subject, which was summarized in a brief essay read and published to a small circle of Theosophists. A continuation of that study has resulted in this volume. Some readers will regard it as a waste of energy, except as a diverting curiosity, the truth or falsehood of reincarnation being to them of little consequence. But a sincere motive underlies it. For reincarnation illuminates the darkest passages in the murky road of life, dispels many haunting enigmas and illusions, and reveals cardinal principles which, if apprehended, will steady the shambling gait of mankind. Virtue, kindliness, and spirituality may thus be seen in their unveiled splendor as the only proper modes of action and thought. The noblest life is discerned to be the only sen-sible kind, and not abandoned to the accidental expression of impulse or sentiment. The cause of all the evils of modern society, the parent of the revolutions of Europe, the source of the labor disturbances aggravating America, is the arch-enemy of the race — materialism. Reincarnation combats that foe by a most subtle and deadly warfare.

The sincere thanks of the writer are due to a number of kind friends, whose assistance has largely facilitated the collection of materials for this book, and also to the authors who have kindly permitted the use of extracts from their writings, (in Chapters IV and V.)

E. D. WALKER

Introduction

Once, the whole civilized world embraced reincarnation, and found therein a complete answer to that riddle of man's descent and destiny which the inexorable sphinx Life propounds to every traveler along her way. But the western branch of the race, in working out the material conquest of the world, has acquired the compensating discontent of a material philosophy. It has lost the old faith and drifted into a shadowy region, where the eagerness for "practical" things rejects whatever cannot be physically proven. Even God and immortality are for the most part conjectures, believed only after demonstration, and not vitally then. The realization of this condition is provoking throughout Christendom a counter-current of spirituality. The growing freedom of thought and the eastward look of many leading minds seem to herald a renaissance more radical, although more subtle and gradual, than the reformations of Columbus, Luther, and Guthenberg. As surely as the occupation and development of the western Eldorado revived Europe into unprecedented vigor, the exploration of Palestine, and beyond into India, for treasures more precious than gold and dominion, shall revitalize the West with an unparalleled growth of spiritual power.

Strangely enough, too, just as the "New World" proved to be geologically the oldest continent, so the "new truths" recently discovered are found to be the most ancient. They are as universal as the ocean, always waiting to be used. The latest philosophies and heterodoxies are only fresh phrasings of early ideas. The most advanced conceptions of art, education, and government are essentially identical with those of Greece and Rome. The newest industries are approaching the lost arts of Egypt. The modern sciences (as electricity and chemistry) are merely ingenious applications of what the schoolmasters of the primitive races knew better in some respects than Edison and Cooke. Geology has just dawned upon us to reveal the sublime synopsis of earth's history hidden for over three thousand years in the first chapter of the Bible. The last great thought of this era — Evolution — is as old as the hills in the East. Professor Crookes's wonderful experiments connected with the instability of certain elements, psychic force, and the fourth dimension of matter (so far in advance of present scientific culture that many physicists deride them) are stumblings upon the outskirts of a domain long familiar to oriental students. After many centuries of tedious jangling with creeds and sects, we are slowly learning that primitive Christianity will make earth a paradise. The permanent edifice of the world's complete education seems to patiently await the time when men shall tire of fashioning useless building stuff from their crumbling theories and revert to the basal granite of which the everlasting foundations are laid, caring only to shape the superstructure by the Architect's plan.

Although commonly rejected throughout Europe and America, reincarnation is unreservedly accepted by the majority of mankind at the present day, as in all the past centuries. From the dawn of history it has prevailed among the largest part of humanity with an unshaken intensity of conviction. Over all the mightiest eastern nations it has held permanent sway. The ancient civilization of Egypt, whose grandeur cannot be overestimated, was built upon this as a fundamental truth, and taught it as a precious secret to Pythagoras, Empedocles, Plato, Virgil, and Ovid, who scattered it through Greece and Italy. It is the keynote of Plato's philosophy, being stated or implied very frequently in his dialogues. "Soul is older than body," he says. "Souls are continually born over again from Hades into this life." In his view all knowledge is reminiscence. To search and learn is simply to revive the images of what the soul saw in its preexistent state in the world of realities. It was also widely spread in the Neo-Platonism of Plotinus and Proclus. The swarming millions of India have made this thought the foundation of their enormous achievements in government, architecture, philosophy, and poetry. It was a cardinal element in the religion of the Persian Magi. Alexander the Great gazed in amazement on the self-immolation by fire to which it inspired the Gymnosophists. Caesar found its tenets propagated among the Gauls. The circle of metempsychosis was an essential principle of the Druid faith, and as such was impressed upon our forefathers the Celts, the Gauls, and the Britons. It is claimed that the people held this doctrine so vitally that they wept around the new-born infant and smiled upon death; for the beginning and end of an earthly life were to them the imprisonment and release of a soul, which must undergo repeated probations to remove its degrading impurities for final ascent into a succession of higher spheres. The Bardic triads of the Welsh are replete with this thought, and a Welsh antiquary insists that an ancient emigration from Wales to India conveyed it to the Brahmans. Among the Arab philosophers it was a favorite idea, and it still may be noticed in many Mohammedan writers. In the old civilizations of Peru and Mexico it prevailed universally. The priestly rites of the Egyptian Isis, the Eleusinian mysteries of Greece, the Bacchic processions of Rome, the Druid ceremonies of Britain, and the Cabalic rituals of the Hebrews, all expressed this great truth with peculiar force for their initiated witnesses. The Jews generally adopted it after the Babylonian captivity through the Pharisees, Philo of Alexandria, and the doctors. John the Baptist was to them a second Elijah. Jesus was commonly thought to be a reappearance of John the Baptist or of one of the old prophets. The Talmud and the Cabala are full of the same teaching. Some of the late Rabbins assert many entertaining things concerning the repeated births of the most noted persons of their nation. Christianity is not an exception to all the other great religions in promulgating the same philosophy. Reincarnation played an important part in the thought of Origen and several other leaders among the early Church Fathers. It was a main portion of the creed of the Gnostics and Manichseans. In the Middle Ages many scholastics and heretical sects advocated it. It has cropped out spontaneously in many western theologians. The elder English divines do not hesitate to inculcate preexistence in their sermons. In the seventeenth century Dr. Henry More and other Cambridge Platonists gave it wide acceptance. The Roman Catholic Purgatory seems to be a make-shift improvised to take its place. Sir Harry Vane is said by Burnet to have maintained this doctrine.

Many philosophers of metaphysical depth, like Scotus, Kant, Schelling, Leibnitz, Schopenhauer, and the younger Fichte, have upheld reincarnation. Geniuses of noble symmetry, like Giordano Bruno, Herder, Lessing, and Goethe, have fathered it. Scientists like Flammarion, Figuier, and Brewster have earnestly advocated it. Theological leaders like Julius Muller, Dorner, Ernesti, Riickert, and Edward Beecher have maintained it. In exalted intuitional natures like Boehme and Swedenborg its hold is apparent. Most of the mystics bathe in it. Of course the long line of Platonists from Socrates down to Emerson have no doubt of it. Nearly all the poets profess it.

Even amid the predominance of materialistic influences in Christendom it has a considerable following. Traces of it are found among the aborigines of North and South America, and in many barbaric tribes. At this time it reigns without any sign of decrepitude over the Burman, Chinese, Japanese, Tartar, Tibetan, and East Indian nations, including at least 750,000,000 of mankind and nearly two thirds of the race. Throughout the East it is the great central thought. It is no mere superstition of the ignorant masses. It is the chief principle of Hindu metaphysics, the basis of all their inspired books. Such a hoary philosophy, held by the venerable authority of ages, ruling from the beginning of time the bulk of the world's thought, cherished in some form by the disciples of every great religion, is certainly worthy of the profoundest respect and study. There must be some vital reality inspiring so stupendous an existence.

But the western fondness for democracy does not hold in the domain of thought. The fact that the majority of the race has agreed upon reincarnation is no argument for it to an occidental thinker. The conceit of modern progress has no more respect for ancient ideas than for the forgotten civilization of old, even though in many essentials they anticipated or outstripped all that we boast of. Therefore we propose to treat this subject largely from a western standpoint.

○ ○ ○ ○ ○ ○ ○ ○ ○

We cannot yet have learned all that we are meant to learn through the body. How much of the teaching even of this world can the most diligent and most favored man have exhausted before he is called to leave it. Is all that remains lost?
— GEORGE MACDONALD.

You cannot say of the soul, it shall be, or is about to be, or is to be hereafter. It is a thing without birth. — BHAGAVAD GITA.

As the inheritance of an illustrious name and pedigree quickens the sense of duty in every noble nature, a belief in preexistence may enhance the glory of the present life and intensify the reverence with which the deathless principle is regarded.
— WILLIAM KNIGHT.

If we except the belief of a future remuneration beyond this life for suffering virtue and retribution for successful crimes, there is no system so simple, and so little repugnant to our understanding, as that of metempsychosis. The pains and pleasures of this life are by this system considered as the recompense or the punishment of our actions in another state. — ISAAC D'ISRAELI.

The experiences gained in one life may not be remembered in their details in the next, but the impressions which they produce will remain. Again and again man passes through the wheel of transformation, changing his lower energies into higher ones, until matter attracts him no longer, and he becomes — what he is destined to be — a god. — HARTMANN.

As billows on the undulating main That swelling fall, and falling swell again, So on the tide of time incessant roll The dying body and the deathless soul.

Chapter I
What Is Reincarnation?

Reincarnation is an extremely simple doctrine rooted in the assurance of the soul's indestructibility. It explains at once the descent and the destiny of the soul by so natural and forcible a method that it has not only dominated the ingenuous minds of all the primitive races, but has become the most widely spread and most permanently influential of all philosophies.

Reincarnation teaches that the soul enters this life, not as a fresh creation, but after a long course of previous existences on this earth and elsewhere, in which it acquired its present inhering peculiarities, and that it is on the way to future transformations which the soul is now shaping. It claims that infancy brings to earth, not a blank scroll for the beginning of an earthly record, nor a mere cohesion of atomic forces into a brief personality soon to dissolve again into the elements, but that it is inscribed with ancestral histories, some like the present scene, most of them unlike it and stretching back into the remotest past. These inscriptions are generally undecipherable, save as revealed in their moulding influence upon the new career; but like the invisible photographic images made by the sun of all it sees, when they are properly developed in the laboratory of consciousness they will be distinctly displayed. The current phase of life will also be stored away in the secret vaults of memory, for its unconscious effect upon the ensuing lives. All the qualities we now possess, in body, mind and soul, result from our use of ancient opportunities. We are indeed "the heirs of all the ages," and are alone responsible for our inheritances. For these conditions accrue from distant causes engendered by our older selves, and the future flows by the divine law of cause and effect from the gathered momentum of our past impetuses. There is no favoritism in the universe, but all have the same everlasting facilities for growth. Those who are now elevated in worldly station may be sunk in humble surroundings in the future. Only the inner traits of the soul are permanent companions. The wealthy sluggard may be the beggar of the next life; and the industrious worker of the present is sowing the seeds of future greatness. Suffering bravely endured now will produce a treasure of patience and fortitude in another life; hardships will give rise to strength; self-denial must develop the will; tastes cultivated in this existence will somehow bear fruit in coming ones; and acquired energies will assert themselves whenever they can by the *lex parsimonice* upon which the principles of physics are based. *Vice versa*, the unconscious habits, the uncontrollable impulses, the peculiar tendencies, the favorite pursuits, and the soul-stirring friendships of the present descend from far-reaching previous activities. Science explains the idiosyncrasies of plants and animals by the environment of previous generations and calls instinct hereditary habit. In the same way there is an evolution of individuality, by which the child opens its new era with characteristics derived from anterior lives, and adds the experience of a new personality to the sum total of his treasured traits. In its passage through earthly personalities the spiritual self, the essential *Ego*, accumulates a fund of individual character which remains as the permanent thread stringing together the separate lives. The soul is therefore an eternal water globule, which sprang in the beginningless past from mother ocean, and is destined after an unreckonable course of meanderings in cloud and rain, snow and steam, spring and river, mud and vapor, to at last return with the garnered experience of all lonely existences into the central Heart of all. Or rather, it is the crystal stream running from a heavenly fountain through one continuous current that often halts in favorite corners, sunny pools, and shady nooks, muddy ponds and clearest lakes, each delay shifting the direction and altering the complexion of the next tide as it issues out by the path of least resistance.

That we have forgotten the causes producing the present sequence of pleasures and pains, talents and defects, successes and failures, is no disproof of them, and does not disturb the justice of the scheme. For temporary oblivion is the anodyne by which the kindly physician is bringing us through the darker wards of sorrow into perfect health.

We do not undertake to trace the details of our earlier stoppages further than is indicated in the uncontrovertible principle, that as long as the soul is governed by material desires it must find its homes in physical realms, and when its inclination is purely spiritual it certainly will inhabit the domain of spirit. The restless wandering of all souls must at last conclude in the peace of God, but that will not be possible until they have gone through all the rounds of experience and learned that only in that Goal is satisfaction. That men ever dwell in bodies of beasts, we deny as irrational, as such a retrogression would contradict the fundamental maxims of nature. That philosophy is a corruption of Reincarnation, in which the masses have coarsely masked the truth.

Granting the permanence of the human spirit amid every change, the doctrine of rebirth is the only one yielding a metaphysical explanation of the phenomena of life. It is already accepted in the physical plane as evolution, and holds a firm ethical value in applying the law of justice to human experience. In confirmation of it there stands the strongest weight of evidence, argumentary, empirical, and historic. It untangles the knotty problem of life simply and grandly. It meets the severest requirements of enlightened reason, and is in deepest harmony with the spirit of Christianity.

○ ○ ○ ○ ○ ○ ○ ○

The house of life hath many chambers. — ROSSETTI.

The soul is not born; it does not die; it was not produced from any one; nor was any produced from it. — EMERSON.

For men to tell how human life began
Is hard: for who himself beginning knew.
      — MILTON.

There is surely a piece of divinity in us — something that was before the elements and owes no homage unto the sun. Whatever hath no beginning may be confident of no end. — SIR THOMAS BROWNE.

For of the soul the body form doth take, For soul is form and doth the body make. — SPENSER.

Secreted and hidden in the heart of the world and the heart of man is the light which can illumine all life, the future and the past. — THROUGH THE GATES OF GOLD.

The soul, if immortal, existed before our birth. What is incorruptible must be ungenerable. Metempsychosis is the only system of immortality that Philosophy can hearken to. — HUME.

Nature is nothing less than the ladder of resurrection which, step by step, leads upward — or rather is carried from the abyss of eternal death up to the apex of life. — SCHLEGEL.

Look nature through; 'tis revolution all,
All change; no death. Day follows night, and night
The dying day; stars rise and set, and set and rise.
Earth takes the example. All to reflourish fades
As in a wheel: all sinks to reascend;
Emblems of man, who passes, not expires.
——YOUNG.

The blending of mind and matter in the bodily structure of the sentient and rational orders, we may be assured, is a method of procedure which, if it be not absolutely indispensable to the final purposes of the creation, subserves the most important ends and carries with it consequences such as will make it the general, if not the universal law of all finite natures, in all worlds. — ISAAC TAYLOR.

Chapter II
Western Evidences of Reincarnation

The old Saxon chronicler, Bede, records that at a banquet given by King Edwin of Northumbria to his nobles, a discussion arose as to how they should receive the Christian missionary Paulinus, who had just arrived from the continent. Some urged the sufficiency of their own Druid and Norse religions and advised the death of the invading heretic. Others were in favor of hearing his message. At length the king asked the opinion of his oldest counsellor. The sage arose and said: "O king and lords. You all did remark the swallow which entered this festal hall to escape the chilling winds without, fluttering near the fire for a few moments and then vanishing through the opposite window. Such is the life of man. Whence it came and whither it goes none can tell. Therefore if this new religion brings light upon so great a mystery, it must be diviner than ours and should be welcomed." The old man's advice was adopted.

We are in the position of those old ancestors of ours. The religion of the churches, called Christianity, is to many earnest souls a dry husk. The germinant kernel of truth as it came from the founder of Christianity, when it is discovered under all its barren wrappings, is indeed sufficient to feed us with the bread of life. It answers all the practical needs of most people even with the husks. But it leaves some vital questions unanswered which impel us to desire something more than Jesus taught — not for mere curiosity, but as food for larger growth. The divine law which promises to fill every vacuum, and to gratify at last every aspiration, has not left us without means of grasping a portion of these grander truths.

The commonest idea of the soul throughout Christendom seems to be that it is created specially for birth on this world, and after its lifetime here it goes to a permanent spiritual realm of infinite continuance. This is a very comfortable belief derived from the appearances of things, and those holding it may very properly say, "My view agrees with the phenomena, and if you think differently the burden of proof rests upon you." We accept this responsibility. But a careful observer knows that the true explanation of facts is as a rule very different from the appearance. Ptolemy thought he could account for all the heavenly motions on his geocentric theory, and his teachings were at once received by his contemporaries. But the deeper studies of Copernicus and Galileo had to wait a century before they were accepted, although they introduced an astronomy of immeasurably nobler scale. Is it not a relic of the old confidence in appearances to consider the physical orbits of human souls as limited to our little view of them?

The theologian seeks to explain life, with its inequalities, its miseries and injustices, by a future condition rewarding and punishing men for the deeds of earth. He concedes that benevolence and justice cannot be proven in God by what is seen of His earthly administration. The final law of creation is said to be Love, but the sin and suffering bequeathed to most of the race through no apparent fault of theirs annuls that dictum in the world's real thought, and compels men to regard life as a ceaseless struggle for existence in which the strongest wins and the weakest fails, and the devil takes the hindermost. But even if the future life will straighten out this by a just judgment, fairness demands that all shall have an even chance here—which only reincarnation assures.

The materialist takes a more plausible ground. On the basis of the soul beginning with the present existence, he regards all the developments of life as results of blind natural forces. He says that the variety of atomic qualities accounts for all the divergencies of life, physical, mental, and moral. But he can give no reason why the same particles of matter should accomplish such stupendous varieties. Moreover Science, the materialist's gospel, instead of disposing of psychic facts, is studying and classifying them as a new branch of supersensuous knowledge.*These investigations will ultimately initiate Science into the surety of non-physical things. Already a strong advance in that direction has been made by

* See the publications of the Society of Psychical Research of London and Boston and New York.

Isaac Taylor's "Physical Theory of a Future Life" and Stewart & Tait's "Unseen Universe." The conception of an Infinite Personality overwhelms all the narrow groove-thinking of every mechanical school, and rises supremely in the strongest scientific philosophy of all time — that of Herbert Spencer. Strangest of all, Evolution, the cornerstone of Spencerian philosophy, is merely a paraphrase of reincarnation.

There are seven arguments for Reincarnation which seem conclusive.

1. That the idea of *immortality* demands it.
2. That *analogy* makes it the most probable.
3. That *science* confirms it.
4. That the *nature of the soul* requires it.
5. That it most completely *answers* the *theological questions* of "original sin" and "future punishment."
6. That it *explains* many *mysterious experiences*.
7. That it alone *solves* the problem of *injustice* and *misery* which broods over our world.

▮. Immortality demands it

Only the positivists and some allied schools of thought, comprising a very small proportion of Christendom, doubt the immortality of the soul. But a conscious existence after death has no better proof than a prenatal existence. It is an old declaration that what begins in time must end in time. We have no right to say that the soul is eternal on one side of its earthly period without being so on the other. Far more rational is the view of certain scientists who, believing that the soul originates with this life, also declare that it ends with this life. That is the logical outcome of their premise. If the soul sprang into existence specially for this life, why should it continue afterward? It is precisely as probable from all the grounds of reason that death is the conclusion of the soul as that birth is the beginning of it. As Cudworth points out, it was this argument which had special weight with the Greek philosophers, whose reasonings upon immortality have led all later generations. They asserted the eternity of the soul in order to vindicate its immortality. For, they held, as nothing which has being can have originated from nothingness, or can vanish into nothingness, and as they were certain of their existence, it was impossible that they could have had a temporal beginning. The present life must be only one stage of a vast number, stretching backward and forward.

Our instinctive belief in immortality implies a subconscious acceptance of this view. We are certain of a persevering life outlasting all the changes of time and death. But birth, as well as death, is one of the temporal shifts belonging to the transitory sphere which is foreign to our spirits. It is only because our backs are toward the earlier change and our faces to the later that we refuse to reason about one on the principles used about the other. If we lived in the reversed world of Fechner's "Dr. Mises," in which old things grow new and men begin life by a reversed dying and end by a reversed birth, we would probably devise arguments for preexistence as zealously as we do now for future existence, and that would lead to reincarnation. For all the indications of immortality point as unfailingly to an eternity preceding this existence: the love of prolonged life; the analogy of nature; the prevailing belief of the most spiritual minds; the permanence of the ego principle; the inconceivability of annihilation or of creation from nothing; the promise of an extension of the present career; the injustice of any other thought.

The ordinary Christian idea of special creation at birth involves the correlative of annihilation at death. What the origin of the soul may have been does not affect this subject, further than that it long antedates the present life. Whether it be a spark from God himself, or a divine emanation, or a cluster of independent energies, its eternal destiny compels the inference that it is uncreated and indestructible. Moreover, it is unthinkable that from an infinite history it enters this world for its first and only physical experience and then shoots off to an endless spiritual existence. The deduction is rather that it assumed many forms before it appeared as we now see it, and is bound to pass through many coming lives before it will be rounded into the full orb of perfection and reach its ultimate goal.

II. Analogy is strongly in favor of reincarnation

Were Bishop Butler to work out the problem of the career of the human soul in the light of modern science, we doubt not that his masterpiece would advocate this "pagan" thought. For many centuries the
literature of nations has discerned a standard simile of the soul's death-
lessness in the transformation of the caterpillar into the butterfly. But
it is known now that once all the caterpillars and butterflies were alike,
and that by repeated incarnations they have reached the bewildering
differences. When they started off from the procession of life on their
own road from one or a few similar species, the progeny scattered into
various circumstances, and the struggles and devices which they went
through for their own purposes, being repeated for thousands of years in
millions of lives, has developed the surprising heterogeneity of feather-
winged insects. And as each undergoes his rapid changes in rehearsal
of his long pedigree, we may trace the succession of his earlier lives.

The violent energy of the present condition argues a previous stage
leading up to it. It is contended with great force of analogy that death
is but another and higher birth. This life is a groping embryo plane
implying a more exalted one. Mysterious intimations reach us from a
diviner sphere,—

> "Like hints and echoes of the world
> To spirits folded in the womb."

But subtle indications rearward argue that birth is the death of an
earlier existence. Even the embryo life necessitates a preparatory one
preceding it. So complete a structure must have a foundation. So swift
a momentum must have traveled far. As Emerson observes: "We wake
and find ourselves on a stair. There are other stairs below us which we
seem to have ascended; there are stairs above us, many a one, which go
upward and out of sight."

The grand order of creation is everywhere proclaiming as the universal
word, "change." Nothing is destroyed, but all is passing from one exis-

tence to another. Not an atom but is dancing in lively march from its present condition to a different form, running a ceaseless cycle through mineral, vegetable, and animal existence, though never losing its individuality, however diverse its apparent alterations. Not a creature but is constantly progressing to something else. The tadpole becomes a fish, the fish a frog, and some of the frogs have turned to birds. It was the keen perception of this principle in nature which gave their vital force to the Greek mythologies and other ancient stories embodying the idea of transmutation of personality through many guises. It was this which animated the metamorphoses of Ovid, whose philosophy is contained in these lines from his poem on Pythagoras:—

> "Death, so called, is but old matter dressed
> In some new form. And in a varied vest
> From tenement to tenement, though tossed,
> The soul is still the same, the figure only lost:
> And as the softened wax new seals receives,
> This face assumes, and that impression leaves,
> Now called by one, now by another name,
> The form is only changed, the wax is still the same.
> Then, to be born is to begin to be
> Some other thing we were not formerly.
> That forms are changed, I grant; that nothing can
> Continue in the figure it began."*

Evolution has remoulded the thought of Christendom, expanding our conception of physiology, astronomy and history. The more it is studied the more universal is found its application. It seems to be the secret of God's life. Now that we know the evolution of the body, it is time that we learned the evolution of the soul. The biologist shows that each of us physically before birth runs through all the phases of animal life — polyp, fish, reptile, dog, ape, and man — as a brief synopsis of how the ages have prepared our tenements. The preponderance of special animal traits

* Dryden's Translation.

in us is due, he says, to the emphasis of those particular stages of our physical growth. So in infancy does the soul move through an unconscious series of existences, recapitulating its long line of descent, until it is fastened in maturity. And why is it not true that our soul traits are the relics of former activities? Evolution proves that the physical part of man is the product of a long series of changes, in which each stage is both the effect of past influences and the cause of succeeding issues. Does not the immaterial part of man require a development equally vast? The fact of an intellectual and moral evolution proceeding hand in hand with the physical can only be explained under the economy of nature by a series of reincarnations.

▉▉▉. Science confirms it

Furthermore, the idea that the soul is specially created for introduction into this world combats all the principles of science. All nature proceeds on the strictest economic methods. Nothing is either lost or added. There is no creation or destruction. Whatever appears to spring suddenly into existence is derived from some sufficient cause — although as unseen as the vapor currents which feed the clouds. There is a growing consensus of opinion among spiritualists and materialists alike, that the quantity both of force and of matter remains constant. The law of conservation of energy holds in the spiritual realm as in physics. The uniform stock of energy in the universe neither declines nor increases, but incessantly changes. The marvelous developments shown in the protean organisms continually entering the procession of life indicate that the new manifestations descend from some patriarchal line, uncreated and immortal, coming through the hidden regions of previous existences. Science allows no such miracle as the theological special resurrection, which is contrary to all experience. But it recognizes the universality of resurrection throughout all nature, which is a matter of common observation. The idea of the soul as a phoenix, eternally continuing through myriad embodiments, is adapted to the whole spirit of modern science.

Especially significant is the axiomatic law of cause and effect. There is no other adequate explanation of the phenomena of life than the purely scientific one, that causes similar to those now operating before our eyes have produced the results we witness. The impelling characteristics of each personality require some earlier experiences of physical life to have generated them. All the sensuous proclivities of human nature point to long earthly experience as their only origin. And the unsatisfied physical inclinations of the soul necessitate a series of material existences to work themselves out. The irrepressible eagerness for all the range of experience seems to be a sufficient reason for a course of incarnations which shall accomplish that result.

Physiologists contend that the wondrous human organism could not have grown up out of mere matter, but implies a preexistent personal idea,* which grouped around itself the organic conditions of physical existence and constrained the material elements to follow its plan. This dynamic agent — or the soul — must have existed independent of the body before the receptacle was prepared. Bouiller and the German scientists Muller, Hartmann, and Stahl, have especially demonstrated in physiology this idea of a preexistent soul monad, whose plastic power unconsciously constructs its own corporeal organism. The Greeks coiled this idea into the word σχῆμα, and the younger Fichte and Lotze have developed it. The doctrine of modern physiology, as presented by the animists, is precisely the ground taken by upholders of reincarna-

* We purposely use the term Personal in preference to spiritual, for the word should be rescued from its confusion of meanings to the old classical one, in connection with the soul. As Hermann Lotze beautifully unfolds, "Personality is the key to existence," using the word in its first sense from persona, a mask, parallel to the Hebrew analogy which calls man the image of Jehovah. Mulford also presents the thought grandly in The Republic of God and The Nation, __] drawing his suggestion from the Germans Stahl and Froshammer. In this sense humanity is the shadow of Deity, the veil through which the Absolute tries to reveal Himself, casting about in the multiplicity of natural forms after an expression through physical means of His own nature. In this sublime conception God is the life of the universe, who, in Schelling's phrase, "sleeps in the stone, breathes in the plant, moves in the animal, and wakes up to consciousness in man." It is this thought which makes Novaks so reverent to a human being as a Microdeus, and elevates the dignity of the soul above all else. For as the purpose of nature is to personify the Invisible, human souls are the Persons (or masks) by which the leading parts are here acted with many changes of scenery.

tion—that as the lower animals fashion ingenious nests with incredible skill, so the unwitting soul blindly frames the fabric of its body in keeping with the laws of its own adaptation. The unconscious agency of the mind or instinct in repairing the body, healing its hurts and guiding its growth, is recognized by most scientists. Plato but expresses the same idea when he says, "The soul always weaves her garment anew." This thought is well worded by Giordano Bruno when he says, "The soul is not in the body locally, but as its intrinsic form and extrinsic mould, as that which makes the members and shapes the whole within and without. The body, then, is in the soul, the soul in the mind (spirit). The Intellect (Spirit) is God."

This conception gives the lie to the materialism which limits the forces of the individual to the complications of a mechanism. A corollary of this moulding power of the independent soul is Plato's proposition that "the soul has a natural strength which will hold out and be born many times." Since the ego is older than the body, the resident who builds its dwelling according to its tastes and materials, and since the purpose of its corporeal habitation cannot possibly be accomplished in a single brief lifetime, it is necessary that it should repeat that experience, always framing its receptacle to suit its growing character, like the epochs of a lobster's enlargement, until it has done with physical life. The new apparitions of men upon the earth thus hail from older scenes.

Evolution may fairly be claimed as a spiritual truth applying to all the methods of life. The gradual development of the soul, by the school of experience, demands a vaster arena of action than one earthly life affords. If it takes ages of time and thousands of lives to form one kind of an animal from another, the expansion of human souls from lower to higher natures surely needs many and many a life for that growth.

Evolutionary science explains the instinctive acts of young animals as inherited tendencies—as past experiences transmitted into fresh forms. Psychic science is learning that the earliest acts of human beings are also derived from remote habits formed in anterior activities, and stored away in the unconscious memory. Herbert Spencer, the philosopher of evolution, speaks of a constant energy manifesting itself through all transformations. This is the one life which runs eternally in protean shapes.

The measure of our acquisition of conceptions from the outer universe resides in the senses. There is no evidence that these have always been five. Nature, never taking a leap, must have put us through all the lower stages before she placed us at our present position. And since nature contains many substances and powers which are partially or wholly beyond these senses, some of which powers are known to other animals, we must assume that our present ascending development will introduce us to higher levels in which the soul shall have as many senses as correspond with the powers of nature.*

IV. Nature of the soul requires it

A much more weighty argument is that the nature of the soul requires reincarnation. The conscious soul cannot feel itself to have had any beginning, any more than it can conceive of annihilation. The sense of persistence overwhelms all the interruptions of forgetfulness and sleep, and all the obstacles of matter. This incessant self-assurance suggests the idea of the soul being independent of the changing body, its temporary prison. Then follows the conception that, as the soul has once appeared in human form, so it may reappear in many others. The eternity of the soul, past and present, leads directly to an innumerable succession of births and deaths, dis-embodiments and re-embodiments.

The identity of the soul surely does not consist in a remembrance of all its past. We are always forgetting ourselves and waking again to recognition. But the sense of individuality bridges all the gaps. In the same way it seems as if our present existence were a somnambulant condition into which we have drowsed from an earlier life, being sleepily oblivious of that former activity, and from which we may after a while be roused into wakefulness.

* This idea is grandly stated in Isaac Taylor's Physical Theory of a Future Life. In demonstrating the assurance that the future existence is in material bodies, and showing the glorious extensions to which the coming bodily powers will probably be developed, the author approaches strangely near the philosophy of reincarnation.

The study of infant psychology confirms this. The nature and extent of the mental furniture with which we begin life, apart from all experience of this world, has obliged many thinkers to resort to preexistence as the necessary explanation.

A careful examination of the rarer facts of life, noticeably those found in dreams, trances, and analogous phenomena, demonstrates that our complete life is largely independent of the body, and consists in a perpetual transfer of the sensuous experiences of self-consciousness into a supersensuous unconsciousness. But this higher storehouse of character might more truly be called our real consciousness, although we are not ordinarily cognizant of it, for it comprises our habits, instincts, and tendencies. This is the essential character of the soul and must persist after death. Now, unless all our earthly possibilities are exhausted in one life, these inherent material qualities of our spiritual nature will find expression in a plurality of earthly existences. And if the purpose of life be the acquisition of experience, it would be unreasonable to suppose a final transfer elsewhere before a full knowledge of earth has been gained. It is apparent that one life cannot accomplish this, even in the longest and most diverse career — to say nothing of the short average, and the curtailed allowance given to the majority. If one earth life answers for all, what a tiny experience suffices for the immense masses who prematurely die as children! Men are willing enough to believe in an eternity of spiritual development after this world; but is it consistent with the thought of Omnipotence to consider that the Divine plan is achieved in preparing for that by a few swift years in one body? In devoting eternity to our education, the infinite Teacher surely will not put us into the highest grade of all until we have well mastered the lessons of all the lower classes.

The philosophy of "innate ideas" is an admission of earlier lives than the present. The intuitionalists emphatically regard the concepts of cause, substance, time, and space as existing in the mind independent of experience. The sensationalists consider them entirely due to our sensations. The Spencerian evolutionalists occupy a middle ground and call them a mental heredity resulting from the experience of the race. It has been well shown, as Edgar Fawcett says, by two impartial critics, that this controversy cannot be solved by any agreement of Western psychologists. Buckle inveighs against these discordant systems as having "thrown the study of the mind into a confusion only to be compared to that in which the study of religion has been thrown by the controversies of the theologians."* And George Henry Lewes, in his "History of Philosophy," deplores this perplexing condition of metaphysics. The solution of the problem comes, along with reincarnation, from the eastern students, who assert that a true conception of the soul is discovered only by the culture of supersensuous faculties. They concede a portion of truth to both extreme schools, declaring that the *primary* acquisition of such ideas was gained by sensation, but that at present they are innate in the infant mind. They are now the generalized experience of former existences rising again into consciousness.

The restlessness of our spirits points to ancient habits of varied action. And a still more forcible indication is the diversity of character in the same person. These wavering uncertainties and contraries in each one of us, which strive for the mastery and are never crushed even by the sternest fixity of habit—rendering the best of us amenable to temptations, and making the strongest vacillate, may well result from meanderings in numerous characters. The main trend of our natures is still often distracted into old forgotten ways.

V. It most completely answers the theological questions of "original sin" and "future punishment"

Reincarnation provides a complete answer to the most perplexing problem of theology—original sin. Properly this point belongs to the preceding section, but its importance justifies a separate mention. The endless controversies centering upon this question show how Christian metaphysics have vainly wrestled with a Grordian knot which cannot possibly be untied from the standpoint considering this life the initial and only earthly one—a knot which reincarnation not simply cuts, but

* H. T. Buckle, *History of Civilization*, vol. i. p. 166.

reveals how it was made. Between the extreme dogmas of Pelagius, who maintained that all men are born in a state of innocence and may therefore live without sin, and of Augustine, who held the total depravity of mankind, arising from their transgression in Adam and their absolute bondage to the devil, there has raged a continual warfare, which has divided Christendom into many sects of thought on this leading doctrine. The modern church creeds still range themselves in conflicting battalions, following the discussions during the Reformation between Erasmus, who denied the power of hereditary sin over free will, and Luther, who insisted that the race is completely in the devil's power by nature. By far the largest part of the Christian world professedly adheres to the latter faith — that men are born entirely corrupt. Even the Arminians, Quakers, and liberal denominations who admit only a germ of sin in humanity are at a loss to account it. The ordinary theological explanation which derives our sin from the transgression of Adam, as apparently taught by St. Paul, although tacitly held by most of the churches and expressed in the majority of creeds, grates so severely on the inner consciousness and common sense that it does not answer the real difficulty. There is a general agreement among mankind, upon which the codes of practical life are based, that Adam's responsibility for our sin is only a makeshift of the theologians: for every sensible man knows that no one but the individual himself can be blamed for his wrong-doing. Adam is accepted as a fable for our older selves. Dismissing all the interminable arguments of theology, which only obscure truth in a cloud of intellectual wranglings, the broad foundation of ethics, grounded in our best instincts, attached sin somehow, though inexplicably, to the sinner; and the only sufficient explanation traces its beginning to earlier lives.

The moral character of children, especially the occurrence of evil in them long before it could have been implanted by this existence, has forced acute observers to assume that the human spirit has made choice of evil in a prenatal sphere similar to this. Every one who knows children rejects the Pelagian theory of their immaculate innocence. As soon as they have the power to do wrong, without any teaching the wrong is done as a natural proceeding.

The germ of sin springs up from some old sowing. But the Augustinian doctrine is equally untrue to human nature. The most incorrigible tendency to evil in an uninfluenced child cannot conceal the good within it, but merely indicates that former ill habits are working themselves out. The depraved criminal at last sees his own folly when his course of sin is run, and becomes so weary of it that the next lease of life must be on a better plan. So evil is discovered to be good in the making, and vice is virtue in the strengthening.

Every person at some stage of growth awakens to the recognition of sin within him, and is certain that it is so radical as to reach back of all his present life, although it is surely foreign to his true nature. We all feel ourselves to have bounded into life like a stag carrying a panther which must be shaken off. Theology attempts to account for this by Adam's sin entailing a hereditary depravity. But our inmost consciousness agrees with the common sense of mankind in holding us alone responsible for our tendency to wrong. Remorse seizes us for the inexplicable evil in us. The only solution is that of the parasite in the butterfly. The insect allowed the pest to enter when it was a worm. This blighted condition cannot be the original state of man. It must be the result of the human will resisting the divine, and choosing wrong in old existences beyond recollection.

A masterly expression of this thought nourished the childhood of Christianity in the teaching of Origen, and flourished with wholesome influence until it was forcibly crushed out of popularity by the Council of Constantinople, to make room for the harsh dogmas which have since darkened the rationale of Christianity. It never was intelligently met and conquered, but was summarily ousted as incompatible with the weight of prejudice. The same treatment of it appears in Dr. Hodge's "Systematic Theology" (under the section on Preexistence). That it is in harmony with Scripture has been shown by Henry More, Soame Jenyns, Chevalier Ramsay, and Professor Bowen, from whom quotations are given in chapter IV., and by other writers mentioned at the close of this book. Julius Müller, Lessing, Edward Beecher, Coleridge, and Kant* also sustain it from a religio-philosophical ground. It is the only rational explanation of the theological idea of sin.

The same is true regarding the church's dogma of future punishments and rewards. A reasonable consideration fails to understand how the jump can be made from this condition of things to an eternity of either suffering or bliss — as ordinary theology demands. The Roman Catholics recognized this difficulty sufficiently to provide Purgatory, and in that tenet they meet the sense of humanity. Reincarnation simply says that there are many purgatories, and one is earth. The more rational Protestants get around the incongruity by permitting many grades of existence in heaven and hell, which approaches the same solution. Reincarnation says also, there are infinite degrees of heaven and hell, and many of them slope down through this life. It is inconceivable how earthly natures (and most of human souls are such) can find their penalties and their rewards elsewhere than on some kind of earth. The scheme of the universe presents everywhere a simple and sublime habit of keeping affinities together, and it certainly seems as if the same economy could apply to souls as to atoms. This idea meets better than any other the principles that punishment for sin cannot continue longer than the sin continues, and that the everlasting mercy of the Supreme will provide some final release for his erring children.

VI. Reincarnation explains many curious experiences

Most of us have known the touches of feeling and thought that seem to be reminders of forgotten things. Sometimes as dim dreams of old scenes, sometimes as vivid lightning flashes in the darkness recalling distant occurrences, sometimes with unutterable depth of meaning. It appears as if nature's opiate which ushered us here had been so diluted that it did not quite efface the old memories, and reason struggles to

---

* Kant's distinction between the character and the Intelligible Empirical or acquired character,which is a metaphysical form of the reincarnation view concerning the eternal Individuality and is shown by Professor Bowen in a later chapter.

decipher the vestiges of a former state. Almost every one has felt the sense of great age. Thinking of some unwonted subject often an impression seizes us that somewhere, long ago, we have had these reflections before. Learning a fact, meeting a face for the first time, we are puzzled with an obscure sense that it is familiar. Traveling newly in strange places we are sometimes haunted with a consciousness of having been there already. Music is specially apt to guide us into mystic depths, where we are startled with the flashing reminiscences of unspeakable verities which we have felt or seen ages since. Efforts of thought reveal the half-obliterated inscriptions on the tablets of memory, passing before the vision in a weird procession. Every one has some such experiences. Most of them are blurred and obscure. But some are so remarkably distinct that those who undergo them are convinced that their sensations are actual recollections of events and places in former lives. It is even possible for certain persons to trace thus quite fully and clearly a part of their bygone history prior to this life.

Sir Walter Scott was so impressed by these experiences that they led him to a belief in preexistence. In his diary was entered this circumstance, February 17, 1828: "I cannot, I am sure, tell if it is worth marking down, that yesterday, at dinner time, I was strangely haunted by what I would call the sense of preexistence, viz. a confused idea that nothing that passed was said for the first time; that the same topics had been discussed and the same persons had stated the same opinions on them... The sensation was so strong as to resemble what is called a *mirage* in the desert and a calenture on board ship. ... It was very distressing yesterday, and brought to my mind the fancies of Bishop Berkeley about an ideal world. There was a vile sense of unreality in all I said or did."* That this was not due to the strain upon his later years is evident from the fact that the same experience is referred to in one of his earliest novels, where this "sentiment of preexistence" was first described. In "Guy Mannering," Henry Bertram says: "Why is it that some scenes awaken thoughts which belong, as it were, to dreams of early and shadowy recollections, such as old Brahmin moonshine would have ascribed to a state

* Lockhart's *Life of Scott* (first edition, vol. vii. p. 114).

of previous existence. How often do we find ourselves in society which we have never before met, and yet feel impressed with a mysterious and ill-defined consciousness that neither the scene nor the speakers nor the subject are entirely new; nay, feel as if we could anticipate that part of the conversation which has not yet taken place."

Bulwer Lytton describes it as "that strange kind of inner and spiritual memory which often recalls to us places and persons we have never seen before, and which Platonists would resolve to be the unquenched and struggling consciousness of a former life." Again, in "Godolphin" (chapter XV.), he writes: "How strange is it that at times a feeling comes over us as we gaze upon certain places, which associates the scene either with some dim remembered and dreamlike images of the Past, or with a prophetic and fearful omen of the Future... Every one has known a similar strange and indistinct feeling at certain times and places, and with a similar inability to trace the cause."

Edgar A. Poe writes (in "Eureka"): "We walk about, amid the destinies of our world existence, accompanied by dim but ever present memories of a Destiny more vast—very distant in the bygone time and infinitely awful... We live out a youth peculiarly haunted by such dreams, yet never mistaking them for dreams. As *memories* we know them. During our youth the distinctness is too clear to deceive us even for a moment. But the doubt of manhood dispels these feelings as illusions."

Explicit occurrences of this class are found in the narratives of Hawthorne, Willis, Coleridge, De Quincey, and many other writers. A striking instance appears in a little memoir of the late William Hone, the Parodist, upon whom the experience made such a profound effect that it roused him from thirty years of materialistic atheism to a conviction of the soul's independence of matter. Being called in business to a house in a part of London entirely new to him, he kept noticing that he had never been that way before. "I was shown," he says, "into a room to wait. On looking around, to my astonishment everything appeared perfectly familiar to me: I seemed to *recognize* every object. I said to myself, what is this? I was never here before and yet I have seen all this, and if so, there is a very peculiar knot in the shutter." He opened the shutter, and there was the knot.

The experience of many persons supports this truth. The sacred Hindu books contain many detailed histories of transmigration. Kapila is said to have written out the Vedas from his recollection of them in a former life. The Vishnu Purana furnishes some entertaining instances of memory retained through successive lives. Pythagoras is related to have remembered his former existences in the persons of a herald named Æthalides, Euphorbus the Trojan, Hermotimus of Clazomenæ, and others. It is stated that he pointed out in the temple of Juno, at Argos, the shield with which, as Euphorbus, he attacked Patroclus in the Trojan war. The life of Apollonius of Tyana gives some extraordinary examples of his recognitions of persons he had known in preceding lives. All these cases are considered fictions by most people, because they trespass the limits of historical accuracy. But there are many facts in our own time that point in the same direction. The Druses have no doubt that this life follows many others. A Druse boy explained his terror at the discharge of a gun by saying, "I was born murdered;" that is, the soul of a man who had been shot entered into his body. A scholarly friend of the writer is satisfied that he once lived among the mountains before his present life, for, though born in a flat country destitute of pines, his first young entrance to a wild pine-grown mountain district roused the deepest sense of familiarity and home-likeness. And his last life, he thinks, was as a woman, because of certain commanding feminine traits which continually assert themselves. And this in spite of an apparently strong masculine nature, which never excites a suspicion of effeminacy.

Another friend of the writer says that his only child, a little girl now deceased, often referred to a younger sister of whom he knew nothing. When corrected with the assurance that she had no sister, she would reply, "Oh, yes, I have! I have a little baby sister in heaven!" The same gentleman tells this anecdote of a neighbor's family where the subject of reincarnation is never mentioned. A group of children was playing in the house at a counting game while their mother watched them. When they reached one hundred they started again at one and climbed up the numbers once more. The brightest boy commented on the proceeding: "We count ten, twenty, thirty, and so on to a hundred. Then we get through and begin all over. Mamma! That's the way people do. They go on and on till they come to the end, and then they begin over again. I hope I have you for a mamma again the next time I begin." Lawrence Oliphant gives in "Blackwood's Magazine" for January, 1881, a remarkable account of a child who remembered experiences of previous lives.

A writer in "Notes and Queries," second series, vol. iv. p. 157, says, "A gentleman of high intellectual attainments, now deceased, once told me that he had dreamed of being in a strange city, so vividly that he remembered the streets, houses, and public buildings as distinctly as those of any place he ever visited. A few weeks afterward he was induced to visit a panorama in Leicester Square, when he was startled by seeing the city of which he had dreamed. The likeness was perfect except that one additional church appeared in the picture. He was so struck by the circumstance that he spoke to the exhibitor, assuming for his purpose the air of a traveler acquainted with the place. He was informed that the additional church was a recent erection." It is difficult to account for such a fact by the hypothesis of the double structure of the brain, or by clairvoyance.

In Lord Lindsay's description of the valley of Kadisha ("Letters," p. 351, ed. 1847) he says: "We saw the river Kadisha descending from Lebanon. The whole scene bore that strange and shadowy resemblance to the wondrous landscape in 'Kubla Khan' that one so often feels in actual life, when the whole scene around you appears to be reacting after a long interval. Your friends seated in the same juxtaposition, the subjects of conversation the same, and shifting with the same dream-like ease, that you remember at some remote and indefinite period of preexistence; you always know what will come next, and sit spellbound, as it were, in a sort of calm expectancy."

Dickens, in his "Pictures from Italy," mentions this instance, on his first sight of Ferrara: "In the foreground was a group of silent peasant girls, leaning over the parapet of the little bridge, looking now up at the sky, now down into the water; in the distance a deep dell; the shadow of an approaching night on everything. If I had been murdered there in some former life I could not have seemed to remember the place more thoroughly, or with more emphatic chilling of the blood; and the real remembrance of it acquired in that minute is so strengthened by the imaginary recollection that I hardly think I could forget it."

A passage in the story of "The Wool-gatherer" shows that James Hogg, the author, shared the same feeling and attributed it to an earlier life on earth. N. P. Willis wrote a story of himself as the reincarnation of an Austrian artist, narrating how he discovered his previous personality, in "Dashes at Life," under the title "A Revelation of a Previous Existence." D. Gr. Rossetti does the same in his story "St. Agnes of Intercession."

The well-known lecturer, Eugene Ashton, recently contributed to a Cincinnati paper these two anecdotes:—

"At a dinner party in New York, recently, a lady, who is one of New York's most gifted singers, said to one of the guests: 'In some reincarnation I hope to perfect my voice, which I feel is now only partially developed. So long as I do not attain the highest of which my soul is capable I shall be returned to the flesh to work out what nature intended me to do.' But, madam, if you expect incarnations, have you any evidence of past ones?' 'Of that I cannot speak positively. I can recall dimly things which seem to have happened to me when I was in the flesh before. Often I go to places which are new to the present personality, but they are not new to my soul; I am sure that I have been there before.'

"A Southern literary woman, who now lives in Brooklyn, speaking of her former incarnations, says: 'I am sure that I have lived in some past time; for instance, when I was at Heidelberg, Germany, attending a convention of Mystics, in company with some friends I paid my first visit to the ruined Heidelberg Castle. As I approached it I was impressed with the existence of a peculiar room in an inaccessible portion of the building. A paper and pencil were provided me, and I drew a diagram of the room even to its peculiar floor. My diagram and description were perfect, when we afterwards visited the room. In some way not yet clear to me I have been connected with that apartment. Still another impression came to me with regard to a book, which I was made to feel was in the old library of the Heidelberg University. I not only knew what the

book was, but even felt that a certain name of an old German professor would be found written in it. Communicating this feeling to one
of the Mystics at the convention, a search was made for the volume,
but it was not found. Still the impression clung to me, and another effort was made to find the book; this time we were rewarded for our
pains. Sure enough, there on the margin of one of the leaves was the
very name I had been given in such a strange manner. Other things at
the same time went to convince me that I was in possession of the soul
of a person who had known Heidelberg two or three centuries ago.'"

The writer knows a gentleman who has repeatedly felt a vivid sense of
some one striking his skull with an axe, although nothing in his own
experience or in that of his family explains it. An extraordinary person
to whom he had never hinted the matter once surprised him by saying
that his previous life was closed by murder in that very way. Another
acquaintance is sure that some time ago he was a Hindu, and recollects
several remarkable incidents of that life.

Objectors ascribe these enigmas to a jumble of associations producing a blurred vision—like the drunkard's experience of seeing double,
a discordant remembrance, snatches of forgotten dreams—or to the
double structure of the brain. In one of the lobes, they say, the thought
flashes a moment in advance of the other, and the second half of the
thinking machine regards the first impression as a memory of something long distant.* But this explanation is unsatisfactory, as it fails to
account for the wonderful vividness of some of these impressions in
well-balanced minds, or the long trains of thought which come independent of any companions, or the prophetic glimpses which anticipate
actual occurrences. Far more credible is it that each soul is a palimpsest
inscribed again and again with one story upon another, and whenever
the all-wise Author is ready to write a grander page on us He washes
off the old ink and pens his latest word. But some of us can trace here

---

* As a physiological explanation of these instances, Dr. Wigan published in
1844 a curious book entitled, "The Duality of the Mind" (London), which
excited animated discussions and called forth a number of circumstances
which the double structure of the brain could not explain.

and there letters of the former manuscript not yet effaced.

A contributor to the "Penn Monthly," of September, 1875, refers to the hypothesis of double mental vision as supposed to account for most of these instances, and then concludes: "Such would be my inference as regards ordinary cases of this sort of reminiscence, especially when they are observed to accompany any impaired health of the organs of mental action. But there are more extraordinary instances of this mental phenomenon, of which I can give no explanation. Three of these have fallen within my own range of observation. A friend's child of about four years old was observed by her older sister to be talking to herself about matters of which she could not be supposed to know anything. 'Why, W —,' exclaimed the older sister, 'what do you know about that? All that happened before you were born!' 'I would have you know, L-, that I grew old in heaven before I was born.' I do not quote this as if it explained what the child meant it to explain, but as a curious statement from the mouth of one too young to have ever heard of preexistence, or to have inferred it from any ambiguous mental experiences of her own. The second case is that of the presence of inexplicable reminiscences, or what seem such in dreams. As everybody knows, the stuff which dreams are ordinarily made of is the every-day experience of life, which we cast into new and fantastic combinations, whose laws of arrangement and succession are still unknown to us. In the list of my acquaintances is a young married lady, a native of Philadelphia, who is repeatedly but not habitually carried back in her dreams to English society of the eighteenth century, seemingly of the times of George II, and to a social circle somewhat above that in which she now lives. Her acquaintance with literature is not such as to give her the least clue to the matter, and the details she furnishes are not such as would be gathered from books of any class. The dress, especially the lofty and elaborate headdresses of the ladies, their slow and stately minuet dancing, the deference of the servants to their superiors, the details of the stiff, square brick houses, in one of which she was surprised to find a family chapel with mural paintings and a fine organ — all these she describes with the sort of detail possible to one who has actually seen them, and not in the fashion in which book-makers write about them. Yet another, a more wide-awake experience, is that of a friend, who remembers having died in youth and in India. He sees the bronzed attendants gathered about his cradle in their white dresses; they are fanning him. And as they gaze he passes into unconsciousness. Much of his description concerned points of which he knew nothing from any other source, but all was true to the life, and enabled me to fix on India as the scene which he recalled."

VII. That it alone solves the problem of injustice and misery which broods over our world

The strongest support of reincarnation is its happy solution of the problem of moral inequality and injustice and evil which otherwise overwhelms us as we survey the world. The seeming chaos is marvelously set in order by the idea of soul-wandering. Many a sublime intellect has been so oppressed with the topsy-turviness of things here as to cry out, "There is no God. All is blind chance." An exclusive view of the miseries of mankind, the prosperity of wickedness, the struggles of the deserving, the oppression of the masses, or, on the other hand, the talents and successes and happiness of the fortunate few, compels one to call the world a sham without any moral law. But that consideration yields to a majestic satisfaction when one is assured that the present life is only one of a grand series in which every individual is gradually going the round of infinite experience for a glorious outcome—that the hedging ills of today are a consequence of what we did yesterday and a step toward the great things of tomorrow. Thus the tangled snarls of earthly phenomena are straightened out as a vast and beautiful scheme, and the total experience of humanity forms a magnificent tapestry of perfect poetic justice.

The crucial test of any hypothesis is whether it meets all the facts better than any other theory. No other view so admirably accounts for the diversity of conditions on earth, and refutes the charge of favoritism on the part of Providence. Hierocles said, and many a philosopher before and since has agreed with him, "Without the doctrine of metempsychosis it is not possible to justify the ways of God." Some of the theologians have found the idea of preexistence necessary to a reasonable explanation of the world, although it is considered foreign to the Bible. Over thirty years ago, Dr. Edward Beecher published "The Conflict of Ages," in which the main argument is this thought. He demonstrates that the facts of sin and depravity compel the acceptance of this doctrine to exonerate God from the charge of maliciousness. His book caused a lively controversy, and was soon followed by "The Concord of Ages," in which he answers the objections and strengthens his position. The same truth is taught by Dr. Julius Müller, a German theologian of prodigious influence among the clergy. Another prominent leader of theological thought, Dr. Dorner, sustains it.

We conclude, therefore, that reincarnation is necessitated by immortality, that analogy teaches it, that science upholds it, that the nature of the soul needs it, that many strange sensations support it, and that it alone grandly solves the problem of life. The fullness of its meaning is majestic beyond appreciation, for it shows that every soul, from the lowest animal to the highest archangel, belongs to the infinite family of God and is eternal in its conscious essence, perishing only in its temporary disguises; that every act of every creature is followed by infallible reactions which constitute a perfect law of retribution; and that these souls are intricately interlaced with mutual relationships. The bewildering maze thus becomes a divine harmony. No individual stands alone, but trails with him the unfinished sequels of an ancestral career, and is so bound up with his race that each is responsible for all and all for each. No one can be wholly saved until all are redeemed. Every suffering we endure apparently for faults not our own assumes a holy light and a sublime dignity. This thought removes the littleness of petty selfish affairs and confirms in us the vastest hopes for mankind.

Chapter III
Objections to Reincarnation

Man has an Eternal Father who sent him to reside and gain experience in the animal principles.—PARACELSUS.

God, who takes millions of years to form a soul that shall understand Him, and be blessed; who never needs to be and never is, in haste; who welcomes the simplest thought of truth or beauty as the return for seed he has sown upon the old fallows of eternity.—GEORGE MACDONALD.

Might not the human memory be compared to a field of sepulture, thickly stocked with the remains of many generations? But of these thousands whose dust heaves the surface, a few only are saved from immediate oblivion, upon tablets and urns; while the many are, at present, utterly lost to knowledge. Nevertheless each of the dead has left in that soul an imperishable germ; and all, without distinction, shall another day start up, and claim their dues.—ISAAC TAYLOR.

The absence of memory of any actions done in a previous state cannot be a conclusive argument against our having lived through it. Forgetfulness of the past may be one of the conditions of an entrance upon a new stage of existence. The body which is the organ of sense-perception may be quite as much a hindrance as a help to remembrance. In that case casual gleams of memory, giving us sudden abrupt and momentary revelations of the past, are precisely the phenomena we would expect to meet with. If the soul has preexisted, what we would a priori *anticipate are only some faint traces of recollection surviving in the crypts of memory.*—PROFESSOR WILLIAM KNIGHT.

○ ○ ○ ○ ○ ○ ○ ○

There are four leading objections to the idea of rebirths:—

1. That we have no memory of past lives.
2. That it is unjust for us to receive now the results of forgotten deeds enacted long ago.
3. That heredity confutes it.
4. That it is an uncongenial doctrine.

1. Why do we not remember something of our previous lives, if we have really been through them?

The reason why there is no universal conviction from this ground seems to be that birth is so violent as to scatter all the details and leave only the net spiritual result. As Plotinus said, "Body is the true river of Lethe; for souls plunged into it forget all." The real soul life is so distinct from the material plane that we have difficulty in retaining many experiences of this life. Who recalls all his childhood? And has any one a memory of that most wonderful epoch—infancy?

Nature sometimes shows us what may be the initial condition of a man's next life in depriving him of his life's experience, and returning him to a second childhood, with only the character acquired during life for his inseparable fortune. The great and good prelate Frederick Christian von Oetingen of Würtemberg (1702-1782) became in his old age a devout and innocent child, after a long life of usefulness. Gradually speech died away, until for three years he was dumb. Leaving his study, where he had written many edifying books, and his library, whose volumes were now sealed to hi in, he would go to the streets and join the children in their plays, and spend all his time sharing their delights. The profound scholar was stripped of his intellect and became a venerable boy, lovable and kind as in all his busy life. He had bathed in the river of Lethe before his time. Similar cases might be produced, where the spirits of strong men have been divested of a lifetime's memory in aged infancy, seeming to be a foretaste of the next existence. They show that the loss of a life's details does not appear strange to nature, and that the nepenthes waters of Styx, which the ancients represented as imbibed by souls about to reenter earthly life to dispel recollection of former experiences, are not wholly fabulous.

"Memory of the details of the past is absolutely impossible. The power of the conservative faculty though relatively great is extremely limited. We forget the larger portion of experience soon after we have passed through it, and we should be able to recall the particulars of our past years, filling all the missing links of consciousness since we entered on the present life, before we were in a position to remember our antenatal experience. Birth must necessarily be preceded by crossing the river of oblivion, while the capacity for fresh acquisition survives, and the garnered wealth of old experience determines the amount and character of the new."

But it has been shown that there are traces of former existences lingering in some memories. These and other exceptional departures from the general rule furnish substantial evidence that the obliteration of previous lives from our consciousness is only apparent. Sleep, somnambulism, trance, and similar conditions open up a world of supersensuous reality to illustrate how erroneous are our common notions of memory. Experimental evidence demonstrates that we actually forget nothing, though for long lapses we are unable to recall what is stored away in the chambers of our soul; and that the Orientals may be right in affirming that as a man's lives become purer he is able to look backward upon previous stages, and at last will view the long vista of the aeons by which he has ascended to God. Many cases reveal that the reach and clearness of memory are greatly increased during sleep and still more greatly during somnambulant trance; so much so that the memory of some sleepings and of most trances is sufficiently distinct from the memory of the same individual in waking consciousness, to seem the faculty of a different person. And, while the memory of sensuous consciousness does not retain the facts of the trance condition, the memory of the trance state retains and includes all the facts of the sensuous consciousness — exemplifying the superior and unsuspected powers of our unconscious selves. Instances are frequent illustrating how the higher consciousness faithfully stores away experiences which are thought to be long forgotten until some vivid touch brings them forth in accurate order.* The higher recollection and the lower sometimes conduct us through a double life. Dreams that vanish during the day are resumed at night in an unbroken course. There is an interesting class of cases on record in which the memory which links our successive dual states of consciousness into a united whole is so completely wanting that in observing only the difference between the two phases of the same person we describe it as "alternating consciousness." These go far toward an empirical proof that one individual can become two distinct persons in succession, making a practical demonstration of reincarnation. Baron Du Prel's "Philosophie der Mystik" cites a number of such authentic instances, of which the following is one, given by Dr. Mitchell in "Archiv fur thierischen Magnetismus," IV.

"Miss *R*——enjoyed naturally perfect health, and reached womanhood without any serious illness. She was talented, and gifted with a remarkably good memory, and learned with great ease. Without any previous warning she fell one day into a deep sleep which lasted many hours, and on awakening she had forgotten every bit of her former knowledge, and her memory had become a complete *tabula rasa*. She again learned to spell, read, write, and reckon, and made rapid progress.

* Leibnitz first directed attention to these singular phenomena. Sir William Hamilton has collected a number of instances of such wonderful revival of memory. Carpenter's *Mental Physiology*, pp. 430 et seq., and Brodie's *Psychological Inquiries*, Second Series, p. 55, mention several cases. Coleridge cited from the German a remarkable illustration, and commented upon it in his *Biographia Literaria*, chapter vi.:—
"This fact (and it would not be difficult to adduce several of the same kind) contributes to make it even probable that all thoughts are in themselves imperishable; and that, if the intelligent faculty should be rendered more comprehensive, it would require only a different and apportioned organization, *the body celestial* instead of *the body terrestrial*, to bring before every human soul the collective experience of its whole past existence. And this—this, perchance, is the dread Book of Judgment, in whose mysterious hieroglyphics every idle word is recorded! Yea, in the very nature of a living spirit, it may be more possible that heaven and earth should pass away than that a single act, a single thought, should be loosened or lost from that living chain of causes to all whose links, conscious or unconscious, the free will, our only absolute Self, is co-extensive and co-present."

Some few months afterward she again fell into a similarly prolonged slumber, from which she awoke to her former consciousness, *i. e.*, in the same state as before her first long sleep, but without the faintest recollection of the existence or events of the intervening period. This double existence now continued, so that in a single subject there occurred a regular alternation of two perfectly distinct personalities, each being unconscious of the other, and possessing only the memories and knowledge acquired in previous corresponding states."

More singular still are cases in which one individual becomes two interchanging persons, of whom one is wholly unconnected with the known history of that individual, like that narrated in Mr. Stevenson's story of "The Adventures of Dr. Jekyl and Mr. Hyde," and Julian Hawthorne's story of "Archibald Malmaison." The newspapers recently published ail account of a Boston clergyman, who strangely disappeared from his city, leaving no trace of his destination. Just before going away he drew some money from the bank, and for weeks his family and friends heard nothing of him, though he had previously been most faithful. Soon after his departure a stranger turned up in a Pennsylvania town and bought out a certain store, which he conducted very industriously for some time.

At length a delirious illness seized him. One day he awoke from it and asked his nurse, "Where am I?" "You are in —— ," she said. "How did I get here? I belong in Boston." "You have lived here for three months and own Mr.—'s store," replied his attendant. "You are mistaken, madam; I am The Rev.——, pastor of the —— church in Boston."

Three months were an absolute blank. He had no memory of anything since drawing the money at his bank. Returning home, he there resumed the broken line of his ministerial life and continued in that character without further interruption.

Numerous similar cases are recorded in the annals of psychological medicine, and justify us in assuming, according to the law of correspondences, that some such alternation of consciousness occurs after the great change known as death. The attempt to explain them as mental aberrations is wholly unsuccessful. Reincarnation shows them to be exceptions proving the rule—the recall of former activities supposed to be forgotten. In these examples of double identity the facts of each state disappear when the other set come forward and are resumed again in their turn. Where did they reside meanwhile? They must have been preserved in a subtler organ than the brain, which is only the medium of translation from that unconscious memory to the world of sense-perception. This must be in the supersensuous part of the soul. This provides that, as a slow and painful training leads to unconscious habits of skill, so the experience of life is stored up in the higher memory, and becomes, when assimilated, the reflex acts of the following life — those operations which we call instinctive and hereditary.

2. The question is raised, is it just that a man should suffer for what he is not conscious of having done?

As just as that he should *enjoy* the results of what he does not remember causing. It is said that justice requires that the offender be conscious of the fault for which he is punished. But the ideas of justice between man and man cannot be applied to the all-wise operations of the Infinite. In human attempts at justice that method is imperative because of our liability to mistake. God's justice is vindicated by the undisturbed sway of the law of causation. If *I* suffer it must be for what *I* have done. The faith in Providence demands this, and it is because of unbelief in reincarnation that the seeming negligence on the part of Providence has obliterated the idea of a Personal God from many minds. Nature is the arena of infallible cause and effect, and there is no such absurdity in the universe as an effect without a responsible cause. A man may suffer from a disease in ignorance of the conditions under which its germs were sown in his body, but the right sequence of cause and effect is not imperiled by his ignorance. To doubt that the experiences we now enjoy and endure properly belong to us by our own choice is to abandon the idea of God. How and why they have come is explained only by reincarnation. The universal Over-Soul makes no mistakes. By veiling our memories the Mother Heart of all, mercifully saves us the horror and burden of knowing all the myriad steps by which we have become what we are. We would be staggered by the sight of all our waywardness, and what we have done well is possessed more richly in the grand total than would be possible in the infinite details. We are in the hands of a generous omniscient banker, who says: " I will save you all the trouble of the accounts. Whenever you are ready to start a new folio, I will strike the balance and turn over your net proceeds with all accrued interests. The itemized records of your deposits and spendings are beyond your calculation."

3. It may be claimed that the facts of heredity bear against reincarnation. As the physical, mental, and moral peculiarities of children come from the parents, how can it be possible that a man is what he makes himself — the offspring of his own previous lives?

Science is certain of the tendency of every organism to transmit its own qualities to its descendants, and the intricate web of ancestral influences is assumed to account for all the aberrations of individual life. But the forces producing this result are beyond the ken of science. The mechanical theory of germ cells multiplying their kind is inadequate: for the germs become more complex and energetic with growth, and exceed the limitations of molecular physics. The facts of heredity demand the existence in nature of supersensuous forces escaping our observation and cognizable only through their effects on the plane of sensuous consciousness. These forces residing in the inaccessible regions of the soul mould all individual aptitudes and faculties and character. Reincarnation includes the facts of heredity, by showing that the tendency of every organism to reproduce its own likeness groups together similar causes producing similar effects, in the same lines of physical relation. Instead of being content with the statement that heredity causes the resemblances of child to parent, reincarnation teaches that a similarity of ante-natal development has brought about the similarity of embodied characteristics. The individual soul seeking another birth finds the path of least resistance in the channels best adapted to its qualities. The Ego selects its material body by a choice more wise than any voluntary selection, by the inherent tendencies of its nature, in fitness for its need, not only in the particular physique best suited for its purpose, but in the larger physical casements of family and nationality. The relation of child and parent is required by the similarity of organisms. This view accounts also for the differences invariably accompanying the resemblances. Identity of character is impossible, and the conditions which made it easy for an individual to be born in a certain family, because of the adaptation of circumstances there to the expression of portions of his nature, would not prevent a strong contrast between him and his relatives in some respects. The facts observed in the life history of twins show that two individuals born under precisely identical conditions, and having exactly the same heredity, sometimes differ completely in physique, in intellect, and in character. The birth of geniuses in humble and commonplace circumstances furnishes abundant evidence that the individual soul outstrips all the trammels of physical birth; and the unremarkable children of great parents exhibit the inefficiency of merely hereditary influences. These conspicuous violations of the laws of heredity confirm reincarnation.

4. At the first impression the idea of rebirths is unwelcome, because —

1. It is interlaced with the theory of transmigration through animals;
2. It destroys the hope of recognizing friends in the coming existence;
3. It seems a cold, irreligious notion.
4. As will be fully shown in chapter XII., the conceit of a transmigration of human souls through animal bodies, although it has been and is cherished by most of the believers in reincarnation, is only a gross metaphor of the germinal truth, and never was received by the enlightened advocates of plural existences.
5. The most thoughtful adherents of a future life agree that there must be there some subtler mode of recognition between friends than physical appearances, for these outer signs cannot endure in the world of spirit. The conviction that "whether there be prophecies they shall fail, whether there be tongues they shall cease, whether

there be knowledge it shall vanish away," but "love never fails," and only character shall remain as the means of identification, is precisely the view entertained by believers in reincarnation. The most intimate ties of this life cannot be explained otherwise than as renewals of old intimacies, drawn together by the spiritual gravitation of love, and enjoying often the sense of a previous similar experience. (A further reference to this point will be found later. See chapter XIII.)

6.   The strongest religious natures have been nourished from time immemorial with the feeling that life is a pilgrimage through which we tread our darkened way back to God. The Scriptures are full of it, and the spiritual manhood of every age has found it a source of invigoration. From Abraham, who reckoned his lifetime as "the days of the years of his pilgrimage," through all the phases of Christian thought to the mightiest book of modern Christendom, "The Pilgrim's Progress," this idea has been universally cherished. A typical expression of it may be seen in the mediaeval churchyard of St. Martin at Canterbury, upon a stone over the remains of Dean Alford bearing these words in Latin, which were inscribed by his own direction: "The inn of a traveler journeying to Jerusalem." Now this pilgrimage philosophy is only a simpler phrasing of reincarnation. Our theory extends the journey in just proportion to the supernal destination, providing many a station by the way, wherein abiding a few days we may more profitably traverse the upward road, gathering so much experience that there will be no occasion to wander again. Instead of being a cold philosophic hypothesis, reincarnation is a living unfoldment of that Christian germ, enlarged to a fullness commensurate with the needs of men and the character of God. It throbs with the warmth of deepest piety combined with noblest intelligence, providing as no other supposition does, for the grandest development of mankind.

Chapter IV
Western Prose Writers on Reincarnation

I think I must once have been masculine, because my love is all for girls.—Louisa M. Alcott.

The greatest guilt of man is that he was born.—Calderon.
I seem often clearly to remember in my soul a presentiment which I have not seen with my present, but with some other eye.—J. E. Von Schubert.

I produced the golden key of preexistence only at a dead lift, when no other method could satisfy me touching the ways of God, that by this hypothesis I might keep my heart from sinking.—Henry More.

The essences of our souls can never cease to be because they never began to be, and nothing can live eternally but that which hath lived from eternity. The essences of our souls were a breath in God before they became living souls; they lived in God before they lived in the created souls, and therefore the soul is a partaker of the eternity of God.—William Law.

If there be no reasons to suppose that we have existed before that period at which our existence apparently commences, then there are no grounds for supposing that we shall continue to exist after our existence has apparently ceased.—Shelley.

The ancient doctrine of transmigration seems the most rational and most consistent with God's wisdom and goodness; as by it all the unequal dispensations of things so necessary in one life may be set right in another, and all creatures serve the highest and lowest, the most eligible and most burdensome offices of life by an equitable rotation; by which means their rewards and punishments may not only be proportioned to their behavior, but also carry on the business of the universe, and thus at the same time answer the purposes both of justice and utility. — SOAME JENYNS.

○ ○ ○ ○ ○ ○ ○ ○

There is a larger endorsement of reincarnation among western thinkers than the world knows. In many of them it springs up spontaneously, while others embrace it as a luminous ray from the East which is confirmed by all the candid tests of philosophy. When Christianity first swept over Europe the inner thought of its leaders was deeply tinctured with this truth. The Church tried ineffectually to eradicate it, and in various sects it kept sprouting forth beyond the time of Erigena and Bonaventura, its mediaeval advocates. Every great intuitional soul, as Paracelsus, Boehine, and Swedenborg, has adhered to it. The Italian luminaries, Giordano Bruno and Campanella, embraced it. The best of German philosophy is enriched by it. In Schopenhauer, Lessing, Hegel, Leibnitz, Herder, and Fichte the younger, it is earnestly advocated. The anthropological systems of Kant and Schelling furnish points of contact with it. The younger Helmont, in "De Bevolutione Animarum," adduces in two hundred problems all the arguments which may be urged in favor of the return of souls into human bodies, according to Jewish ideas. Of English thinkers the Cambridge Platonists defended it with much learning and acuteness, most conspicuously Henry More; and in Cudworth and Hume it ranks as the most rational theory of immortality. Glanvil's "Lux Orientalis" devotes a curious treatise to it. It captivated the minds of Fourier and Leroux. Andre Pezzani's book on "The Plurality of the Soul's Lives" works out the system on the Roman Catholic idea of expiation. Modern astronomy has furnished material for the elaborate speculations of a reincarnation extending through many worlds, as published in Fontenelle's volume "The Plurality of Worlds," Huygens's "Cosmotheoros," Brewster's "More Worlds than One; the Philosopher's Faith and the Christian's Hope," Jean Reynaud's "Earth and Heaven," Flammarion's "Stories of Infinity" and "The Plurality of Inhabited Worlds," and Figuier's "The Tomorrow of Death." With various degrees of fancy and probability these writers trace the soul's progress among the heavenly bodies. The astronomer Bode wrote that we start from the coldest planet of our solar system and advance from planet to planet, nearer the sun, where the most perfect beings, he thinks, will live. Emmanuel Kant, in his "General History of Nature," says that souls start imperfect from the sun, and travel by planet stages, farther and farther away to a paradise in the coldest and remotest star of our system. Between these opposites many *savants* have formulated other theories. In theology reincarnation has retained a firm influence from the days of Origen and Porphyry, through the scholastics, to the present day. In Soame Jenyns's works, which long thrived as the best published argument for Christianity, it is noticeable. Chevalier Ramsay and William Law have also written in its defense. Julius Müller warmly upholds it in his profound work on "The Christian Doctrine of Sin," as well as Dr. Dorner. Another means of its dissemination through a good portion of the ministry is Dr. Edward Beecher's espousal of it, in the form of preexistence, in "The Conflict of Ages" and "The Concord of Ages." English and Irish bishops* have not hesitated to promulgate it. Henry Ward Beecher and Phillips Brooks have dared to preach it. James Freeman Clarke speaks strongly in its favor. Professor William Knight, the Scotch metaphysician of St. Andrews, and Professor Francis Bowen of Harvard University, clearly show the logical probabilities in which reincarnation compares favorably with any other philosophy.†

The following extracts from the most interesting of these and other Western authors who refer to the matter may represent the unsuspected prevalence of this thought in our own midst.

1. Schopenhauer's powerful philosophy includes reincarnation as one of its main principles, as these extracts show, from his chapter on "Death"

---

* A noble passage from one of the greatest of these may be found in Scott's *Christian Life*, chapter iii. section i. See also Dr. Henry More's *Immortality of the Soul*, Book II. Chapter xvi., and Sir Kenehn Digby's remarks on Sir Thomas Browne's *Religio Medici*.

† A full list of the principal western writers on this subject is given in the Appendix.

in "The World as Will and Idea":—*

"What sleep is for the individual, death is for the will [character]. It would not endure to continue the same actions and sufferings throughout an eternity, without true gain, if memory and individuality remained to it. It flings them off, and this is lethe; and through this sleep of death it reappears refreshed and fitted out with another intellect, as a new being—'a new day tempts to new shores.'"

"These constant new births, then, constitute the succession of the life-dreams of a will which in itself is indestructible, until, instructed and improved by so much and such various successive knowledge in a constantly new form, it abolishes or abrogates itself"—[becomes in perfect harmony with the Infinite].

"It must not be neglected that even empirical grounds support a palingenesis of this kind. As a matter of fact, there does exist a connection between the birth of the newly appearing beings and the death of those that are worn out. It shows itself in the great fruitfulness of the human race which appears as a consequence of devastating diseases. When in the fourteenth century the Black Death had for the most part depopulated the old world, a quite abnormal fruitfulness appeared among the human race, and twin-births were very frequent. The circumstance was also remarkable that none of the children born at this time obtained their full number of teeth; thus nature, exerting itself to the utmost, was niggardly in details. This is related by F. Schnurrer, 'Chronik der Seuchen,' 1825. Casper also, 'Ueber die Wahrscheinliche Lebensdauer des Menschen,' 1835, confirms the principle that the number of births in a given population has the most decided influence upon the length of life and mortality in it, as this always keeps pace with the mortality: so that always and everywhere the deaths and the births increase and decrease in like proportion; which he places beyond doubt by an accumulation of evidence collected from many lands and their various provinces. And yet it is impossible that there can be a *physical* causal connection between my early death and the fruitfulness of a marriage with which I have nothing to do, or conversely. Thus here the metaphysi-

* Haldane and Kemp's Translation, vol. iii. pp. 299-306.

cal appears undeniable and in a stupendous manner as the immediate ground of explanation of the physical. Every new-born being comes fresh and blithe into the new existence, and enjoys it as a free gift: but there is, and can be, nothing freely given. Its fresh existence is paid for by the old age and death of a worn-out existence which has perished, but which contained the indestructible seed out of which the new existence has arisen: they are *one* being. To show the bridge between the two would certainly be the solution of a great riddle.

"The great truth which is expressed here has never been entirely unacknowledged, although it could not be reduced to the exact and correct meaning, which is only possible through the doctrine of the primary and metaphysical nature of the will, and the secondary, merely organic nature of the intellect. We find the doctrine of metempsychosis, springing from the earliest and noblest ages of the human race, always spread abroad in the earth as the belief of the great majority of mankind; nay, really as the teaching of all religions, with the exception of that of the Jews and the two which have proceeded from it: in the most subtle form however, and coming nearest to the truth in Buddhism. Accordingly, while Christians console themselves with the thought of meeting again in another world, in which one regains one's complete personality and knows one's self at once, in those other religions the meeting again is going on now, only incognito. In the succession of births, and by virtue of metempsychosis or palingenesis, the persons who now stand in close connection or contact with us will also be born again with us at the next birth, and will have the same or analogous relations and sentiments towards us as now, whether these are of a friendly or a hostile description. Recognition is certainly here limited to an obscure intimation—a reminiscence, which cannot be brought to distinct consciousness, and refers to an infinitely distant time; with the exception, however, of Buddha himself, who has the prerogative of distinctly knowing his own earlier births and those of others—as this is described in the 'Jataka.' But in fact, if at a favorable moment one contemplates, in a purely objective manner, the action of men in reality, the intuitive conviction is forced upon one that it not only is and remains constantly the same, according to the [Platonic] Idea, but also that the present generation, in its true inner nature, is precisely and substantially identical with every generation that has been before it. The question simply is, in what this true being consists. The answer which my doctrine gives to this question is well known. The intuitive conviction referred to may be conceived as arising from the fact that the multiplying-glasses, time and space, lose for a moment their effect. With reference to the universality of the belief in metempsychosis, Obry says rightly in his excellent book 'Du Nirvana Indien,' p. 13, 'Cette vieille croyance a fait le tour du monde, et tellement répandue dans la haute antiquité qu'un docte Anglican l'avait jugée sans père, sans mère, et sans généalogie.' Taught already in the 'Vedas' as in all the sacred books of India, metempsychosis is well known to be the kernel of Brahmanism and Buddhism. It accordingly prevails at the present day in the whole of non-Mohammedan Asia, thus among more than half the whole human race, as the firmest conviction, and with an incredibly strong practical influence. It was also the belief of the Egyptians, from whom it was received with enthusiasm by Orpheus, Pythagoras, and Plato. The Pythagoreans, however, specially retained it. That it was also taught in the mysteries of the Greeks undeniably follows from the ninth book of Plato's Laws. The 'Edda' also, especially in the 'Voluspa,' teaches metempsychosis. Not less was it the foundation of the religion of the Druids. Even a Mohammedan sect in Hindustan, the Bohrahs, of which Colebrooke gives a full account in the 'Asiatic Researches,' believes in metempsychosis, and accordingly refrains from all animal food. Also among American Indians and Negro tribes, nay, even among the natives of Australia, traces of this belief are found... According to all this the belief in metempsychosis presents itself as the natural conviction of man whenever he reflects at all in an unprejudiced manner. It would really seem to be that which Kant falsely asserts of his three pretended ideas of the reason, a philosopheme natural to human reason, which proceeds from its forms; and when it is not found it must have been displaced by positive religious doctrines coming from a different source. I have also remarked that it is at once obvious to every one who hears of it for the first time. Let any one only observe how earnestly Lessing defends it in the last seven paragraphs of his 'Erziehung des Menschengeschlechts.'* Lichtenberg also says in his 'Selbstcharacteristik': 'I cannot get rid of the thought that I died before I was born.' Even the excessively empirical Hume says in his skeptical essay on immortality, 'The metempsychosis is therefore the only system of this kind that philosophy can hearken to.' What resists this belief is Judaism, together with the two religions which have sprung from it, because they teach the creation of man out of nothing, and they have the hard task of linking on to this belief an endless existence *a parte post*. They certainly have succeeded, with fire and sword, in driving out of Europe and part of Asia that consoling primitive belief of mankind; it is still doubtful for how long. Yet how difficult this was is shown by the oldest church histories. Most of the heretics were attached to this belief; for example, Simonists, Basilidians, Valentinians, Marcionists, Gnostics, and Manicheans. The Jews themselves have in part fallen into it, as Tertullian and Justinus inform us. In the Talmud it is related that Abel's soul passed into the body of Seth, and then into that of Moses. Even the passage of the Bible, Matt, XVI, 13-15, only obtains a rational meaning if we understand it as spoken under the assumption of the dogma of metempsychosis... In Christianity, however, the doctrine of original sin, *i.e.*, the doctrine of punishment for the sins of another individual, has taken the place of the transmigration of souls, and the expiation in this way of all the sins committed in an earlier life. Both identify the existing man with one who has existed before: the transmigration of souls does so directly, original sin indirectly."

2. In the remarkable little treatise on "The Divine Education of the Human Race," by Lessing, the German philosopher, a book so sublimely simple in its profound insight that it has had enormous influence and was translated into English as a labor of love by the Rev. Frederick W. Robertson, the author outlines the gradual instruction of mankind and shows how the enlightenment is still progressing through many important lessons. His thought mounts to a climax in suggesting the stupendous programme by which God is developing the individual just

* Translated in section 2 of this chapter.

as he has been educating the race:—

"The very same way by which the race reaches its perfection must every individual man—one sooner, another later—have traveled over. Have traveled over in one and the same life? Can he have been in one and the selfsame life a sensual Jew and a spiritual Christian? Can he in the selfsame life have overtaken both?

"Surely not that: but why should not every individual man have existed more than once upon this world?

"Is this hypothesis so laughable merely because it is the oldest? Because the human understanding, before the sophistries of the schools had dissipated and debilitated it, lighted upon it at once?

"Why may not even I have already performed those steps of my perfecting which bring to men only temporal punishments and rewards? And once more, why not another time all those steps to perform which, the views of eternal rewards so powerfully assist us?

"Why should I not come back as often as I am capable of acquiring fresh knowledge, fresh expertness? Do I bring away so much from once that there is nothing to repay the trouble of coming back?

"Is this a reason against it? Or, because I forget that I have been here already? Happy is it for me that I do forget. The recollection of my former condition would permit me to make only a bad use of the present. And that which even I must forget *now*, is that necessarily forgotten forever?

"Or is it a reason against the hypothesis that so much time would have been lost to me? Lost? And how much then should I miss? Is not a whole eternity mine?"

3. "The Destiny of Man," by J. G. Fichte, whose great thoughts still heave the heart of Germany and grandly mould the world, contains these paragraphs:

"These two systems, the purely spiritual and the sensuous—which last may consist of an immeasurable series of particular lives—exist in me from the moment when my active reason is developed, and pursue their parallel course. The former alone gives to the latter meaning and purpose and value. I *am* immortal, imperishable, eternal, so soon as I form the resolution to obey the law of reason. After an existence of myriad lives the supersensuous world cannot be more present than at this moment. Other conditions of my sensuous existence are to come, but these are no more the true life than the present condition is.

"Man is not a product of the world of sense; and the end of his existence can never be attained in that world. His destination lies beyond time and space and all that pertains to sense.

"Mine eye discerns this eternal life and motion in all the veins of sensible and spiritual nature, through what seems to others a dead mass. And it sees this life forever ascend and grow and transfigure itself into a more spiritual expression of its own nature. The sun rises and sets, the stars vanish and return again, and all the spheres hold their cycle dance. But they never return precisely such as they disappeared; and in the shining fountains of life there is also life and progress.

"All death in nature is birth; and precisely in dying, the sublimation of life appears most conspicuous. There is no death-bringing principle in nature, for nature is only life, throughout. Not death kills, but the more living life, which is hidden behind the old, begins and unfolds itself. Death and birth are only the struggles of life with itself to manifest itself in ever more transfigured form, more like itself.

"Even because Nature puts me to death she must quicken me anew. It can only be my higher life, unfolding itself in her, before which my present life disappears; and that which mortals call death is the visible appearing of another vivification."

4. Among the wealth of German geniuses, there is none more lofty and broad than Herder, whom Jean Paul admiringly pronounced, "a Poem made by some purest Deity—combining the boldest freedom of philosophy concerning nature and God with a most pious faith." One of the most suggestive of this master's works is a series of "Dialogues on Metempsychosis," in which two friends discuss the theme together. As the outcome of their colloquy is a stanch vindication of that hypothesis, it is not unfair to group together a few of the paragraphs on one side of the conversation:—

"Do you not know great and rare men who cannot have become what they are at once, in a single human existence? who must have often existed before in order to have attained that purity of feeling, that instinctive impulse for all that is true, beautiful, and good, in short, that elevation and natural supremacy over all around them?

"Do not these great characters appear, for the most part, all at once? Like a cloud of celestial spirits, descended from on high; like men risen from the dead born again, who brought back the old time?

"Have you never had remembrances of a former state, which you could find no place for in this life? In that beautiful period when the soul is yet a half-closed bud, have you not seen persons, been in places, of which you were ready to swear that you had seen those persons, or had been in those places before? And yet it could not have been in this life? The most blessed moments, the grandest thoughts, are from that source. In our more ordinary seasons, we look back with astonishment on ourselves, we do not comprehend ourselves. And such are *we*; we who, from a hundred causes, have sunk so deep and are so wedded to matter, that but few reminiscences of so pure a character remain to us. The nobler class of men who, separated from wine and meat, lived in perfect simplicity according to the order of nature, carried it further, no doubt, than others, as we learn from the example of Pythagoras, of Iarchas, of Apollonius, and others, who remembered distinctly what and how many times they had been in the world before. If we are blind, or can see but two steps beyond our noses, ought we therefore to deny that others may see a hundred or a thousand degrees farther, even to the bottom of time, into the deep, cool well of the fore-world, and there discern everything plain and bright and clear?"

To this last strain the listener responds:—

"I will freely confess to you that those sweet dreams of memory are known to me also, among the experiences of my childhood and youth. I have been in places and circumstances of which I could have sworn that I had been in them before. I have seen persons with whom I seemed to have lived before; with whom I was, as it were, on the footing of an old acquaintance." He then attempts to explain them as returned dreams, which his interlocutor answers with more wonderful impressions necessarily requiring a former life.

"Have you never observed that children will sometimes, on a sudden, give utterance to ideas which make us wonder how they got possession of them; which presuppose a long series of other ideas and secret self-communings; which break forth like a full stream out of the earth, an infallible sign that the stream was not produced in a moment from a few raindrops, but had long been flowing concealed beneath the ground, and, it may be, had broken through many a rock, and contracted many defilements?

"You know the law of economy which rules throughout nature. Is it not probable that the Deity is guided by it in the propagation and progress of human souls? He who has not become ripe in one form of humanity is put into the experience again, and, some time or other, must be perfected.

"I am not ashamed of my half-brothers the brutes; on the contrary, as far as they are concerned, I am a great advocate of metempsychosis. I believe, for a certainty, that they will ascend to a higher grade of being, and am unable to understand how any one can object to this hypothesis, which seems to have the analogy of the whole creation in its favor.

"All the life of nature, all the tribes and species of animated creation — what are they but sparks of the Godhead, a harvest of incarnate stars, among which the two human sexes stand forth like sun and moon? We overshine, we dim the other figures, but, doubtless, we lead them onward in a chorus invisible to ourselves. Oh, that an eye were given us to trace the shining course of this divine spark; to see how life flows to life, and ever refining, impelled through all the veins of creation, wells up into a purer, higher life.

"And yet Pythagoras, too, spoke of a Tartarus and an Elysium. When you stand before the statue of a high-hearted Apollo, do you not feel what you lack of being that form? Can you ever attain to it here below, though you should return ten times? And yet that was only the idea of an artist — a dream which our narrow breast also inclosed. Has the almighty Father no nobler forms for us than those in which our heart now heaves and groans? The soul lies captive in its dungeon, bound as with a sevenfold chain, and only through a strong grating, and only through a pair of light and air-holes, can it breathe and see, and always it sees the world on one side only, while there are a million other sides before us and in us, had we but more and other senses, and could we but exchange this narrow hut of our body for a freer prospect. That restless discontent shall some time finally release us from our repeated sojourns on earth, through which the Father is training us for a complete divorce from sense-life. When even at the sweetest fountains of friendship and love, we so often pine, thirsty and sick, seeking union and finding it not, what noble soul does not lift itself up and despise tabernacles and wanderings in the circle of earthly deserts.

"Purification of the heart, the ennobling of the soul, with all its propensities and cravings, this, it seems to me, is the true palingenesis of this life, after which, I doubt not, a happy, more exalted, but yet unknown metempsychosis awaits us."

5. Dr. Henry More, the learned and lovable Platonist of the seventeenth century, wrote a charming treatise on the "Immortality of the Soul," in which (chapter XII) he argues for preexistence as follows:—

"If it be good for the souls of men to be at all, the sooner they are, the better. But we are most certain that the wisdom and goodness of God will do that which is the best; and therefore if they can enjoy themselves before they come to these terrestrial bodies, they must be before they come into these bodies. For nothing hinders but that they may live before they come into the body, as well as they may after going out of it. Wherefore the preexistence of souls is a necessary result of the wisdom and goodness of God.

"Again, the face of Providence in the work seems very much to suit with this opinion, there being not any so natural and easy account to be given of those things that seem the most harsh in the affairs of men, as from this hypothesis: that these souls did once subsist in some other state; where, in several manners and degrees, they forfeited the favor of their Creator, and so, according to that just Nemesis that He has interwoven in the constitution of the universe and of their own natures, they undergo several calamities and asperities of fortune and sad drudgeries of fate, as a punishment inflicted, or a disease contracted from the several obliquities of their *apostasy*. Which key is not only able to unlock that recondite mystery of some particular men's almost fatal averseness from all religion and virtue, their stupidity and dullness and even invincible slowness to these things from their very childhood, and their incorrigible propension to all manner of vice; but also of that squalid forlornness and brutish barbarity that whole nations for many ages have lain under, and many do still lie under at this very day: which sad scene of things must needs exceedingly cloud and obscure the ways of Divine Providence, and make them utterly unintelligible; unless some light be let in from the present hypothesis.

"And as this hypothesis is rational in itself, so has it also gained the suffrage of all philosophers of all ages, of any note, that have held the soul of man incorporeal and immortal. I shall add, for the better countenance of the business, some few instances herein, as a pledge of the truth of my general conclusion. Let us cast our eye, therefore, into what corner of the world we will, that has been famous for wisdom and literature, and the wisest of those nations you shall find the asserters of this opinion.

"In Egypt, that ancient nurse of all hidden sciences, that this opinion was in vogue amongst the wisest men there, the fragments of Trismegist do sufficiently witness: of which opinion, not only the Gymnosophists, and other wise men of Egypt, were, but also the Brahmans of India, and the Magi of Babylon and Persia. To these you may add the abstruse philosophy of the Jews, which they call their Cabbala, of which the soul's preexistence makes a considerable part, as all the learned of the Jews do confess.

"And if I should particularize in persons of this opinion, truly they are such of so great fame for depth of understanding, and abstrusest science, that their testimony alone might seem sufficient to bear down any ordinary modest man into an assent to their doctrine. And, in the first place, if we believe the Cabbala of the Jews, we must assign it to Moses, the greatest philosopher certainly that ever was in the world; to whom you may add Zoroaster, Pythagoras, Epicharmus, Cebes, Euripides, Plato,

Euclid, Philo, Virgil, Marcus Cicero, Plotinus, Iamblichus, Proclus, Boethius, Pfellus, and several others, which it would be too long to recite. And if it were fit to add fathers to philosophers, we might enter into the same list Synesius and Origen; the latter of whom was surely the greatest light and bulwark that ancient Christianity had. But I have not yet ended my catalogue; that admirable physician Johannes Fernelius is also of this persuasion, and is not to be so himself only, but discovers those two grand-masters of medicine, Hippocrates and Galen, to be so, too. Cardan, also, that famous philosopher of his age, expressly concludes that the rational soul is both a distinct being from the soul of the world, and that it does preexist before it comes into the body; and lastly, Pomponatius, no friend to the soul's immortality, yet cannot but confess that the safest way to hold it is also therewith to acknowledge her preexistence.

"And we shall evince that Aristotle, that has the luck to be believed more than most authors, was of the same opinion, in his treatise 'De Anima,' where he says, 'for every art must use its proper instruments, and every soul its body.' He speaks something more plainly in his 'De Generatione Anima?.''There are generated,' said he, 'in the earth, and in the moisture thereof, plants and living creatures, and in the whole universe an animal heat; insomuch that in a manner all places are full of souls.' We will add a third place still more clear, out of the same treatise, where he starts that very question of the preexistency of souls, of the sensitive and rational especially, and he concludes thus: 'It remains that the rational or intellectual soul only enters from without, as being only of a nature purely divine; with whose actions the actions of this gross body have no communication.' Concerning which point he concludes like an orthodox scholar of his excellent master Plato; to whose footsteps the closer he keeps, the less he ever wanders from the truth. For in this very place he does plainly profess what many would not have him so apertly guilty of, that the soul of man is immortal, and can perform her proper functions without the help of this terrestrial body."

6. Sir Thomas Browne explains and defends his own heresies, by suggesting the added heresy of reincarnation:—

"For, indeed, heresies perish not with their authors: but like the river Arethusa, though they lose their currents in one place, they rise up again in another. One general council is not able to extirpate one single heresy: it may be canceled for the present: but revolution of time and the like aspects from heaven will restore it, when it will flourish till it be condemned again. For, as though there were a metempsychosis, and the soul of one man passed into another, opinions do find, after certain revolutions, men and minds like those that first begat them. To see ourselves again, we need not look for Plato's year; every man is not only himself: there have been many Diogeneses, and as many Timons, though but few of that name; men are lived over again; the world is now as it was in ages past; there was none then, but there had been some one since, that parallels him, and is, as it were, his revived self."

7. One of the rare volumes of the early eighteenth century is Chevalier Ramsay's remarkable work entitled "The Philosophical Principles of Natural and Revealed Religion," in which he elaborates the idea that "the sacred mysteries of our holy faith are not new fictions unheard of by the philosophers of all nations," but that "on the contrary Christianity is as old as the creation." In this "History of the human mind in all ages, nations, and religions, concerning the most divine truths," he shows that reincarnation is the common possession of Christianity and of all the other great systems of sacred thought:—

"The holy oracles always represent Paradise as our native country, and our present life as an exile. How can we be said to have been banished from a place in which we never were? This argument alone would suffice to convince us of preexistence, if the prejudice of infancy inspired by the schoolmen had not accustomed us to look upon these expressions as metaphorical, and to believe, contrary to Scripture and to reason, that we were exiled from a happy state, only for the fault of our first parents. Atrocious maxim that sullies all the conduct of Providence, and that shocks the understandings of the most intelligent children of all nations. The answers ordinarily made to them throw into their tender minds the seeds of a lasting incredulity.

"In Scripture, the wise man says, speaking of the eternal Logos, and his preexistent humanity: 'The Lord possessed me from the beginning of his ways, before his works of old; I was set up from everlasting, from the beginning or ever the earth was! All this can be said only of the eternal Logos. But what follows may be applied to the preexistent humanity of the Messiah: 'When he prepared the heavens I was there, when he encircled the force of the deep, when he established the clouds above, when he appointed the foundations of the earth, then I was by him, as one brought up with him, and I was daily his delight, rejoicing always before him, rejoicing in the habitable parts of the earth, and my delights were with the sons of men.' It is visible that Solomon speaks here of a time soon after the creation of the world, of a time when the earth was inhabited only by a pure, innocent race. Can this be said after the fall, when the earth was cursed? It is only a profound ignorance of the ancient, primitive tradition of preexistence that can make men mistake the true sense of this sublime text.

"Our Saviour seems to approve the doctrine of preexistence in his answer to his disciples when they interrogate him thus about the man born blind: 'Master, who did sin, this man or his parents, that he was born blind?'* It is clear that this question would have been ridiculous and impertinent, if the disciples had not believed that the man born blind had sinned before his corporeal birth, and, consequently, that he had preexisted in another state. Our Saviour's answer is remarkable: 'Neither hath this man sinned, nor his parents; but that the works of God should be made manifest in him.' Jesus Christ could not mean that neither this man nor his parents had ever sinned, for this can be said of no mortal; but the meaning is, that it was neither for the sins committed by this man in a state of preexistence, nor for those of his parents, that he was born blind, but in order to manifest one day the power of God. Our Lord, therefore, far from blaming and redressing this error in his disciples, answers in a way that seems to confirm them in the doctrine of preexistence. If he had looked upon this opinion as a capital error, would it have been compatible with his wisdom to pass it over so slightly, and taciturnly authorize it? On the contrary, does not his

* Gospel of John IX. 2.

silence indicate that he looked upon this doctrine, which was a received maxim of the Jewish church, as the true explication of original sin?

"St. Paul says, in speaking of the origin of mortal and physical evil, 4 By one man sin entered into the world, and death by sin; and death passed upon all men, for that all have sinned."* If all have sinned, then all have voluntarily cooperated with Adam in the breach of the eternal law: for where there is no deliberate act of will, there can be no sin. The Apostle does not say that Adam's sin was imputed to all. The doctrine of imputation, by which God attributes Adam's sin to his innocent posterity, cannot be the meaning of St. Paul, for, besides that this doctrine is incompatible with the divine perfection, the Apostle adds: 'For as by one man's disobe dience many were made sinners, so by the obedience of one shall all be made righteous.'† Now it is certain that men can only be made righteous by their personal, deliberate, and voluntary cooperation with the spirit of grace, or the second Adam. The Apostle assures us in the same passage that 'all did not sin after the similitude of Adam's transgression.' This sin was really committed in a preexistent state by the individuals of the present human race. The meaning is that one pair gave the bad example, and all the human race coexistent with them in Paradise soon imitated this crime of disobedience against the eternal law, by the false love of natural knowledge and sensible pleasure. St. Paul seems to confirm this when he says: For the children being not yet born, having neither done good nor evil, it was said unto Eebecca, 'Jacob have I loved, but Esau have I hated.' God's love and hatred depend upon the moral dispositions of the creature. Since God says that he loved Jacob and hated Esau before they were born, and before they had done good or evil in this mortal life, it follows clearly that they must have preexisted in another state. This would have appeared to be the natural sense of the text, if prejudices imbibed from our infancy, more or less, had not blinded the mind of Christian doctors to the same degree as Judaical prejudices darkened those of the ancient Pharisees.

* Romans V. 12.
† Ibid. V. 19.

"If it be said that these texts are obscure; that preexistence is only drawn from them by induction, and that this opinion is not revealed in Scripture by express words, I answer, that the doctrines of the immortality of the soul are nowhere revealed expressly in the sacred oracles of the Old or New Testament, but because all their morals and doctrines are founded upon these great truths. We may say the same of preexistence. The doctrine is nowhere expressly revealed, but it is evidently supposed, as without it original sin becomes not only inexplicable, but absurd, repugnant, and impossible.

"There is nothing: in the fathers nor councils that contradicts this doctrine; yea, while the fifth general council and all the fathers after the sixth century condemn a false idea of preexistence in which the ancient tradition was adulterated by the Origenists and Priscillianists, the true doctrine of preexistence was not condemned by the church. This supposes that all the individuals of the human species composed of soul and body were created in Paradise, that they all cooperated in Adam's disobedience, partook of his crime, and so were justly punished. This was the constant tradition of the Jewish church, and confirmed by the Scriptures. This opinion of preexistence was also very ancient in the Christian church, before the Origenists spoiled it with the Pythagorean and Platonic fictions.

"It is against the impious degradation of transmigration [through animal bodies] that the fathers declaim, and not the true Scripture doctrine of degraded [human] intelligences. This the schoolmen confound with the false disguises — mixtures of the pagans. This great principle is the true key by which we can understand the meaning of several passages of Scripture, and the sense of many sublime articles of faith. Thus only can we shelter Christianity from the railleries of the incredulous."

8. Among Soame Jenyns's "Disquisitions on Several Subjects" is a "Disquisition on a Preexistent State," from which we quote the following:—

"That mankind had existed in some state previous to the present was the opinion of the wisest sages of the most remote antiquity. It was held by the Gymnosophists of Egypt, the Brahmans of India, the Magi of

Persia, and the greatest philosophers of Greece and Rome; it was likewise adopted by the fathers of the Christian Church, and frequently enforced by her primitive writers. Why it has been so little noticed, so much overlooked rather than rejected, by the divines and metaphysicians of later ages, I am at a loss to account for, as it is undoubtedly confirmed by reason, by all the appearances of nature, and the doctrines of revelation.

"In the first place, then, it is confirmed by reason, which teaches us that it is impossible that the conjunction of a male and female can create, or bring into being, an immortal soul: they may prepare a material habitation for it, but there must be an immaterial preexistent inhabitant ready to take possession. Reason assures us that an immortal soul, which will eternally exist after the dissolution of the body, must have eternally existed before the formation of it; for whatever has no end can never have had any beginning, but must exist in some manner which bears no relation to time, to us totally incomprehensible; if, therefore, the soul will continue to exist in a future life, it must have existed in a former. Reason likewise tells us that an omnipotent and benevolent Creator would never have formed such a world as this, and filled it with inhabitants, if the present was the only, or even the first, state of their existence, a state which, if unconnected with the past and the future, seems calculated for no one purpose intelligible to our understandings; neither of good or evil, of happiness or misery, of virtue or vice, of reward or punishment, but a confused jumble of them all together, proceeding from no visible cause and tending to no end. But, as we are certain that infinite power cannot be employed without effect, nor infinite wisdom without design, we may rationally conclude that this world could be designed as nothing more than a prison, in which we are awhile confined to receive punishment for the offenses committed in a former, and an opportunity of preparing ourselves for the enjoyment of happiness in a future, life.

"Secondly, these conclusions of reason are sufficiently confirmed by the force of nature and the appearance of things. This world is evidently formed for a place of punishment as well as probation—a prison, or

house of correction, to which we are committed, some for a longer, and
some for a shorter time; some to the severest labor, others to more indul-
gent tasks; and if we consider it under this character, we shall perceive it
admirably fitted for the end for which it was intended. It is a spacious,
beautiful, and durable structure; it contains many various apartments,
a few very comfortable, many tolerable, and some extremely wretched;
it is inclosed with a fence so impassable that none can surmount it but
with the loss of life. Its inhabitants likewise exactly resemble those of
other prisons: they come in with malignant dispositions and unruly
passions, from whence, like other confined criminals, they receive great
part of their punishment by abusing and injuring each other. As we
may suppose that they have not all been equally guilty, so they are not
all equally miserable; the majority are permitted to procure a tolerable
subsistence by their labor, and pass through their confinement without any extraordinary penalties, except from paying their fees at their
discharge by death. Others, who perhaps stand in need of more severe
chastisement, receive it by a variety of methods, some by the most tedious pains and diseases; some by disappointments, and many by success in their favorite pursuits; some by being condemned to situations
peculiarly unfortunate, as to those of extreme poverty or superabundant
riches, of despicable manners or painful preeminence, of galley-slaves
in a despotic, or ministers in a free, country.

"Lastly, the opinion of preexistence is no less confirmed by revelation
than by reason and the appearance of things; for although, perhaps, it
is nowhere in the New Testament explicitly enforced, yet throughout
the whole tenor of those writings it is everywhere implied. In them
mankind are constantly represented as coming into the world under
a load of guilt — as condemned criminals, the children of wrath, and
objects of divine indignation, placed in it for a time by the mercies of
God, to give them an opportunity of expiating their guilt by sufferings,
and regaining by a pious and virtuous conduct their lost estate of happiness and innocence; this is styled working out their salvation, not
preventing their condemnation, for that is already past, and their only
hope now is redemption, that is, being rescued from a state of captivity

and sin, in which they are universally involved. This is the very essence of the Christian dispensation, and the grand principle in which it differs from the religion of nature; in every other respect they are nearly similar. They both enjoin the same moral duties and prohibit the same vices; but Christianity acquaints us that we are admitted into this life oppressed by guilt and depravity, which we must atone for by suffering its usual calamities, and work off by acts of positive virtue, before we can hope for happiness in another. Now, if by all this a preexistent state is not constantly supposed, in which this guilt was incurred and this depravity contracted, there can be no meaning at all, or such a meaning as contradicts every principle of common sense—that guilt can be contracted without acting, or that we can act without existing. So undeniable is this inference that it renders any positive assertion of a preexistent state totally useless; as, if a man at the moment of his entrance into a new country was declared a criminal, it would surely be unnecessary to assert that he had lived in some other before he came there.

"In all our researches into abstruse subjects there is a certain clue, without which, the further we proceed the more we are bewildered; but which, being fortunately discovered, leads us at once through the whole labyrinth, puts an end to our difficulties, and opens a system perfectly clear, consistent, and intelligible. The doctrine of preexistence, or the acknowledgment of some past state of disobedience, I take to be this very clue; which, if we constantly carry along with us, we shall proceed unembarrassed through all the intricate mysteries both of nature and revelation, and at last arrive at so clear a prospect of the wise and just dispensations of our Creator, as cannot fail to afford complete satisfaction to the most inquisitive skeptic.

"Thus is a preexistent state, I think, clearly demonstrated by the principles of reason, the appearance of things, and the sense of revelation; all which agree that this world is intended for a place of punishment, as well as probation, and must therefore refer to some former period. For as probation implies a future life, for which it is preparatory, so punishment must imply a former state, in which offenses were committed for which it is due; and indeed there is not a single argument drawn from the justice of God, and the seemingly undeserved sufferings of many in the present state, which can be urged in proof of a future life, which proves not with superior force the existence of another which is already past."

9. One of the chapters in Joseph Glanvil's "Lux Orientalis," a treatise attempting to demonstrate the truth of Platonic preexistence, and strengthened by the elaborate annotations of Dr. Henry More, is an extension of the following —

"Seven Pillars on which the Hypothesis of Preexistence stands.

"1. All the divine designs and actions are carried on by pure and infinite goodness.

"2. There is an exact geometrical justice that runs through the universe, and is interwoven in the contexture of things.

"3. Things are carried to their proper place and state by the congruity of their natures; where this fails we may suppose some arbitrary management.

"4. The souls of men are capable of living in other bodies besides terrestrial; and never act but in some body or other.

"5. The soul in every state has such a body as is fittest to those faculties and operations that it is most inclined to exercise.

"6. The powers and faculties of the soul are either spiritual or intellectual, or sensitive or plastic.

"7. By the same degrees that the higher powers are invigorated, the lower are abated, as to their proper exercise."

10. In Dowden's "Life of Shelley" (vol. I. p. 80), the following anecdote of the poet is quoted from his friend Hogg: "One morning we had been reading Plato together so diligently that the usual hour of exercise passed away unperceived. We sallied forth hastily to take the air for half an hour before dinner. In the middle of Magdalen Bridge we met a woman with a child in her arms. Shelley was more attentive at that instant to our conduct in a life that was past or to come than to a decorous regulation of his behavior according to the established usages of society. With abrupt dexterity he caught hold of the child. The mother, who well might fear that it was about to be thrown over the parapet

of the bridge into the sedgy waters below, held it fast by its long train. 'Will your baby tell us anything about preexistence, madam?' he asked in a piercing voice and with a wistful look. The mother made no answer, but perceiving that Shelley's object was not murderous, but altogether harmless, she dismissed her apprehension and relaxed her hold. 'Will your baby tell us anything about preexistence, madam?' he repeated, with unabated earnestness. 'He cannot speak, sir,' said the mother seriously. 'Worse, worse,' cried Shelley with an air of disappointment, shaking his long hair most pathetically about his young face. 'But surely the babe can speak if he will, for he is only a few weeks old. He may fancy that he cannot, but it is only a silly whim. He cannot have forgotten the use of speech in so short a time. The thing is absolutely impossible.' 'It is not for me to dispute with you, gentlemen,' the woman meekly replied, 'but I can safely declare I never heard him speak, nor any child of his age.' It was a fine placid boy. So far from being disturbed by the interruption, he looked up and smiled. Shelley pressed his fat cheeks with his fingers. We commended his healthy appearance and his equanimity, and the mother was allowed to proceed, probably to her satisfaction, for she would doubtless prefer a less speculative nurse. Shelley sighed as we walked on. 'How provokingly close are these newborn babes!' he ejaculated; 'but it is not the less certain, notwithstanding the cunning attempts to conceal the truth, that all knowledge is reminiscence. The doctrine is far more ancient than the times of Plato, and as old as the venerable allegory that the muses are the daughters of memory; not one of the muses was ever said to be the child of invention.'"

11. Hume's skeptical essay on "The Immortality of the Soul" argues thus:—

"Reasoning from the common course of nature, and without supposing any new interposition of the supreme cause, which ought always to be excluded from philosophy, what is incorruptible must also be ungenerable. The soul, therefore, if immortal, existed before our birth, and if the former existence noways concerns us, neither will the latter...

"The metempsychosis is, therefore, the only system of this kind that philosophy can hearken to."

12. Southey says in his published "Letters": "I have a strong and lively faith in a state of continued consciousness from this stage of existence, and that we shall recover the consciousness of some lower stages through which we may previously have passed seems to me not impossible...

"The system of progressive existence seems, of all others, the most benevolent; and all that we do understand is so wise and so good, and all we do or do not, so perfectly and overwhelmingly wonderful, that the most benevolent system is the most probable."

13. From a letter written by that curious genius William Blake (the artist) to his friend John Flaxman (the sculptor):*—

"In my brain are studies and chambers filled with books and pictures of old which I wrote and painted in ages of eternity before my mortal life; and these works are the delight and study of archangels.

"You, O dear Flaxman, are a sublime archangel, my friend and companion from eternity. I look back into the regions of reminiscence and behold our ancient days before this earth appeared and its vegetative mortality to my mortal vegetated eyes. I see our houses of eternity which can never be separated, though our mortal vehicles should stand at the remotest corners of heaven from each other."

14. In the "Fortnightly Review" for September, 1878, Professor William Knight writes:—

"It seems surprising that in the discussions of contemporary philosophy on the origin and destiny of the soul there has been no explicit revival of the doctrines of Preexistence and Metempsychosis. Whatever may be their intrinsic worth or evidential value, their title to rank on the roll of philosophical hypotheses is undoubted. They offer quite as remarkable a solution of the mystery which all admit as the rival theories of Creation, Traduction, and Extinction.

"If we reject the doctrine of Preexistence, we must either believe in non-existence or fall back in one or other of the two opposing theories of Creation and Traduction; and as we reject Extinction, we may find Preexistence has fewer difficulties to face than the rival hypotheses. Creation is the theory that every moment of time multitudes of souls

* See Scoones's *English Letters*, p. 361.

are simultaneously born—not sent down from a celestial source, but freshly made out of nothing and placed in bodies prepared for them by natural growth. To the Platonist the theory of Traduction seemed even worse, as it implied the derivation of the soul from at least two sources—from both parents—and a substance thus derived was apparently composite and quasi-material.

"Stripped of all extravagance and expressed in the modest terms of probability, the theory has immense speculative interest and great ethical value. It is much to have the puzzle of the origin of evil thrown back for an indefinite number of cycles of lives; to have a workable explanation of *Nemesis*, and of what we are accustomed to call the moral tragedies and the untoward birth of a multitude of men and women. It is much also to have the doctrine of immortality lightened of its difficulties; to have our immediate outlook relieved by the doctrine that in the soul's eternity its preexistence and its future existence are one. The retrospect may assuredly help the prospect."

"Whether we make use of it or not, we ought to realize its alternatives. They are these. Either all life is extinguished and resolved through an absorption and reassumption of the vital principle everywhere, or a perpetual miracle goes on in the incessant and rapid increase in the amount of spiritual existence within the universe; and while human life survives, the intelligence and the affection of the lower animals perish everlastingly."

15. Professor W. A. Butler's celebrated lectures upon "The History of Ancient Philosophy" lean strongly toward an endorsement of Plato's philosophy of reincarnation:—

"It must be allowed that there is much in the hypothesis of preexistence (at least) which might attract a speculator busied with the endeavor to reduce the moral system of the world under intelligible laws. The solution which it at once furnishes of the state and fortunes of each individual, as arising in some unknown but direct process from his own voluntary acts, though it throws, of course, no light on the ultimate question of the existence of moral evil (which it only removes a single step), does yet contribute to satisfy the mind as to the equity of that immediate manifestation of it, and of its physical attendants, which we unhappily witness. There is internally no greater improbability that the present may be the result of a former state now almost wholly forgotten, than that the present should be followed by a future form of existence in which, perhaps, or in some departments of which, the oblivion may be as complete. And if to that future state there are already discernible faint longings and impulses which to many men have seemed to involve a direct proof of its reality, hopes that will not be bounded by the grave, and desires that grasp eternity, others have found within them, it would seem, faint intimations scarcely less impressive of the past, as if the soul vibrated the echoes of a harmony not of this world. Wordsworth has told us that such convictions seem to be a part, though a neglected part, of the heritage of our race."

16. The novelist Bulwer thus expresses his opinion of this truth: "Eternity may be but an endless series of those migrations which men call deaths, abandonments of home after home, even to fairer scenes and loftier heights. Age after age the spirit may shift its tent, fated not to rest in the dull Elysium of the heathen, but carrying with it evermore its two elements, activity and desire."*

17. Pezzani, the author of "The Plurality of the Soul's Lives,"† writes: "The earthly sojourn is only a new probation, as was said by Dupont de Nemours, that great writer who, in the eighteenth century, outstripped all modern thought. Now, if this be so, is it not plain that the recollection of former lives would seriously hinder probations, by removing most of their difficulties, and consequently of their deserts, as well as of their spontaneity? We live in a world where freewill is all-powerful, the inviolable law of advancement and progress among men. If past lives were remembered, the soul would know the significance and import of the trials which are reserved for it here below: indolent and careless, it would harden itself against the purposes of Providence, and become paralyzed by the hopelessness of mastering them, or even, if of a better quality and more manly, it would accept and work them out with-

* Other extracts from Bulwer appear on page 37.
† Paris, 1865, third edition, p. 405.

out fail. Well, neither of these suppositions is necessary; the struggle must be free, voluntary, safe from the influences of the past; the field of combat must seem new, so that the athlete may exhibit and practice his virtues upon it. The experience he has already acquired, the forces he has learned how to conquer, serve him in the new strife; but in such a manner that he does not suspect it, for the imperfect soul undergoes reincarnations in order to develop the qualities that it has already manifested, to free itself from the vices and faults which are in opposition to the ascensional law. What would happen if all men remembered their former lives? The order of the earth would be overthrown; at least, it is not now established on such conditions. Lethe, as well as freewill, is a law of the actual world."

18. One of Emerson's earliest essays ("The Method of Nature") contains this paragraph: "We cannot describe the natural history of the soul, but we know that it is divine. I cannot tell if these wonderful qualities which house today in this mortal frame shall ever reassemble in equal activity in a similar frame, or whether they have before had a natural history like that of this body you see before you; but this one thing I know, that these qualities did not now begin to exist, cannot be sick with my sickness nor buried in my grave; but that they circulate through the universe: before the world was, they were. Nothing can bar them out, or shut them in, but they penetrate the ocean and land, space and time, form and essence, and hold the key to universal nature."

19. James Freeman Clarke writes (in "Ten Great Religions," II. 190): "That man has come up to his present state of development by passing through lower forms is the popular doctrine of science today. What is called evolution teaches that we have reached our present state by a very long and gradual ascent from the lowest animal organizations. It is true that the Darwinian theory takes no notice of the evolution of the soul, but only of the body. But it appears to me that a combination of the two views would remove many difficulties which still attach to the theory of natural selection and the survival of the fittest. If we are to believe in evolution, let us have the assistance of the soul itself in this development of new species. Thus science and philosophy will cooper-

ate, nor will poetry hesitate to lend her aid."

20. The noblest work of modern times, and probably of all time, upon immortality, is a large volume by the Rev. William R. Alger, entitled "A Critical History of the Doctrine of a Future Life." It was published in 1860, and still remains the standard authority upon that topic throughout Christendom. This book is substantially indebted to it. The author is a Unitarian minister, who devoted half his lifetime to the work, undermining his health thereby. In the first edition (1860) the writer characterizes reincarnation as a plausible delusion, unworthy of credence. For fifteen years more he continued studying the subject, and the last edition (1878) gives the final result of his ripest investigations in heartily endorsing and advocating reincarnation. No more striking argument for the doctrine could be advanced than this fact. That a Christian clergyman, making the problem of the soul's destiny his life's study, should become so overpowered by the force of this pagan idea as to adopt it for the climax of his scholarship is extremely significant. And the result is reached by such a sincere course of reasoning that the seminaries in all denominations are compelled to accept his book as the masterpiece. From one of the supplemental chapters we quote the following by his permission:—

"Besides the various distinctive arguments of its own, every reason for the resurrection holds with at least equal force for transmigration. The argument from analogy is especially strong. It is natural to argue from the universal spectacle of incarnated life that this is the eternal scheme everywhere, the variety of souls finding in the variety of worlds an everlasting series of adventures in appropriate organisms; there being, as Paul said, one kind of flesh of birds, another of beasts, another of men, another of angels, and so on. Our present lack of recollection of past lives is no disproof of their actuality. Every night we lose all knowledge of the past, but every day we reawaken to a memory of the whole series of days and nights. So in one life we may forget or dream, and in another recover the whole thread of experience from the beginning.

"In every event, it must be confessed that of all the thoughtful and refined forms of the belief in a future life none has had so extensive and prolonged a prevalence as this. It has the vote of the majority, having for ages on ages been held by half the human race with an intensity of conviction almost without a parallel. Indeed, the most striking fact about the doctrine of the repeated incarnations of the soul, its form and experience in each successive embodiment being determined by its merits and demerits in the preceding ones, is the constant reappearance of that faith in all parts of the world, and its permanent hold on certain great nations.

"Another striking fact connected with this doctrine is that it seems to be a native and ineradicable growth of the oriental world, but appears in the western world only in scattered instances, and rather as an exotic form of thought. In the growing freedom and liberality of thought, which, no less than its doubt and denial, now characterize Christendom, it seems as if the full time had come for a greater mental and aesthetic hospitality on the part of Christians towards Hindus. The advocates of the resurrection should not confine their attention to the repellent or the ludicrous aspects of metempsychosis, but do justice to its claim and its charm."

After reviewing and strengthening the evidences in favor of plural births, Mr. Alger continues: "The above translation of the ecclesiastical doctrine of the resurrection into a form scientifically credible, and reconciled with the immemorial tenet of transmigration, may seem to some a fanciful speculation, a mere intellectual toy. Perhaps it is so. It is not propounded with the slightest dogmatic animus. It is advanced solely as an illustration of what may possibly be true, as suggested by the general evidence of the phenomena of history and the facts of experience. The thoughts embodied in it are so wonderful, the method of it so rational, the region of contemplation into which it lifts the mind is so grand, the prospects it opens are of such universal reach and import, that the study of it brings us into full sympathy with the sublime scope of the idea of immortality, and of a cosmopolitan vindication of Providence uncovered to every eye. It takes us out of the littleness of petty themes and selfish affairs, and makes it easier for us to believe in the vastest hopes mankind have ever known. It causes the most magnificent conceptions of human destiny to seem simply proportional to the native magnitude and beauty of the powers of the mind which can conceive such things. After traversing the grounds here set forth, we feel that if the view based on them be not the truth, it must be because God has in reserve for us a sequel greater and lovelier, not meaner, than our brightest dream hitherto."

21. In the "Princeton Review" for May, 1881, Professor Francis Bowen (of Harvard University) publishes a very interesting article on "Christian Metempsychosis," in which he urges the Christian acceptance of reincarnation. By his consent we quote a large portion of it, because it is so able an appeal for the adoption of this truth, from both a metaphysical and a Christian standpoint:—

"Our life upon earth is rightly held to be a discipline and a preparation for a higher and eternal life hereafter. But if limited to the duration of a single mortal body, it is so brief as to seem hardly sufficient for so grand a purpose. Threescore years and ten must surely be an inadequate preparation for eternity. But what assurance have we that the probation of the soul is confined within so narrow limits? Why may it not be continued, or repeated, through a long series of successive generations, the same personality animating one after another an indefinite number of tenements of flesh, and carrying forward into each the training it has received, the character it has formed, the temper and dispositions it has indulged, in the stage of existence immediately preceding? It need not remember its past history, even while bearing the fruits and the consequences of that history deeply ingrained into its present nature. How many long passages of any one life are now completely lost to memory, though they may have contributed largely to build up the heart and the intellect which distinguish one man from another! Our responsibility surely is not lessened by such forgetfulness. We are still accountable for the misuse of time, though we have forgotten how or on what we wasted it. We are even now reaping the bitter fruits, through enfeebled health and vitiated desires and capacities, of many forgotten acts of self-indulgence, willfulness, and sin—forgotten just because they were so numerous. Then a future life even in another frail body upon this earth may well be a state of just and fearful retribution.

"Why should it be thought incredible that the same soul should inhabit in succession an indefinite number of mortal bodies, and thus prolong its experience and its probation till it has become in every sense ripe for heaven or the final judgment? Even during this one life our bodies are perpetually changing, though by a process of decay and restoration which is so gradual that it escapes our notice. Every human being thus dwells successively in many bodies, even during one short life. This physiological fact seems to have been known by Plato, as in a well-known passage of the Phsedo, a clear statement of it is put into the mouth of Cebes, who argues, however, that this fact affords no sufficient proof of the immortality of the soul. 'You may say with reason,' Cebes is made to argue, 'that the soul is lasting, and the body weak and short-lived in comparison. And every soul may be said to wear out many bodies, especially in the course of a long life. For if, while the man is alive, the body deliquesces and decays, and yet the soul always weaves her garment anew and repairs the waste, then of course, when the soul perishes, she must have on her last garment, and this only will survive her; but then, again, when the soul is dead, the body will at last show its native weakness and soon pass into decay.' And again: 'Suppose we admit also that, after death, the souls of some are existing still, and will exist, and will be born and die again and again, and that there is a natural strength in the soul which will hold out and be born many times—for all this, we may still be inclined to think that she will be weary In the labor of successive births, and may at last succumb in one of her deaths and utterly perish.*

"If every birth were an act of absolute creation, the introduction to life of an entirely new creature, we might reasonably ask why different souls are so variously constituted at the outset. We do not all start fair in the race that is set before us, and therefore all cannot be expected, at the close of one brief mortal pilgrimage, to reach the same goal, and to be equally well fitted for the blessings or the penalties of a fixed state hereafter. The commonest observation assures us that one child is born

* *Jowett's translation*, Am. ed. vol. I. p. 416.

with limited capacities and perhaps a wayward disposition, strong passions, and a sullen temper; that he has tendencies to evil which are almost sure to be soon developed. Another, on the contrary, seems happily endowed from the start; he is not only amiable, tractable, and kind, but quick-witted and precocious, a child of many hopes. The one seems a perverse goblin, while the other has the early promise of a Cowley or a Pascal. The differences of external condition also are so vast and obvious that they seem to detract much from the merit of a well-spent life and from the guilt of vice and crime. One is so happily nurtured in a Christian home, and under so many protecting influences, that the path of virtue lies straight and open before him — so plain, indeed, that even the blind could safely walk therein; while another seems born to a heritage of misery, exposure, and crime. The birthplace of one is in Central Africa, and of another in the heart of civilized and Christian Europe. Where lingers eternal justice then? How can such frightful inequalities be made to appear consistent with the infinite wisdom and goodness of God?

"If metempsychosis is included in the scheme of the divine government of the world, this difficulty disappears altogether. Considered from this point of view, every one is born into the state which he has fairly earned by his own previous history. He carries with him from one stage of existence to another the habits or tendencies which he has formed, the dispositions which he has indulged, the passions which he has not chastised, but has voluntarily allowed to lead him into vice and crime. No active interference of retributive justice is needed, except in selecting for the place of his new birth a home with appropriate surroundings — perhaps such a home as through his evil passions he has made for others. The doctrine of inherited sin and its consequences is a hard lesson to be learned. We submit with enforced resignation to the stern decree, corroborated as it is by every day's observation of the ordinary course of this world's affairs, that the iniquity of the fathers shall be visited upon the children even to the third and fourth generation. But no one can complain of the dispositions and endowments which he has inherited, so to speak, from himself; that is, from his former self in a previous stage of existence. If, for instance, he has neglected his opportunities and fostered his lower appetites in his childhood, if he was then wayward and self-indulgent, indolent, deceitful, and vicious, it is right and just that, in his manhood and old age, he should experience the bitter consequences of his youthful follies. If he has voluntarily made himself a brute, a brute he must remain. The child is father of the man, who often inherits from him a sad patrimony. There is an awful meaning, if we will but take it to heart, in the solemn announcement of the angel in the apocalyptic vision : 'He that is unjust, let him be unjust still; and he which is filthy, let him be filthy still; and he that is righteous, let him be righteous still; and he that is holy, let him be holy still!' And it matters not, so far as the justice of the sentence is concerned, whether the former self, from whom we receive this heritage, was the child who, not many years ago, bore the same name with our present self, or one who bore a different name, who was born in another age and perhaps another hemisphere, and of whose sad history we have not now the faintest remembrance. We know that our personal identity actually extends farther back, and links together more passages of our life, than what is now present to consciousness; though it is true that we have no direct evidence of this continuity and sameness of being beyond what is attested by memory. But we may have indirect evidence of it from the testimony of others in the case of our own infancy, or from revelation, or through reasoning from analogy and from the similarity of cases and characters. The soul, said the Hindus, is in the body like a bird in a cage, or like a pilot who steers a ship, and seeks a new vessel when the old one is worn out.

"Nothing prevents us, however, from believing that the probation of any one soul extends continuously through a long series of successive existences upon earth, each successive act in the whole life-history being retributive for what went before. For this is the universal law of being, whether of matter or mind; everything changes, nothing dies in the sense of being annihilated. What we call death is only the resolution of a complex body into its constituent parts, nothing that is truly one and indivisible being lost or destroyed in the process. In combustion or any other rapid chemical change, according to the admission of the materialists themselves, not an atom of matter is ever generated or ever ceases to be; it only escapes from one combination to enter upon another. Then the human soul, which, as we know from consciousness, is absolutely one and indivisible, only passes on after the dissolution of what was once its home to animate another body. In this sense we can easily accept the doctrine of the resurrection of the body. Our future life is not, at any rate not while the present administration of this world's affairs continues, to be some inconceivable form of merely spiritual being. It will be clothed again with a body, which may or may not be in part the same with the one which it has just left. Leibnitz held that the soul is never entirely divorced from matter, but carries on some portion of what was its earthly covering into a subsequent stage of existence... We can easily imagine and believe that every person now living is a representation of someone who lived perhaps centuries ago under another name, in another country, it may be not with the same line of ancestry, and yet one and the same with him in his inmost being and essential character. His surroundings are changed; the old house of flesh has been torn down and rebuilt; but the tenant is still the same. He has come down from some former generation, bringing with him what may be either a help or a hindrance; namely, the character and tendencies which he there formed and nurtured. And herein is retribution; he has entered upon a new stage of probation, and in it he has now to learn what the character which he there formed naturally leads to when tried upon a new and perhaps broader theatre. If this be not so, tell me why men are born with characters so unlike and with tendencies so depraved. In a sense far more literal than was intended by the poet, it may be true of every country churchyard, that

'Some mute inglorious Milton there may rest,
Some Cromwell guiltless of his country's blood.'

"They bring with them no recollection of the incidents of their former life, as such memory would unfit them for the new part which they have to play. But they are still the same in the principles and modes of conduct, in the inmost springs of action, which the forgotten incidents of their former life have developed and strengthened. They are the same in all the essential points which made them formerly a blessing or a curse to all with whom they came immediately in contact, and through which they will again become sources of weal or woe to their environment. Of course, these inborn tendencies may be either exaggerated or chastised by the lessons of a new experience, by the exercise of reflection, and by habitually heeding or neglecting the monitions of conscience. But they still exist as original tendencies, and as such they must make either the upward or the downward path more easy, more natural, and more likely to reach a goal so remote that it would otherwise be unattainable.

"To make this more clear, let me refer to the pregnant distinction so admirably illustrated by Kant between what he calls the Intelligible Character and the Empirical or acquired Character. The former is the primitive foundation on which the latter, which directly determines our conduct for the time being, is built. To a great extent, though not entirely, we are what we are through the influence of what have been our surroundings — through our education, our companions, our habits, and our associations. But these influences must have had a primitive basis to work upon, and can only modify the operation of the native germs, not change their nature; and they will modify these more or less profoundly according as they are more or less amenable to outside influences and manifest more or less decidedly a bias in one direction or another. What the future plant will be depends much more on the specific nature of the seed which is sown than on the fertility or barrenness of the soil into which it is cast. The latter only determine whether it shall be a vigorous plant or a weak one, whether in fact it shall grow at all or only rot in the ground; but they do not determine the specific direction of its development, whether it shall be an oak, a willow, or an ivy-bush. The Empirical or acquired Character, as it is open to observation, is a phenomenon; it is what the man *appears* to be, or what he has become under the shaping influence of the circumstances to which he has been exposed. But the Intelligible Character, the inmost kernel of his real being, is a noumenon, and escapes external observation; we can judge of its nature only indirectly from its effects; that is to say, from the conduct which it has cooperated to produce. A change taking place in any substance must be the joint result of two factors; namely, its proper cause operating upon it from without, and the thing's own nature or internal constitution. Thus the same degree of heat acts very differently upon different substances, say, on wax, iron, water, clay, or powder. In like manner, a given motive, say, the desire of wealth, when acting on different persons, though with the same strength or intensity, may lead to very dissimilar results; it makes one man a thief and another a miser, renders one envious and another energetic and industrious. If frequently indulged, it forms a fixed habit, and thus becomes an element in the acquired or empirical character.

"Now Kant, with the bias of a necessitarian, places our freedom and our responsibility in the realm of noumena, attributing them exclusively to our Intelligible Character. As to the acquired character when once formed, he says we *must* act in accordance with it, and therefore we are not accountable for the particular act to which it led, since that we could not help. After I have once formed a habit of lying or stealing, should an opportunity and temptation recur, I *must* repeat the offense. But our inborn character, which expresses what we really are, as a noumenon, lies outside of time, space, and causality, and therefore cannot be led astray by temptation or external circumstances, but is entirely free. Herein solely consists our merit or our guilt. Hence Kant would make us responsible not for the particular crime, which we could not help committing, but for being such a person as to be capable of that crime. We are accountable not for what we do, but for what we are. We are to be punished not for stealing this horse, but for being a rogue, or thief in grain, for being naturally inclined to stealing...

"I know not how it may seem to others, but to me there is something inexpressibly consolatory and inspiring in the thought that the great and good of other days have not finally accomplished their earthly career, have not left us desolate, but that they are still with us, in the flesh, though we know them not, and though in one sense they do not really know themselves, because they have no remembrance of a former life in which they were trained for the work which they are now doing. But they are essentially the same beings, for they have the same intellect and character as before, and sameness in these two respects is all that constitutes our notion of personal identity. We are unwilling to believe that their beneficent activity was limited to one short life on earth, at the close of which there opened to them an eternity without change, without farther trial or action, and seemingly having no other purpose than unlimited enjoyment. Such a conception of immortality is exposed to Schopenhauer's sarcasm, that if effort and progress are possible only in the present life, and no want or suffering can be endured except as the penalties of sin, there remains for heaven only the weariness of nothing to do. An eternity either of reward or punishment would seem to be inadequately earned by one brief period of probation. It is far more reasonable to believe that the future life which we are taught to expect will be similar to the present one, and will be spent in this world, though we shall carry forward to it the burden or the blessing entailed upon us by our past career. Besides the spiritual meaning of the doctrine of regeneration, besides the new birth which is 'of water and of the Spirit,' there may be a literal meaning in the solemn words of the Saviour, 'Except a man be born again, he cannot see the kingdom of God.'...

"I should be sorry to believe that that remarkable group of excellent scholars, thinkers, and divines, the Port-Koyalists, who upheld the cause of Jansenism for three quarters of a century, have finally passed away from earth. On the contrary, if anywhere in these later times the model of a Christian scholar and historian could be found, we might well say that the spirit of Tillemont lives again in him. If we could find one who united in himself all the best qualities of a Christian teacher, stainless in heart and life, we might well believe that it was Lancelot in another earthly form. For either Pascal or Arnauld, it must be admitted that we should not know where to look; if their spirits are yet in this world, they must be in the obscurity of some lowly station.*

"All this speculation, I repeat, is completely fanciful, and can serve no other purpose than to show, even if the doctrine of metempsychosis were true, that we should not be able to identify one person in any two of his successive appearances upon earth. We surely could not know of him in this respect any more than he knows of himself; and, as already said, the total break in memory at the beginning of every successive life must prevent the newly born from recognizing the oneness of his own being with any former existence in an earthly shape.

"Curiously enough this want of self-knowledge is confessed in the only case in which we have a direct assertion in Scripture (if language is to be interpreted in its ordinary literal meaning and not strained into a figurative sense), that one of the heroes of the olden time had reappeared upon earth under a new name, as the forerunner of a new dispensation. At the time of the Saviour there appears to have been a general expectation among the Jews that the coming of the Messiah was to be heralded by the reappearance upon earth of the prophet Elijah, this expectation being founded upon the text in Malachi: 'Behold, I will send you Elijah the prophet before the coining of the great and dreadful day of the Lord.'

Early in the public ministry of John the Baptist, we read that the belief prevailed among his hearers that this prophecy was fulfilled in him. But when directly asked, 'Art thou Elias?' he replied, 'I am not. Art thou that prophet? And he answered, No.' He had no memory of his former life under that name; and though he must have been aware of the popular belief upon the subject, and of the many points of similarity between his own career and that of the great restorer of the worship of the true God at an earlier period, he was too honest to claim an authority which he did not positively know to belong to him.

"Yet we learn that our Lord subsequently twice declared, in very distinct language, that Elijah and John the Baptist were really one and the same person. Once, while John was still alive but in prison, Jesus told the multitude who thronged around him, 'Among them that are born

* See Matthew Arnold's poem upon his father, Dr. Arnold, page 168.

of women there hath not risen a greater than John the Baptist;' and he directly goes on to assert, 'If ye will receive it, this is *Elias*, which was for to come.' (Matt. XI. 14.) And again, after John was beheaded, Jesus said to his disciples, 'Elias is come already and they knew him not, but have done unto him whatsoever they listed.' 'Then the disciples under-stood that he spake unto them of John the Baptist.' (Matt. XVII. 12, 13.) Still again, in the scene on the mount of Transfiguration: 'Behold there talked with him two men, which were Moses and Elias;' and it is said of the three disciples who were then in company with Jesus that, 'When they were awake, they saw his glory and the two men that stood with him.' (Luke IX. 30, 32.) That the commentators have not been willing to receive, in their obvious and literal meaning, assertions so di-rect and so frequently repeated as these, but have attempted to explain them away in a non-natural and metaphorical sense, is a fact which proves nothing but the existence of an invincible prejudice against the doctrine of the transmigration of souls...

"Assuming the doctrine to be well founded, it is for every person to determine with what character he will leave the world at the close of one stage of his earthly being, believing that with this same character thus trained for weal or woe he is inevitably at once to begin a new life, and thus either to rise or fall farther than ever. It seems to me that the dogma of a future life, so prolonged through a countless succession of other lives on earth until it becomes an immortality, is thus brought home to one with a force, a vividness and certainty, of which in no other form it is susceptible. It has been said that no prudent man, if the election were offered to him, would choose to live his present live over again; and as he whom the world calls *prudent* does not usually cherish any lofty aspirations, the saying is probably true. We are all so conscious of the many errors and sins that we have committed that the retrospect is a saddening one; and worldly wisdom would probably whisper, 'It is best to stop here, and not try such a career over again.' But every one would ardently desire a renewal of his earthly experience if assured that he could enter upon it under better auspices, if he believed that what we call death is not the end of all things even here below, but that the

soul is then standing upon the threshold of a new stage of earthly existence, which is to be brighter or darker than the one it is just quitting,
according as there is carried forward into it a higher or lower purpose...

"This doctrine also suggests, as it seems to me, a clearer and more
satisfactory explanation than would otherwise be possible of the fall of
man through disobedience and its consequences, as narrated in Genesis
and interpreted by St. Paul. Certainly the primeval man, the Adam of
each one of us, when he first through the inspiration of Deity 'became
a living soul,' was born into a paradise, an Eden, of entire purity and
innocence, and in that state he talked directly with God. There was also
given to him through his conscience the revelation of a divine law, an
absolute command, to preserve this blessed state through restraining his
appetites and lower impulses to action, and making the love of holiness
superior even to the love of knowledge. But man was tempted by his
appetites to transgress this law; he aspired after a knowledge of good
and evil, which can be attained only through experience of evil, and he
thereby fell from innocence into a state of sin, which necessarily corrupted his whole future being. The habit of disobedience once formed,
sin in the same person has a self-continuing and self-multiplying power.
The stain carried down from a former life becomes darker and more
inveterate in the life that follows. We have no reason to complain of the
corruption of human nature, for the world is what we have made it to
be by our own act. The burden has not been transmitted to us by others,
but has been inherited from ourselves; that is, from our former selves.
Redemption from it by man's own effort thus became impossible. This
is death, moral death, the only death of which a human soul is capable.

"Thus far we have considered metempsychosis as a means of retribution; that is, of awarding to each soul in the next future life upon
which it is entering that compensation either of weal or woe which it
has earned for itself—has in fact necessarily entailed upon itself by its
conduct in the life which it has just completed. But the transmigration
of souls may be regarded also in another light, as that portion of the
divine government of this world's affairs which maintains distributive
justice, since, through its agency, in the long run, all inequalities of con-

dition and favoring or unfavoring circumstances may be compensated, and each person may have his or her equitable share of opportunities for good and of the requisite means for discipline and improvement. If our view be confined within the limits of a single earthly life, it must be confessed that the inequality is glaring enough, so that it seems to justify the honest doubts of the trembling inquirer, while it has offered a broad mark for the scoffs and declamation of the confirmed unbeliever.

"This hypothesis—and I do not claim for it any other character than that of a highly probable and consolatory hypothesis—also throws a new and welcome light upon the deep and dark problem of the origin of evil. In the first place, according to the views which have now been taken, the sufferings which are the immediate consequence and punishment of sin are properly left out of the account, since these evince the goodness of God no less than the happiness resulting from virtue, the purpose in both cases being to advance man's highest interests by the improvement of his moral character; just as the affectionate parent rewards the obedience and punishes the faults of his child, love equally constraining him to adopt either course. And how many of the evils borne both by individuals and by communities are attributable directly to their own misconduct, to their willful disregard of the monitions of conscience! The body which is now languid from inaction through sloth, and enfeebled or racked by disease, might have been active, vigorous, and sound, prompt to second every wish of its owner, and ministering to his enjoyment through every sense and limb. And could we know all, could we extend our vision over the whole history of our former self, how would our estimate of this purely retributive character of our present suffering be enlarged and confirmed! It would then be evident that no portion of it is gratuitous or purposeless. And the community which is now torn with civil dissension, desolated by war, or prostrated in an unequal strife with its rivals, might have been peaceful, affluent, and flourishing, if rulers and ruled had heeded the stern calls of duty, instead of blindly following their own tumultuous passions. And as nations, too, have a continuous life, like that of a river, through a constant change of their constituent parts, many of their woes are clearly attributable to the misdeeds of their former selves. Once admit the great truth that virtue, not happiness, is man's highest interest, and most of the pains of this life indicate the goodness and justice of God quite as much as its pleasures.

"But according to the theory which we are now considering, a still larger deduction must be made from the amount of apparent evil at any one time visible in the world. All the inequalities in the lot of mankind, which have prompted what are perhaps the bitterest of all complaints, and have served skeptics like Hume and J. S. Mill as a reason for the darkest imputations upon divine justice in the government of the world, disappear from the picture altogether. Excepting only what we have just considered, the retributive consequences of more or less sin, there are no inequalities. All start from the same point, and journey through the same vicissitudes of existence, exhausting sooner or later all varieties of condition. Prince and peasant, bond and free, barbarian and cultured, all share alike whatever weal or woe there is in the world, because all must at some future time change places with each other. But after these two large deductions from the amount complained of, what remains? Very little, certainly, which we cannot even now see through; that is, which we cannot assign an adequate reason for; and to the eye of faith nothing remains. The world becomes a mirror which reflects without blot or shadow the infinite goodness of its Creator and Governor. Death remains; but that is no evil, for what we call death is only the introduction to another life on earth, and if this be not a higher and better life than the one just ended, it is our own fault. Our life is really continuous, and the fact that the subsequent stages of it lie beyond our present range of immediate vision is of no more importance, and no more an evil, than the corresponding fact that we do not now remember our previous existence in antecedent ages. Death alone, or in itself considered, apart from the antecedent dread of it which is irrational, and apart from the injury to the feelings of the survivors, which is a necessary consequence of that attachment to each other from which so much of our happiness springs, is not even an apparent evil; it is mere change and development, like the passage from the embryonic to the adult condition, from the blossom to the fruit."

22. In "Ways of the Spirit, and other Essays," by Professor Frederick Henry Hedge, the twelfth chapter, upon "The Human Soul," strongly advocates reincarnation. By the publishers' consent we reprint the pages referring to it:—

"We reach back with our recollection and find no beginning of existence. Who of us knows anything except by report of the first two years of earthly life? No one remembers the time when he first said 'I,' or thought 'I.' We began to exist for others before we began to exist for ourselves. Our experience is not coextensive with our being, and memory does not comprehend it. We bear not the root, but the root bears us.

"What is the root? We call it soul. *Our* soul, we call it; properly speaking, it is not ours, but we are its. It is not a part of us, but we are a part of it. It is not one article in an inventory of articles which together make up our individuality, but the root of that individuality. It is larger than we are, and other than we are—that is, than our conscious self. The conscious self does not begin until some time after the birth of the individual. It is not aboriginal, but a product—as it were, the blossoming of an individuality. We may suppose countless souls which never bear this product, which never blossom into self. And the soul which does so blossom exists before that blossom unfolds.

"How long before, it is impossible to say; whether the birth, for example, of a human individual is the soul's beginning to be; whether a new soul is furnished to each new body, or the body given to a preexisting soul. It is a question on which theology throws no light, and which psychology but faintly illustrates. But so far as that faint illustration reaches it favors the supposition of preexistence. That supposition seems best to match the supposed continued existence of the soul hereafter. Whatever had a beginning in time, it should seem must end in time. The eternal destination which faith ascribes to the soul presupposes an eternal origin. On the other hand, if the preexistence of the soul were assured it would carry the assurance of immortality.

"An obvious objection, and one often urged against this hypothesis, is the absence of any recollection of a previous life. If the soul existed before its union with this present organization, why does it never recall any circumstance, scene, or experience of its former state? There have been those who professed to remember a past existence; but without regarding those pretended reminiscences, or regarding them only as illusions, I answer that the previous existence may not have been a conscious existence. In that case there would have been no recorded experience, and consequently nothing to recall. But suppose a conscious existence antecedent to the present, the soul could not preserve the record of a former organization. The new organization with its new entries must necessarily efface the record of the old, for memory depends on the continuity of association. When the thread of that continuity is broken, the knowledge of the past is gone. If, in a state of unconsciousness, one were taken entirely out of his present surroundings; if falling asleep in one set of circumstances, like Christopher Sly in the play, he were to wake in another, were to wake to entirely new conditions; especially if during that sleep his body were to undergo a change—he would lose on waking all knowledge of the former life for want of a connecting link between it and the new. And this, according to the supposition, is precisely what has happened to the soul at birth. The birth into the present was the death of the old—'a sleep and a forgetting.' The soul went to sleep in one body, it woke in a new. The sleep is a gulf of oblivion between the two.

"And a happy thing, if the soul preexisted, it is for us that we remember nothing of its former life. The memory of a past existence would be a drag on the present, engrossing our attention much to the prejudice of this life's interests and claims. The backward-looking soul would dwell in the past instead of the present, and miss the best uses of life.

"But though on the supposition of a former existence the soul would not be likely to preserve the record of that existence, it would nevertheless retain the effect. It would not, on assuming its present conditions, be as though it had never before been. Its past experience would essentially modify it; it would take a character from its former state. If a moral and intellectual being, it would bring into the world of its present destination certain tendencies and dispositions, the growth of a previous life. And thus the moral law and the moral nature of the soul would assert themselves with retributions transcending the limits of a single existence, and reaching on from life to life of the pilgrim soul.

"It is commonly conceded that there are native differences of character in men — different propensities, tempers, not wholly explained by difference of circumstances or education. They show themselves where circumstances and education have been the same; they seem to be innate. These are sometimes ascribed to organization. But organization is not final. That, again, requires to be explained. According to my thinking, it is the soul that makes organization, not organization the soul. The supposition of a previous existence would best explain these differences as something carried over from life to life — the harvest of seed that was sown in other states, and whose fruit remains, although the sowing is remembered no more.

"This was the theory of the most learned and acute of the Christian Fathers (Origen), and though never adopted and sanctioned by the church, has been occasionally revived in later time. Of all the theories respecting the origin of the soul it seems to me the most plausible, and therefore the one most likely to throw light on the question of a life to come."

23. Sir Humphry Davy, in his "Consolations in Travel" (Dialogue IV., The Proteus or Immortality), arguing for the necessity of the continuance of some kind of a body for the human spirit after death, says: —

"The external world is to us nothing but a cluster of sensations, and in looking back to the memory of our being we find one principle which may be called the monad or self, constantly present, intimately associated with a particular class of sensations, which we call our body, or organs. These organs are connected with other sensations, and move, as it were, with them in circles of existence, quitting for a time some trains of sensation to return to others, but the monad is always present. We can fix no beginning to its operations, we can place no limit to them. We sometimes in sleep lose the beginning and end of a dream, and recollect the middle of it, and one dream has no connection with another, and yet we are conscious of an infinite variety of dreams, and there is a strong analogy for believing in an infinity of past existences which must have been connected; and human life may be regarded as a type of infinite and immortal life, and its succession of sleep and dreams as a type of the changes of death and birth to which from its nature it is liable... The whole intellect is a history of change, according to a certain law, and we retain the memory only of those changes which may be useful to us. The child forgets what happened to it in the womb. The recollections of the infant likewise, before two years, are soon lost; yet many of the habits acquired in that age are retained for life. The sentient principle gains thoughts by material instruments, and its sensations change as those instruments change; and in old age the mind, as it were, falls asleep, to awake in a new existence. With its present organization the intellect of man is naturally limited and imperfect, but this depends upon its material machinery, and in a higher organized form it may be imagined to possess infinitely higher powers. It does not, however, appear improbable to me that some of the more refined machinery of thought may adhere, even in another state, to the sentient principle, for though the organs of gross sensation, the nerves and brain, are destroyed by death, yet something of the more ethereal value may be less destructible, and I sometimes imagine that many of those powers which have been called instinctive belong to the more refined clothing of the spirit. Conscience, indeed, seems to have some undefined source, and may bear relations to a former state of being."

Chapter V
The Poetry of Reincarnation in Western Literature

Poets, the first instructors of mankind.—HORACE.

Poets are the truest diviners of nature.—BULWER-LYTTON.

Poets utter great and wise things which they do not themselves understand.
—Plato.

*Poets should be lawgivers; that is, the boldest lyric inspiration should not
chide and insult, but should announce and lead.*—EMERSON.

*We call those poets who are first to mark Through earth's dull mist the com-
ing of the dawn, Who see in twilight's gloom the first pale spark While others
only note that day is gone.*—HOLMES.

> *O brave poets, keep back nothing,*
> *Nor mix falsehood with the whole.*
> *Look up Godward! Speak the truth in*
> *Worthy song from earnest soul!*
> *Hold, in high poetic duty*
> *Truest Truth, the fairest beauty.*
> > MRS. BROWNING.

> *The spirit of the Poets came at morn*
> *To Sinai, summoned by the Lord's command,*
> *Singers and Seers; those born and those unborn*
> *The chosen souls of men, a solemn band.*
> *The noble army ranged, in viewless might*
> *Around that mountain peak which pierces heaven;*

Greater and lesser teachers, sons of light,
Their number was ten thousand score and seven.
Then Allah took a covenant with his own,
Saying, " My wisdom and my word receive.
Speak of me unto men, known or unknown,
Heard or unheard: bid such as will believe."
"Bear witness then," spake Allah, "souls most dear,
I am your Lord, and ye heralds of mine."
Thenceforward through all lands his Poets bear
The message of the mystery divine.

EDWIN ARNOLD.

○ ○ ○ ○ ○ ○ ○ ○

The poets are the seers of the race. Their best work comes from the intuitional heights where they dwell, conveying truths beyond reason, not understood even by themselves, but merely transmitted through them. They are the few tall pines towering above the common forest to an extraordinary exaltation, where they catch the earliest and latest sunbeams which prolong their day far beyond the limits below, and penetrating into the rare upper currents whose whisperings seldom descend to the crowd.

However diverse the forms of their expression, the heart of it is thoroughly harmonious. They are always prophets voicing a divine message received in the mount, and in these modern days they are almost the only prophets we have. Therefore it is not a mere pleasantry to collect their testimony upon an unusual theme. When it is found that, though working independently, they are in deep accord upon reincarnation, the inevitable conclusion is that their common inspiration means something—namely, that their gospel is worth receiving.

It may be objected that these poems are merely dreamy effusions along the same line of lunacy, with no real attachment to the solid foundations upon which all wholesome poetry is based; that they are kinks in the intellects of genius displaying the weakness of men otherwise strong.

But so universal a feeling cannot be disposed of in that way, especially when it is found to contribute to the solution of life's mystery. All the poets believe in immortality, though unaided reason and observation cannot demonstrate it. Some inexperienced people deride the fact that nearly all poetry centres upon the theme of Love—the most illogical and airy of sentiments. But the deepest sense of the world is nourished by the certainty of these "vague" truths. So the presence of reincarnation in the creed of the poets may give us courage to confide in our own impressions, for "all men are poets at heart." What they have dared publish we may venture to believe and will find a source of strength.

It is well known that the idea of reincarnation abounds in oriental poetry. But as our purpose is to demonstrate the prevalence of the same thought among our own poets, most of whom are wholly independent of eastern influence, we shall here confine our attention to the spontaneous utterances of American and European poets. We shall find that the great majority of the highest occidental poets lean toward this thought, and many of them unhesitatingly avow it. For convenience we divide our study into four parts, comprising forty-two authors.

Part   I. American Poets, (thirteen)
         II. British Poets, (seventeen)
         III. Continental Poets, (six)
         IV. Platonic Poets, (seven)

PART I. AMERICAN POETRY

PREEXISTENCE
BY PAUL HAMILTON HAYNE

While sauntering through the crowded street
Some half-remembered face I meet,
Albeit upon no mortal shore
That face, methinks, hath smiled before.
Lost in a gay and festal throng
I tremble at some tender song
Set to an air whose golden bars
I must have heard in other stars.
In sacred aisles I pause to share
The blessing of a priestly prayer,
When the whole scene which greets mine eyes
In some strange mode I recognize,
As one whose every mystic part
I feel prefigured in my heart.
At sunset as I calmly stand
A stranger on an alien strand
Familiar as my childhood's home
Seems the long stretch of wave and foam.
A ship sails toward me o'er the bay
And what she comes to do and say
I can foretell. A prescient lore
Springs from some life outlived of yore.
O swift, instructive, startling gleams
Of deep soul-knowledge: not as dreams
For aye ye vaguely dawn and die,
But oft with lightning certainty
Pierce through the dark oblivious brain
To make old thoughts and memories plain:
Thoughts which perchance must travel back

Across the wild bewildering track
Of countless seons; memories far
High reaching as yon pallid star,
Unknown, scarce seen, whose flickering grace
Faints on the outmost rings of space.

A MYSTERY
BY J. G. WHITTIER

The river hemmed with leaving trees
  Wound through the meadows green,
A low blue line of mountain showed
  The open pines between.
One sharp tall peak above them all
  Clear into sunlight sprang,
I saw the river of my dreams,
  The mountain that I sang.
No clue of memory led me on,
  But well the ways I knew,
A feeling of familiar things
  With every footstep grew.
Yet ne'er before that river's rim
  Was pressed by feet of mine,
Never before mine eyes had crossed
  That broken mountain line.
A presence strange at once and known
  Walked with me as my guide,
The skirts of some forgotten life
  Trailed noiseless at my side.
Was it a dim-remembered dream
  Or glimpse through aeons old?
The secret which the mountains kept
  The river never told.

THE METEMPSYCHOSIS OF THE PINE
BY BAYARD TAYLOR

As when the haze of some wan moonlight makes
Familiar fields a land of mystery,
Where, chill and strange, a ghostly presence wakes
   In flower or bush or tree,
Another life, the life of day o'erwhelms,
The past from present consciousness takes hue
As we remember vast and cloudy realms
   Our feet have wandered through:
So, oft, some moonlight of the mind makes dumb
The stir of outer thought: wide open seems
The gate where through strange sympathies have come
   The secret of our dreams:
The source of fine impressions, shooting deep
Below the falling plummet of the sense
Which strike beyond all Time and backward sweep
   Through all intelligence.
We touch the lower life of beast and clod
And the long progress of the ages see
From blind old Chaos, before the breath of God
   Moved it to harmony.
All outward vision yields to that within
Whereof nor creed nor canon holds the key;
We only feel that we have ever been
   And evermore shall be.
And thus I know, by memories unfurled
In rarer moods, and many a nameless sign
That once in Time and somewhere in the world
   I was a towering pine.
Some blind harmonic instinct pierced the rind
Of that slow life which made me straight and high,
And I became a harp for every wind,

A voice for every sky.
And thus for centuries my rhythmic chant
Rolled down the gorge or surged about the hill,
Gentle or stern or sad or jubilant,
    At every season's will.
No longer memory whispers whence arose
The doom that tore me from my place of pride,
Whether by storms that load the peak with snows,
    Or hands of men I died.
Yet still that life awakens, brings agaki
Its airy anthems, resonant and long,
Till earth and sky transfigured fill my brain
    With rhythmic sweeps of song.
Thence am I made a poet; thence are sprung
Those shadowy motions of the soul that reach
Beyond all grasp of art — for which the soul
    Is ignorant of speech.
And if some wild full-gathered harmony
Rolls its unbroken music through my line,
There lives and murmurs, faintly though it be,
    The spirit of the pine.

THE POET IN THE EAST
BY BAYARD TAYLOR

The poet came to the land of the East
    When spring was in the air,
The East was dressed for a wedding feast
    So young she seemed and fair,
And the poet knew the land of the East
    His soul was native there.
All things to him were the visible forms
    Of early and precious dreams,
Familiar visions that mocked his quest

    Beside the western streams,
Or gleamed in the gold of the clouds unrolled
    In the sunset's dying beams.

INTIMATIONS OF PREVIOUS EXISTENCE
BY L. E. LANDOJST

Methinks we must have known some former state
More glorious than our present, and the heart
Is haunted with dim memories, shadows left
By past magnificence; and hence we pine
With vain aspirings, hopes that fill the eyes
With bitter tears for their own vanity.
Remembrance makes the poet: 't is the past
Lingering within him, with a keener sense
Than is upon the thoughts of common men,
Of what has been, that fills the actual world
With unreal likenesses of lovely shapes
That were and are not; and the fairer they,
The more their contrast with existing things,
The more his power, the greater is his grief.
We are then fallen from some nobler state
Whose consciousness is as an unknown curse,
And we feel capable of happiness
Only to know it is not of our sphere.

THE METEMPSYCHOSIS
BY T. B. ALDRICH

I know my own creation was divine.
Strewn on the breezy continents I see
The veined shells and burnished scales which once
Enclosed my being — husks that had their use;
I brood on all the shapes I must attain

Before I reach the Perfect, which is God,
And dream my dream, and let the rabble go;
For I am of the mountains and the sea,
The deserts, and the caverns in the earth,
The catacombs and fragments of old worlds.

    I was a spirit on the mountain-tops,
A perfume in the valleys, a simoom
On arid deserts, a nomadic wind
Roaming the universe, a tireless Voice.
I was before Romulus and Remus were;
I was before Nineveh and Babylon;
I was, and am, and evermore shall be,
Progressing, never reaching to the end.

    A hundred years I trembled in the grass,
The delicate trefoil that muffled warm
A slope on Ida; for a hundred years
Moved in the purple gyre of those dark flowers
The Grecian women strew upon the dead.
Under the earth, in fragrant glooms, I dwelt;
Then in the veins and sinews of a pine
On a lone isle, where, from the Cyclades,
A mighty wind, like a leviathan,
Ploughed through the brine, and from those solitudes
Sent Silence, frightened. To and fro I swayed,
Drawing the sunshine from the stooping clouds.
Suns came and went, and many a mystic moon,
Orbing and waning, and fierce meteors,
Leaving their lurid ghosts to haunt the night.
I heard loud voices by the sounding shore,
The stormy sea-gods, and from fluted conchs
Wild music, and strange shadows floated by,
Some moaning and some singing.
So the years Clustered about me, till the hand of God
Let down the lightning from a sultry sky,

Splintered the pine and split the iron rock;
And from my odorous prison-house a bird,
I in its bosom, darted: so we flew,
Turning the brittle edge of one high wave,
Island and tree and sea-gods left behind!
　　Free as the air from zone to zone I flew,
Far from the tumult to the quiet gates
Of daybreak; and beneath me I beheld
Vineyards, and rivers that like silver threads
Ran through the green and gold of pasture-lands,
And here and there a hamlet, a white rose,
And here and there a city, whose slim spires
And palace-roofs and swollen domes uprose
Like scintillant stalagmites in the sun;
I saw huge navies battling with a storm
By ragged reefs along the desolate coasts —
And lazy merchantmen, that crawled, like flies,
Over the blue enamel of the sea To India or the icy Labradors.
　　A century was as a single day.
What is a day to an immortal soul?
A breath, no more. And yet I hold one hour
Beyond all price — that hour when from the sky
I circled near and nearer to the earth,
Nearer and nearer, till I brushed my wings
Against the pointed chestnuts, where a stream,
That foamed and chattered over pebbly shoals,
Fled through the briony, and with a shout
Leapt headlong down a precipice; and there,
Gathering wild-flowers in the cool ravine,
Wandered a woman more divinely shaped
Than any of the creatures of the air,
Or river-goddesses, or restless shades
Of noble matrons marvellous in their time
For beauty and great suffering; and I sung,

I charmed her thought, I gave her dreams, and then
Down from the dewy atmosphere I stole
And nestled in her bosom. There I slept
From moon to moon, while in her eyes a thought
Grew sweet and sweeter, deepening like the dawn —
A mystical forewarning! When the stream,
Breaking through leafless brambles and dead leaves,
Piped shriller treble, and from chestnut-boughs
The fruit dropt noiseless through the autumn night,
I gave a quick, low cry, as infants do:
We weep when we are born, not when we die!
So was it destined; and thus came I here,
To walk the earth and wear the form of Man,
To suffer bravely as becomes my state,
One step, one grade, one cycle nearer God.

IDENTITY
BY T. B. ALDRICH

Somewhere — in desolate wind-swept space —
    In twilight-land — in no-man's land,
Two hurrying shapes met face to face
    And bade each other stand.
"And who are you? "cried one agape,
    Shuddering in the gloaming light.
"I know not," said the other shape,
    "I only died last night."

ONE THOUSAND YEARS AGO
BY CHARLES G. LELAXD

Thou and I in spirit land
    One thousand years ago,
Watched the waves beat on the strand,

Ceaseless ebb and flow,
Vowed to love and ever love,
  One thousand years ago.
Thou and I in greenwood shade
  Nine hundred years ago
Heard the wild dove in the glade
  Murmuring soft and low,
Vowed to love for evermore
  Nine hundred years ago.
Thou and I in yonder star
  Eight hundred years ago
Saw strange forms of light afar
  In wildest beauty glow.
All things change, but love endures
  Now as long ago.
Thou and I in Norman halls
  Seven hundred years ago
Heard the warden on the walls
  Loud his trumpets blow,
"Ton amors sera tojors,"
  Seven hundred years ago.
Thou and I in Germany,
  Six hundred years ago.
Then I bound the red cross on,
  "True love, I must go,
But we part to meet again
  In the endless flow."
Thou and I in Syrian plains
  Five hundred years ago
Felt the wild fire in our veins
  To a fever glow.
All things die, but love lives on
  Now as long ago.
Thou and I in shadow land

Four hundred years ago
Saw strange flowers bloom on the strand,
  Heard strange breezes blow.
In the ideal, love is real,
  This alone I know.
Thou and I in Italy
  Three hundred years ago
Lived in faith and died for God,
  Felt the fagots glow,
Ever new and ever true,
  Three hundred years ago.
Thou and I on Southern seas
  Two hundred years ago
Felt the perfumed even-breeze,
  Spoke in Spanish by the trees,
Had no care or woe.
  Life went dreamily in song,
Two hundred years ago.
Thou and I'mid Northern snows
  One hundred years ago
Led an iron silent life
  And were glad to flow
Onward into changing death,
  One hundred years ago.
Thou and I but yesterday
  Met in fashion's show.
Love, did you remember me,
  Love of long ago?
Yes: we kept the fond oath sworn
  One thousand years ago.

THE FINAL THOUGHT
BY MAURICE THOMPSON

What is the grandest thought
Toward which the soul has wrought?
Has it the spirit form,
And the power of a storm?
Comes it of prophecy
(That borrows light of uncreated fires)
Or of transmitted strains of memory
Sent down through countless sires?
- - - - - - - - -

Which way are my feet set?
Through infinite changes yet
Shall I go on,
Nearer and nearer drawn
To thee,
God of eternity?
How shall the Human grow,
By changes fine and slow,
To thy perfection from the life-dawn sought?
What is the highest thought?
Ah! these dim memories,
Of when thy voice spake lovingly to me,
Under the Eden trees,
Saying, "Lord of all creation thou shalt be,"—
How they haunt me and elude—
How they hover, how they brood
On the horizon, fading yet dying not!
What is the final thought?
What if I once did dwell
In the lowest dust germ-cell,
A faint fore-hint of life called forth of God,
Waxing and struggling on,

Through the long flickering dawn,
The awful while His feet earth's bosom trod?
What if He shaped me so,
And caused my life to blow
Into the full soul-flower in Eden-air?
Lo! now I am not good,
And I stand in solitude,
Calling to Him (and yet He answers not):
What is the final thought?
What myriads of years up from the germ!
What countless ages back from man to worm!
And yet from man to God—oh, help me now!
A cold despair is beading on my brow!
I may see Him, and seeing know Him not!
What is the highest thought?

- - - - - - - - - -

So comes, at last,
The answer from the Vast...
Not so, there is a rush of wings—
Earth feels the presence of invisible things,
Closer and closer drawn
In rosy mists of dawn!
One dies to conquer Death
And to burst the awful tomb—
Lo, with his dying breath
He blows love into bloom!
Love! Faith is born of it!
Death is the scorn of it!
It fills the earth and thrills the heavens above:
And God is love,
And life is love, and, though we heed it not,
Love is the final thought.

FROM "A POEM READ AT BROWN UNIVERSITY
BY N. P. WILLIS

But what a mystery this erring mind?
It wakes within a frame of various powers
A stranger in a new and wondrous world.
It brings an instinct from some other sphere,
For its fine senses are familiar all,
And with the unconscious habit of a dream
It calls and they obey. The priceless sight
Springs to its curious organ, and the ear
Learns strangely to detect the articulate air
In its unseen divisions, and the tongue
Gets its miraculous lesson with the rest,
And in the midst of an obedient throng
Of well trained ministers, the mind goes forth
To search the secrets of its new found home.

FROM "BEYOND"
BY J. T. TROWBRIDGE

From her own fair dominions
Long since, with shorn pinions
My spirit was banished.
But above her still hover in vigils and dreams
Ethereal visitants, voices and gleams
That forever remind her
Of something behind her
Long vanished.
Through the listening night
With mysterious flight
Pass winged intimations;
Like stars shot from heaven, their still voices call to me
Far and departing they signal and call to me,

Strangely beseeching me,
Chiding yet teaching me
Patience.

FROM "RAIN IN SUMMER"
BY H. W. LONGFELLOW

Thus the seer, with vision clear,
Sees forms appear and disappear
In the perpetual round of strange
Mysterious change
From birth to death, from death to birth,
From earth to heaven, from heaven to earth,
Till glimpses more sublime
Of things unseen before
Unto his wondering eyes reveal
The universe, as an immeasurable wheel
Turning for evermore
In the rapid rushing river of time.

FROM "THE TWILIGHT"
BY JAMES RUSSELL LOWELL

Sometimes a breath floats by me,
    And odor from Dreamland sent,
Which makes the ghost seem nigh me
    Of a something that came and went,
Of a life lived somewhere,
    I know not In what diviner sphere:
Of mem'ries that come not and go not;
    Like music once heard by an ear
That cannot forget or reclaim it;
A something so shy, it would shame it

To make it a show.
A something too vague, could I name it,
    For others to know:
As though I had lived it and dreamed it,
As though I had acted and schemed it
    Long ago.
And yet, could I live it over,
  This Life which stirs in my brain;
Could I be both maiden and lover,
Moon and tide, bee and clover,
  As I seem to have been, once again —
Could I but speak and show it,
  This pleasure more sharp than pain,
  Which baffles and lures me so —
  The world would not lack a poet,
    Such as it had
    In the ages glad,
    Long ago.

FROM "FACING WEST FROM CALIFORNIA'S SHORES" BY WALT WHITMAN

Facing west from California's shores,
Inquiring, tireless, seeking what is yet unfound,
I, a child, very old, over waves, towards the house of maternity,
    the land of migrations, look afar,
Look off the shores of my
Western sea, the circle almost circled:
For starting westward from Hindustan, from the vales of
    Kashmere,
From Asia, from the north, from the God, the sage, and the
hero,
From the south, from the flowery peninsulas and the spice
islands,

Long having wander'd since, round the earth having wander'd,
Now I face home again, very pleas'd and joyous.
(But where is what I started for so long ago? And why is it yet
    unfound?)

FROM "LEAVES OF GRASS"
BY WALT WHITMAN

I know I am deathless.
I know that this orbit of mine cannot be swept by a carpenter's
    compass;
And whether I come to my own today, or in ten thousand or
    ten million years,
I can cheerfully take it now or with equal cheerfulness I can
wait.

- - - - - - - - - -

As to you, Life, I reckon you are the leavings of many deaths.
No doubt I have died myself ten thousand times before.

- - - - - - - - - -

Believing I shall come again upon the earth after five thousand
    years.

- - - - - - - - - -

Births have brought us richness and variety, and other births
have
        brought us richness and variety.

STANZAS
BY THOMAS W. PARSONS

"We are such stuff as dreams are made of."
We have forgot what we have been,
And what we are we little know;
We fancy new events begin,
But all has happened long ago.

Through many a verse life's poem flows,
But still, though seldom marked by men,
At times returns the constant close,
Still the old chorus comes again.
The childish grief—the boyish fear—
The hope in manhood's breast that burns;
The doubt—the transport, and the tear—
Each mood, each impulse, oft returns.
Before mine infant eyes had hailed
The new-born glory of the day,
When the first wondrous morn unveiled
The breathing world that round me lay;
The same strange darkness o'er my brain
Folded its close mysterious wings,
The ignorance of joy or pain,
That each recurring midnight brings.
Full oft my feelings make me start,
Like footprints on a desert shore,
As if the chambers of my heart
Had heard their shadowy step before.
So looking into thy fond eyes,
Strange memories come to me, as though
Somewhere—perchance in Paradise—
I had adored thee lone: ago.

PART II. BRITISH POETRY

FROM "INTIMATIONS OF IMMORTALITY" BY WILLIAM WORDSWORTH

Our birth is but a sleep and a forgetting;
The soul that rises with us, our life's star,
Hath had elsewhere its setting,
And cometh from afar.

Not in entire forgetfulness
And not in utter nakedness
But trailing clouds of glory do we come
From God who is our home.
Heaven lies about us in our infancy;
Shades of the prison house begin to close
Upon the growing boy;
But he beholds the light, and whence it flows
He sees it in his joy.
The youth who daily farther from the East
Must travel, still is nature's priest,
And by the vision splendid
Is on his way attended.
At length the man perceives it die away
And fade into the light of common day.

Edmund W. Gosse treats the idea of Wordsworth's "Intimations" in a way directly opposite to the older poet, acknowledging the previous life, but rejoicing in the speedy forgetting of it, in these verses:—

TO MY DAUGHTER
BY EDMUND W. GOSSE

Thou hast the colors of the Spring,
The gold of king cups triumphing,
    The blue of wood-bells wild;
But winter thoughts thy spirit fill,
And thou art wandering from us still,
    Too young to be our child.
Yet have thy fleeting smiles confessed,
Thou dear and much desired guest,
    That home is near at hand.
Long lost in high mysterious lands,
Close by our door thy spirit stands,
    In journey wellnigh past.

Oh, sweet bewildered soul, I watch
The fountains of thine eyes, to catch
   New fancies bubbling there;
To feel one common light, and lose
The flood of strange ethereal hues
   Too dire for us to share!
Fade, cold immortal lights, and make
This creature human for my sake,
   Since I am nought but clay;
An angel is too fine a thing
To sit behind my chair and sing
   And cheer my passing day.
I smile, who could not smile, unless
The air of rapt unconsciousness
   Passed with the fading hours;
I joy in every childish sign
That proves the stranger less divine
   And much more meekly ours.

A REMEMBRANCE
BY DEAN ALFORD

Methtnks I can remember when a shade
All soft and flowery was my couch, and I
A little naked child, with fair white flesh
And wings all gold bedropt, and o'er my head
Bright fruits were hanging and tall balmy shrines
Shed odorous gums around me, and I lay
Sleeping and waking in that wondrous air
Which seemed infused with glory, and each breeze
Bore as it wandered by, sweet melodies;
But whence, I knew not. One delight was there,
Whether of feeling or of sight or touch
I know not now—which is not in this earth,

Something all-glorious and all-beautiful,
Of which our language speaketh not, and which
Flies from the eager grasping of my thought
As doth the shade of a forgotten dream.
All knowledge had I, but I cared not then
To search into my soul and draw it thence.
The blessed creatures that around me played
I knew them all, and where their resting was,
And all their hidden symmetry I knew,
And how the form is linked into the soul —
I knew it all, but thought not on it then,
I was so happy.
                    And once upon a time
I saw an army of bright beaming shapes
Fair-faced and rosy-cinctured and gold-winged
Approach upon the air. They came to me
And from a crystal chalice silver brimmed
Put sparkling potion to my lips and stood
All around me, in the many blooming shades,
Shedding into the centre where I lay
A mingling of soft light; and then they sang
Songs of the land they dwelt in; and the last
Lingereth even till now upon mine ear:
            Holy and blest
            Be the calm of thy rest,
            For thy chamber of sleep
            Shall be dark and deep;
            They shall dig thee a tomb
            In the dark deep womb,
            In the warm dark womb.
Spread ye, spread the dewy mist around him,
Spread ye, spread till the thick dark night surround him,
Till the dark long night has bound him
Which bindeth all before their birth

Down upon the nether earth.
The first cloud is beaming and bright,
The next cloud is mellowed in light,
The third cloud is dim to sight,
And it stretches away into gloomy night.
Twine ye. twine the mystic threads around him,
Twine ye, twine, till the fast firm fate surround him,
Till the firm cold fate hath bound him
Which bindeth all before their birth
Down upon the nether earth.
The first thread is beaming and bright,
The next thread is mellowed in light,
The third thread is dim to sight,
And it stretches away into gloomy night.
Sing ye, sing the fairy songs around him,
Sing ye, sing, till the dull warm sleep surround him,
Till the warm damp sleep hath bound him
Which bindeth all before their birth
Down upon the nether earth.
The first dream is beaming and bright,
The next dream is mellowed in light,
The third dream is dim to sight,
And it stretches away into gloomy night.
Then dimness passed upon me, and that song
Was sounding o'er me when I woke
To be a pilgrim on the nether earth.

RETURNING DREAMS
BY R. M. MILNES (LORD HOUGHTON)

As in that world of Dream whose mystic shades
Are cast by still more mystic substances,
We ofttimes have an unreflecting sense,
A silent consciousness of some things past,

So clear that we can wholly comprehend
Others of which they are a part, and even
Continue them in action, though no stress
Of after memory can recognize
That we have had experience of those things
Or sleeping or awake:
                                    Thus in the dream,
Our universal Dream, of Mortal Life,
The incidents of an anterior dream,
Or it may be, Existence, noiselessly intrude
Into the daily flow of earthly things,
Instincts of good — immediate sympathies,
Places come at by chance, that claim at once
An old acquaintance — single random looks
That bare a stranger's bosom to our eyes;
We *know* these things are so, we ask not why,
But act and follow as the Dream goes on.

BIRTH
BY ALFRED TENNYSON

Out of the deep, my child, out of the deep,
Where all that was to be, in all that was,
Whirled for a million aeons thro' the vast
Waste dawn of multitudinous eddying light —
Out of the deep, my child, out of the deep,
Thro' all this changing world of changeless law,
And every phase of ever heightening life,
And nine long months of ante-natal gloom,
Thou comest.
Tennyson also writes in "The Two-Voices":—
For how should I for certain hold
Because my memory is so cold,
That I *first* was in human mould?

It may be that no life is found
Which only to one engine bound
Falls off, but cycles always round.
But, if I lapsed from nobler place,
Some legend of a fallen race
Alone might hint of my disgrace.
Or, if through lower lives I came —
Tho' all experience past became
Consolidate in mind and frame —
I might forget my weaker lot;
For is not our first year forgot?
The haunts of memory echo not.
Some draughts of Lethe doth await,
As old mythologies relate,
The slipping through from state to state.
Moreover, something is or seems,
That touches me with mystic gleams,
Like glimpses of forgotten dreams —
Of something felt, like something here;
Of something done, I know not where;
Such as no language may declare.

More interesting still, from Tennyson, is an early sonnet which has
been omitted from the later editions of his collected poetry: —

As when with downcast eyes we muse and brood
And ebb into a former life, or seem
To lapse far back in a confused dream
To states of mystical similitude,
If one but speaks or hems or stirs a chair
Ever the wonder waxeth more and more,
So that we say, all this hath been before,
All this *hath* been, I know not when or where;
So, friend, when first I looked upon your face
Our thoughts gave answer each to each, so true,
Opposed mirrors each reflecting each —

Although I knew not in what time or place,
Methought that I had often met with you,
And each had lived in other's mind and speech.

I have been here before,
  But when or how I cannot tell;
I know the grass beyond the door,
  The sweet keen smell,
The sighing sound, the lights around the shore.
You have been mine before—
  How long ago I may not know:
But just when at that swallow's soar
  Your neck turned so,
  Some veil did fall—I knew it all of yore.
Then, now, perchance again!
  O round mine eyes your tresses shake!
Shall we not lie as we have lain
  Thus for Love's sake,
And sleep, and wake, yet never break the chain?

ETERNITY—thou pleasing, dreadful thought,
Through what variety of untried being,
Through what new scenes and dangers must we pass?
The wide, th' unbounded prospect lies before me,
But shadows, clouds, and darkness rest upon it.

FROM "THE MYSTIC"
BY PHILIP JAMES BAILEY

Who dreams not life more yearful than the hours
Since first into this world he wept his way
Erreth much, may be. Called of God, man's soul
In patriarchal periods, comet-like,
Ranges, perchance, all spheres successive, and in each
With nobler powers endowed and senses new
Set season bideth.

FROM "A RECORD"
BY WILLIAM SHARP

None sees the slow and upward sweep
By which the soul from life-depths deep
Ascends—unless, mayhap, when free,
With each new death we backward see
The long perspective of our race
Our multitudinous past lives trace.
The following occurs in Tupper's "Proverbial Philosophy":—

OF MEMORY

Be ye my judges, imaginative minds, full-fledged to soar into the sun,
Whose grosser natural thoughts the chemistry of wisdom hath sub-
limed,
Have ye not confessed to a feeling, a consciousness strange and vague,
That ye have gone this way before, and walk again your daily life,
Tracking an old routine, and on some foreign strand,
Where bodily ye have never stood, finding your own footsteps?
Hath not at times some recent friend looked out an old familiar,
Some newest circumstance or place teemed as with ancient memories?
A startling sudden flash lighteth up all for an instant.

And then it is quenched, as in darkness, and leaveth the cold spirit trembling.

Throughout Browning the truth of reincarnation finds frequent utterance, though not always so distinctly as in these three extracts.

FROM "PARACELSUS"

> At times I almost dream
> I too have spent a life the sages' way,
> And tread once more familiar paths. Perchance
> I perished in an arrogant self-reliance
> An age ago; and in that act, a prayer
> For one more chance went up so earnest, so
> Instinct with better light let in by Death,
> That life was blotted out—not so completely
> But scattered wrecks enough of it remain,
> Dim memories; as now, when seems once more
> The goal in sight again.

FROM "ONE WORD MORE"

> I shall never, in the years remaining,
> Paint you pictures, no, nor carve you statues.
> This of verse alone one life allows me;
> Other heights in other lives, God willing.

FROM "CHRISTINA"

> THERE are flashes struck from midnights, there are fire-flames
>   noondays kindle,
> Whereby piled-up honors perish, whereby swollen ambitions dwindle;
> While just this or that poor impulse which for once had play unstifled,
> Seems the sole work of a lifetime that away the rest have trifled.

FROM "EVELYN HOPE"

Delayed it may be for more lives yet
Through worlds I must traverse, not a few
Much is to learn and much to forget
Ere the time be come for taking you.
Doubt you if, in some such moment, as she fixed me, she felt
clearly,
Ages past the soul existed, here an age 't is resting merely,
And hence fleets again for ages; while the true end, sole and
single,
It stops here for is, this lone way, with some other soul to
mingle.

In Dr. Leyden's beautiful "Ode to Scottish Music" is this stanza:—

Ah, sure, as Hindoo legends tell,
When music's tones the bosom swell
  The scenes of former life return,
Ere sunk beneath the morning star,
We left our parent climes afar,
  Immured in mortal forms to mourn.

Coleridge confesses his fondness for the same idea in the sonnet which he composed "On a homeward journey upon hearing of the birth of a son":—

Oft in my brain does that strange fancy roll
  Which makes the present (while the flash does last)
  Seem a mere semblance of some unknown past,
Mixed with such feelings as perplex the soul
Self-questioned in her sleep: and some have said
  We lived, before yet this robe of flesh we wore.
  O my sweet baby! when I reach my door
If heavy looks should tell me thou art dead
(As sometimes through excess of hope I fear),
  I think that I should struggle to believe
Thou wert a spirit, to this nether sphere

Sentenced for some more venial crime to grieve;
Didst scream, then spring to meet Heaven's quick reprieve,
While we wept idly o'er thy little bier.

The following poem has a peculiar history. Though one of the most beautiful of the entire group, it is the work of a seventeen-year-old girl. In 1846 this child, Emma Tatham, attracted the attention of a London clergyman as a poetic genius, and she read to him, at his frequent visits, her phenomenal compositions, with playful frankness devoid of all affectation or consciousness of brilliancy. She was very delicate, but of ruddy countenance, and her bright winning simplicity carried no suggestion of a sickly prodigy. But she was an intimate friend of the best poets through their books, and her critical judgment of their works was surprisingly mature and keen. From the age of sixteen to that of seventeen and a half, she rapidly wrote an abundance of exquisite poems. Her extreme modesty would not permit their publication until 1854 — seven years later. Issued in the quietest way by a provincial publisher, they met with a singular unanimity of applause, though the extreme youth of their author was unknown. Her rich religious experience directed most of them into the vein of lofty piety, but the general press, and even "The Athenaeum," that severest censor of new writers, spoke commandingly of them. The first edition sold in a few weeks. An exceptionally brilliant career was predicted for the young poet, but in less than a year from the announcement of her book, she died.

"The Dream of Pythagoras," the initial poem of the volume, from which the collection is named, is given here entire (from the fifth edition, 1872), as it is familiar to few Americans.

THE DREAM OF PYTHAGORAS
BY EMMA TATHAM

"The soul was not then imprisoned in a gross mortal body, as it is now: it was united to a luminous, heavenly, ethereal body, which served it as a vehicle to fly through the air, rise to the stars, and wander over all the regions of immensity." — PYTHAGORAS, in *Travel of Cyprus*

PYTHAGORAS, amidst Crotona's groves,
One summer eve, sat; whilst the sacred few
And favour'd at his feet reclin'd, entranc'd,
List'ning to his great teachings. O'er their heads
A lofty oak spread out his hundred hands
Umbrageous, and a thousand slant sunbeams
Play'd o'er them; but beneath all was obscure
And solemn, save that, as the sun went down,
One pale and tremulous sunbeam, stealing in
Through the unconscious leaves her silent way,
Fell on the forehead of Pythagoras
Like spiritual radiance; all else wrapt
In gloom delicious; while the murmuring wind,
Oft moving through the forest as in dreams,
Made melancholy music. Then the sage
Thus spoke: "My children, listen; let the soul
Hear her mysterious origin, and trace
Her backward path to heaven. 'Twas but a dream;
And yet from shadows may we learn the shape
And substance of undying truth. Methought
In vision I beheld the first beginning
And after-changes of my soul. O joy!
She is of no mean origin, but sprang
From loftier source than stars or sunbeams know.
Yea, like a small and feeble rill that bursts
From everlasting mountain's coronet,
And, winding through a thousand labyrinths
Of darkness, deserts, and drear solitudes,
Yet never dies, but, gaining depth and power,
Leaps forth at last with uncontrollable might
Into immortal sunshine and the breast
Of boundless ocean — so is this my soul.
I felt myself spring like a sunbeam out
From the Eternal, and my first abode

Was a pure particle of light, wherein,
Shrined like a beam in crystal, I did ride
Gloriously through the firmament on wings
Of floating flowers, ethereal gems, and wreaths
Of vernal rainbows. I did paint a rose
With blush of day-dawn, and a lily-bell
With mine own essence; every morn I dipt
My robe in the full sun, then all day long
Shook out its dew on earth, and was content
To be unmark'd, unworshipp'd, and unknown,
And only lov'd of heaven. Thus did my soul
Live spotless like her Source. 'Twas mine to illume
The palaces of nature, and explore
Her hidden cabinets, and, raptur'd, read
Her joyous secrets. O return, thou life
Of purity! I flew from mountain-top
To mountain, building rainbow-bridges up—
From hill to hill, and over boundless seas:
Ecstasy was such life, and on the verge
Of ripe perfection. But, alas! I saw
And envied the bold lightning, who could blind
And startle nations, and I long'd to be
A conqueror and destroyer, like to him.
Methonght it was a glorious joy, indeed,
To shut and open heaven as he did,
And have the thunders for my retinue,
And tear the clouds, and blacken palaces,
And in a moment whiten sky, and sea,
And earth: therefore I murmur'd at my lot,
Beautiful as it was, and that one murmur
Despoil'd me of my glory. I became
A dark and tyrant cloud driven by the storm,
Too earthly to be blight, too hard of heart
To drop in mercy on the thirsty land;

And so no creature lov'd me. I was felt
A blot where'er I came. Fair Summer scorn'd
And spurn'd me from her blueness, for, she said,
I would not wear her golden fringe, and so
She could not rank me in her sparkling train.
Soft Spring refused me, for she could not paint
Her rainbows on a nature cold as mine,
Incapable of tears. Autumn despised
One who could do no good. Dark Winter frown'd,
And number'd me among his ruffian host
Of racers. Then unceasingly I fled
Despairing through the murky firmament,
Like a lone wreck athwart a midnight sea,
Chased by the howling spirits of the storm,
And without rest. At last, one day I saw
In my continual flight, a desert blank
And broad beneath me, where no water was;
And there I mark'd a weary antelope,
Dying for thirst, all stretched out on the sand,
With her poor trembling lips in agony
Press'd to a scorch'd-up spring; then, then, at last
My hard heart broke, and I could weep. At once
My terrible race was stopp'd, and I did melt
Into the desert's heart, and with my tears
I quench'd the thirst of the poor antelope.
So having pour'd myself into the dry
And desolate waste, I sprang up a wild flower
In solitary beauty. There I grew
Alone and feverish, for the hot sun burn'd
And parch'd my tender leaves, and not a sigh
Came from the winds. I seem'd to breathe an air
Of fire, and had resign'd myself to death,
When lo! a solitary dewdrop fell
Into my burning bosom; then, for joy,

My spirit rush'd into my lovely guest,
And I became a dewdrop. Then, once more,
My life was joyous, for the kingly sun
Carried me up into the firmament,
And hung me in a rainbow, and my soul
Was robed in seven bright colors, and became
A jewel in the sky. So did I learn
The first great lessons; mark ye them, my sons.
Obedience is nobility; and meek
Humility is glory; self alone
Is base; and pride is pain; patience is power;
Beneficence is bliss. And now first brought
To know myself and feel my littleness,
I was to learn what greatness is prepar'd
For virtuous souls, what mighty war they wage,
What vast impossibilities o'ercome,
What kingdoms, and infinitude of love,
And harmony, and never-ending joy,
And converse, and communion with the great
And glorious Mind unknown — are given to high
And godlike souls.
                      Therefore the winds arose,
And shook me from the rainbow where I hung,
Into the depths of ocean; then I dived
Down to the coral citadels, and roved
Through crystal mazes, among pearls and gems,
And lovely buried creatures, who had sunk
To find the jewel of eternal life.
Sweet babes I saw clasp'd in their mothers' arms;
Kings of the north, each with his oozy crown;
Pale maidens, with their golden streaming hair
Floating in solemn beauty, calm and still,
In the deep, silent, tideless wave; I saw
Young beauteous boys wash'd down from reeling masts

By sudden storm; and brothers sleeping soft,
Lock'd in each other's arms; and countless wealth,
And curling weed, and treasur'd knots of hair,
And mouldering masts, and giant hulls that sank
With thunder sobbing; and blue palaces
Where moonbeams, hand in hand, did dance with me
To the soft music of the surging shells,
Where all else was at rest. Calm, calm, and hush'd,
And stormless, were those hidden deeps, and clear
And pure as crystal. There I wander'd long
In speechless dreamings, and wellnigh forgot
My corporal nature, for it seem'd
Melting into the silent infinite
Around me, and I peacefully began
To feel the mighty universe commune
And converse with me; and my soul became
One note in nature's harmony. So sweet
And soothing was that dream-like ecstasy,
I could have slept into a wave, and roll'd
Away through the blue mysteries forever,
Dreaming my soul to nothing; I could well
Have drown'd my spark of immortality
In drunkenness of peace; I knew not yet
The warrior life of virtue, and the high
And honourable strife and storm that cleanse
And exercise her pinions. I was now
To learn the rapture of the struggle made
For immortality and truth; therefore
The ocean toss'd me to his mountain chains,
Bidding me front the tempest; fires of heaven
Were dancing o'er his cataracts, and scared
His sounding billows; glorious thunders roll'd
Beneath, above, around; the strong winds fought,
Lifting up pyramids of tortur'd waves,

Then dashing them to foam. I saw great ships
As feathers on the opening sepulchres
And starting monuments,
And the gaunt waves leap'd up like fountains fierce,
And snatch'd down frighten'd clouds, then shouting—fell,
And rose again. I, whirling on their tops,
Dizzy flew over masts of staggering ships,
Then plunged into black night. My soul grew mad
Ravish'd with the intense magnificence
Of the harmonious chaos, for I heard
Music amidst the thunders, and I saw
Measure in all the madness of the waves
And whirlpools; yea, I lifted up my voice
In praise of the Eternal, for I felt
Rock'd in His hand, as in a cradling couch;
Rejoicing in His strength; yea, I found rest
In the unbounded roar, and fearless sang
Glad echo to the thunder, and flash'd back
The bright look of the lightning, and did fly
On the dark pinions of the hurricane spirit
In rapturous repose; till suddenly
My soul expanded, and I sprang aloft
Into the lightning flame, leaping for joy
From cloud to cloud. Then, first I felt my wings
Wave into immortality, and flew
Across the ocean with a shouting host
Of thunders at my heels, and lit up heaven,
And earth and sea, with one quick lamp, and crown'd
The mountains with a momentary gold,
Then cover'd them with blackness. Then I glanced
Upon the mighty city in her sleep,
Pierced all her mysteries with one swift look,
Then bade my thunders shout. The city trembled;
And charm'd with the sublime outcry, I paus'd

And listen'd. Yet had I to rise and learn
A loftier lesson. I was lifted high
Into the heavens, and there became a star,
And on my new-form'd orb two angels sat.
The one thus spoke: 'O spirit, young and pure!
Say, wilt thou be my shrine? I am of old,
The first of all things, and of all the greatest;
I am the Sovereign Majesty, to whom
The universe is given, though for a while
I war with rebels strong; my name is Truth.
I am the Spirit of wisdom, love, and power,
And come to claim thee; and if thou obey
My guiding, I will give thee thy desire,
Even eternal life.' He ceas'd, and then
The second angel spoke. 'Ask not,) soul!
My name; I bid thee free thyself, and know
Thou hast the fount of life in thy own breast,
And need'st no guiding: be a child no longer;
Throw off thy fetters, and with me enjoy
Thy native independence, and assert
Thy innate majesty; Truth binds not me,
And yet I am immortal; be thou, too,
A god unto thyself.'
        "But I had learn'd
My own deep insufficiency, and gazed
Indignant on th' unholy angel's face,
And pierced its false refulgence, knowing well
Obedience only is true liberty
For spirits form'd to obey; so best they reign.
Straight the base rebel fled, and, ruled by
Truth, I roll'd unerring on my shining road
Around a glorious centre; free, though bound,
Because love bound me, and my law became
My life and nature; and my lustrous orb

Pure spirits visited: I wore a light
That shone across infinitude, and serv'd
To guide returning wanderers. I sang
With all my starry sisters, and we danced
Around the throne of Time, and wash'd the base
Of high Eternity like golden sands.
There first my soul drank music, and was taught
That melody is part of heaven, and lives
In every heaven-born spirit like her breath;
There did I learn, that music without end
Breathes, murmurs, swells, echoes, and floats, and peals
And thunders through creation, and in truth
Is the celestial language, and the voice
Of love; and now my soul began to speak
The speech of immortality. But yet
I was to learn a lesson more severe—
To shine alone in darkness, and the deeps
Of sordid earth. So did I fall from heaven
Far into night, beneath the mountains' roots,
There, as a diamond burning amidst things
Too base for utterance. Then, alas! I felt
The stirrings of impatience, pining sore
For freedom, and communion with the fires
And majesties of heaven, with whom erewhile
I walk'd, their equal. I had not yet learn'd
That our appointed place is loftiest,
However lowly. I was made to feel
The dignity of suffering. O, my sons!
Sorrow and joy are but the spirit's life;
Without these she is scarcely animate;
Anguish and bliss ennoble: either proves
The greatness of its subject, and expands
Her nature into power; her every pulse
Beats into new-born force, urging her on

To conquering energy.—Then was I cast
Into hot fires and flaming furnaces,
Deep in the hollow globe; there did I burn
Deathless in agony, without murmur,
Longing to die, until my patient soul
Fainted into perfection: at that hour,
Being victorious, I was snatch'd away
To yet another lesson. I became
A date-tree in the desert, to pour out
My life in dumb benevolence, and full
Obedience to each wind of heaven that blew.
The traveller came—I gave him all my shade,
Asking for no reward; the lost bird flew
For shelter to my branches, and I hid
Her nest among my leaves; the sunbeams ask'd
To rest their hot and weary feet awhile
On me, and I spread out my every arm
T'embrace them, fanning them with all my plumes.
Beneath my shade the dying pilgrim fell
Praying for water; I cool dewdrops caught
And shook them on his lip; I gave my fruit
To strengthen the faint stranger, and I sang
Soft echoes to the winds, living in nought
For self; but in all things for others' good.
The storm arose, and patiently I bore
And yielded to his tyranny; I bow'd
My tenderest foliage to his angry blast,
And suffer'd him to tear it without sigh,
And scatter on the waste my all of wealth.
The billowing sands o'erwhelm'd me, yet I stood
Silent beneath them; so they roll'd away,
And rending up my roots, left me a wreck
Upon the wilderness.
                    "'Twas thus, my sons,

I dream'd my spirit wander'd, till at length,
As desolate I mourn'd my helpless woe,
My guardian angel took me to his heart,
And thus he said: 'Spirit, well tried and true!
Conqueror I have made thee, and prepar'd
For human life; behold! I wave the palm
Of immortality before thine eyes:
'Tis thine; it shall be thine, if thou aright
Acquit thee of the part which yet remains,
And teach what thou hast learn'd.'
                                    "This said, he smil'd,
And gently laid me in my mother's arms.
Thus far the vision brought me — then it fled,
And all was silence. Ah! 't was but a dream;
This soul in vain struggles for purity;
This self-tormenting essence may exist
For ever; but what joy can being give
Without perfection! vainly do I seek
That bliss for which I languish. Surely yet
The Day-spring of our nature is to come;
Mournful we wait that dawning; until then
We grovel in the dust — in midnight grope,
For ever seeking, never satisfied."
Thus spake the solemn seer, then pausing, sigh'd,
For all was darkness.

See how the orient dew,
Shed from the bosom of the morn
Into the blowing roses,
Yet careless of its mansion new
For the clear region where 't was born,

Round in itself encloses
And in its little globe's extent
Frames, as it can its native element.
How it the splendid flower does slight,
Scarcely touching where it lies
But gazing back upon the skies,
Shines with a mournful light,
Like its own tear,
Because so long divided from its sphere.
Restless it rolls and insecure,
Trembling lest it grow impure,
Till the warm sun pities its pain
And to the skies exhales it back again.
So the soul, that drop, that ray
Of the clear fountain of eternal day,
Could it within the human flower be seen,
Lamenting still its former height,
Shuns the sweet flowers and the radiant green,
And recollecting its own light
Does in its pure and circling thoughts express
The greater heaven in the heaven less.

Dr. Donne, in a long poem called "The Progress of the Soul," traces the Pythagorean course of an immortal being through an apple (by which Eve was tempted), a plant, a sparrow, a fish, a mouse (which climbed an elephant's proboscis to the brain,

"the soul's bedchamber,
And gnawed the life-cords there like a whole town
Till, undermined, the slain beast tumbled down;
With him the murderer dies, whom envy sent to kill.")

Then the soul enters a wolf, an ape, and at last a woman—Themech, the sister and wife of Cain.

Mortimer Collins's poem, "The Inn of Strange Meetings," is an interesting expression of reincarnation, but it is too long to reprint here. Similar glimpses of this thought occur in Byron, Pope, Southey,

Swinburne, and others, but it is difficult to select from them a distinct and continuous wording of it.

PART III. CONTINENTAL POETRY

Ever since the time of Virgil, whose sixth iEneid (verses 724-) contains a sublime version of reincarnation, and of Ovid, whose Metamorphoses beautifully present the old Greek mythologies of metempsychosis, this theme has attracted many European poets beside those of England. While the Latin poets obtained their inspiration from the East, through Pythagoras and Plato, the Northern singers seem to express it independently, unless it came to them with the Teutonic migration from the Aryan cradle of the race, and shifted its form with all their people's wanderings so that it has lost all traces of connection with its Indian source. The old Norse legends teem with many guises of soul-journeying. In sublime and lovely stories, ballads, and epics, these vikings and their kindred perpetuated their belief that the human individuality travels through a great series of embodiments, which physically reveal the spiritual character. The Icelandic Sagas also delight in these fables of transmigration, and still fire the heart of Scandinavia and Denmark. It permeated the Welsh triads, and among the early Saxons this thought animated their Druid ceremonies and their noblest literature. The scriptures of those magnificent races whom Tacitus found in the German forests, whose intrepid manliness conquered the mistress of the world, and from whom are descended the modern ruling race, were inspired with this same doctrine. The treasures of these ancient writings are buried away from our sight, but a suggestion of their grandeur is found in the heroic qualities of the nations who were bred upon them. A beautiful German version of Giordano Bruno's Pythagorean Latin verses on the relation of the soul to the body is contained in Professor Carriere's Weltanschauung (p. 452). Calderon, the Spanish poet, touches fondly on this idea in his drama " Life is a Dream." Bjornsen has written a superb Danish poem on transmigration called " Salme," but it has never been translated. The following selections are representative of the chief

branches of Continental Europeans. Boyesen, although an American cit-
izen, is really a modernized Norwegian. Goethe stands for the Teutonic
race, and Schiller keeps him good company. Victor Hugo and Beranger
speak for France, and Campanlla represents Italy.

TRANSMIGRATION
BY HJALMAR HJORTH BOYESEN

My spirit wrestles in anguish
With fancies that will not depart;
A ghost who borrowed my semblance
Has hid in the depth of my heart.
A dim, resistless possession
Impels me forever to do
The phantom deeds of this phantom
That lived ages ago.
The thoughts that I think seem hoary
And laden with dust and gloom;
My voice sounds strange, as if echoed
From centuries long in the tomb.
Methinks that e'en through my laughter
Oft trembles a strain of dread;
A shivering ghost of laughter
That is loth to rise from the dead.
My tear has its fount in dead ages,
And choked with their dust is my sigh;
I weep for the pale, dead sorrows
Of the wraith that once was I.
Ah, Earth! thou art old and weary,
With weight of centuries bent;
Thy pristine creative gladness
In youthful aeons was spent.
Perchance, in the distant ages,
My soul, from Nirvana's frost,

"Will gather its scattered life-germs
And quicken the life I lost.
And then, like a song forgotten
That haunts, yet eludes the ear,
Or cry that chills the darkness
With a vague, swift breath of fear,
A faint remembrance shall visit
That sun of earth and sky
In whom the flame shall rekindle
Of the soul which once was I.
From Victor Hugo's poem, "A celle qui est voilée."

"TO THE INVISIBLE ONE"

I AM the drift of a thousand tides,
   The captive of destiny;
The weight of all darkness upon me abides,
   But it cannot bury me.
My spirit endures like a rocky isle
   Amid the ocean of fate,
The thunderstorm is my domicile,
   The hurricane is my mate.
I am the fugitive who far
   From home has taken flight;
Along with the owl and evening star
   I moan the song of night.
Art thou not, too, like unto me
   A torch to light earth's gloom,
A soul, therefore a mystery,
   A wanderer bound to roam?
Seek for me in the sea bird's home,
   Descend to my release!
My depths of cavernous shadows dumb
   Illume, angel of peace!

As night brings forth the rosy morn,
  Perhaps 'tis heaven's law
That from thy mystic smile is born
  A glory I ne'er saw.
In this dark world where now I stay
  I scarce can see myself;
Thy radiant soul shines on my way
  As my fair guiding elf.
With loving tones and beckoning hand
  Thou say'st, "Beyond the night
I catch a glimpse upon the strand
  Of thy mansion gleaming bright."
Before I came upon this earth
  I know I lived in gladness
For ages as an angel. Birth
  Has caused my present sadness.
My soul was once a heavenly dove.
  Do thou, in heaven's domains,
Let fall a pinion from above
  Upon this bird's remains!
Yes, 'tis my dire misfortune now
  To hang between two ties,
To hold within my furrowed brow
  The earth's clay, and the skies.
Alas the pain of being man,
  Of dreaming o'er my fall,
Of finding heaven within my span,
  Yet being but a pall;
Of toiling like a galley slave,
  Of carrying the load
Of human burdens, while I rave
  To fly unto my God;
Of trailing garments black with rust,
  I, son of heaven above!

Of being only graveyard dust,
   E'en though my name is—Love.

THE TRANSMIGRATION OF SOULS
(La Métempsycose)
BY BETANGER

In philosophic mood, last night, as idly I was lying,
That souls may transmigrate, methought there could be no denying:
So, just to know to what I owe propensities so strong,
I drew my soul into a chat—our gossip lasted long.
"A votive offering," she observed, "well might I claim from thee;
For thou in being hadst remained a cipher, but for me: Yet not a virgin
soul was I when first in thee enshrined."—
Ah! I suspected, little soul, thus much that I should find!
"Yes," she continued, "yes, of old—I recollect it now—
In humble ivy was I wreathed round many a joyous brow.
More subtle next the essence was that I essayed to warm,
A bird's, that could salute the skies, a little bird's my form:
Where thickets made a pleasant shade, where shepherdesses strolled,
I fluttered round, hopped on the ground, my simple lays I trolled;
My pinions grew whilst still I flew in freedom on the wind."—
Ah! I suspected, little soul, thus much that I should find!
"Medor, my name, I next became a dog of wondrous tact,
The guardian of a poor blind man, his sole support in fact;
The trick of holding in my mouth a wooden bowl I knew—
I led my master through the streets, and begged his living too.
Devoted to the poor, to please the wealthy was my care,
Gleaning, as sustenance for one, what others well could spare;
Thus good I did, since to good deeds so many I inclined."—
Ah! I suspected, little soul, thus much that I should find!
"Next, to breathe life into her charms, in a young girl I dwelt;
There, in soft prison, snugly housed, what happiness I felt!
Till to my hiding-place a swarm of Cupids entrance gained,

And after pillaging it well, in garrison remained.
Like old campaigners, there the rogues all sorts of mischief did:
And night and day, whilst still I lay in little corner hid,
How oft I saw the house on fire I scarce can call to mind."—
Ah! I suspected, little soul, thus much that I should find.
"Some light on thy propensities may now upon thee break;
But prithee hark! one more remark I still," says she, "would make.
'T is this—that having dared one day with Heaven to make too free,
God for my punishment resolved to shut me up in thee:
And what with sittings up at night, with work and woman's art,
Tears and despair—for I forbear some secrets to impart—
A poet is a very hell for soul thereto consigned!
Ah! I suspected, little soul, thus much that I should find.

THE SONG OF THE EARTH SPIRITS IN GOETHE'S "FAUST"

The soul of man
Is like the water:
From heaven it cometh,
To heaven it mounteth,
And thence at once
It must back to earth,
Forever changing.

THE SECRET OF REMINISCENCE FROM SCHILLER

What unveils to me the yearning glow
Fix'd forever to thy lips to grow?
What the longing wish thy breath to drink—
In thy Being blest, in death to sink
                    When thy look steals o'er me
As when Slaves without resistance yield

To the Victor in the battle-field,
So my Senses in the moment fly
O'er the bridge of Life tumultuously
                    When thou stand'st before me!
Speak! Why should they from their Master roam?
Do my Senses yonder seek their home?
Or do sever'd brethren meet again,
Casting off the Body's heavy chain,
                    Where thy foot hath lighted?
Were our Beings once together twin'd?
Was it therefore that our bosoms pin'd?
Were we in the light of suns now dead,
In the days of rapture long since fled,
                    Into One united?
Aye, we were so! — thou wert link'd with me
In Æone that has ceas'd to be;
On the mournful page of vanish'd time,
By my Muse were read these words sublime:
                    Nought thy love can sever!
And in Being closely twin'd and fair,
I too wondering saw it written there —
We were then a Life, a Deity —
And the world seem'd order'd then to lie
                    'Neath our sway forever.
And, to meet us, nectar-fountains still
Pour'd forever forth their blissful rill;
Forcibly we broke the seal of Things,
And to Truth's bright sunny hills our wings
Joyously were soaring.
Laura, weep! — this Deity hath flown —
Thou and I his ruins are alone;
By a thirst unquenchable we 're driven
Our lost Being to embrace; — tow'rd Heaven
                    Turns our gaze imploring.

Therefore, Laura, is this yearning glow
Fix'd forever to thy lips to grow,
And the longing wish thy breath to drink,
In thy Being blest, in death to sink
                    When thy look steals o'er me!
And as Slaves without resistance yield
To the Victor in the battle-field,
Therefore do my ravish'd Senses fly
O'er the bridge of Life tumultuously,
                    When thou stand'st before me!
Therefore do they from their Master roam!
Therefore do my Senses seek their home!
Casting off the Body's heavy chain,
Those long-sever'd brethren kiss again,
                    Hush'd is all their sighing!
And thou, too — when on me fell thine eye,
What disclos'd thy cheek's deep-purple dye?
Tow'rd each other, like relations dear,
As an exile to his home draws near,
                    Were we not then flying?

A SONNET ON CAUCASUS
BY T. CAMPANELLA

I fear that by my death the human race
  Would gain no vantage. Thus I do not die.
  So wide is this vast cage of misery
That flight and change lead to no happier place.
Shifting our pains, we risk a sorrier case:
  All worlds, like ours, are sunk in agony:
  Go where we will, we feel; and this my cry
I may forget like many an old disgrace.
Who knows what doom is mine? The Omnipotent
  Keeps silence; nay, I know not whether strife

Or peace was with me in some earlier life.
Philip in a worse prison me hath pent
These three days past — but not without God's will.
Stay we as God decrees: God doth no ill.

PART IV. PLATONIC POETS

The largest inspiration of all western thought is nourished by the Academe. Not only idealism, but the provinces of philosophy and literature hostile to Plato are really indebted to him. The noble loftiness, the ethereal subtlety, the poetic beauty of that teaching has captivated most of the line intellects of mediaeval and modern times, and it is impossible to trace the invisible course of exalted thought which has radiated from this greatest Greek, the king of a nation of philosophers.

Adopting Emerson's words, "Out of Plato come all things that are still written and debated among men of thought. Great havoc makes he among our originalities. We have reached the mountain from which all these drift boulders were detached. The Bible of the learned for twenty-two centuries, every brisk young man who says fine things to each reluctant generation, is some reader of Plato translating into the vernacular his good things... How many great men nature is incessantly sending up out of the night to be *his men* — Platonists! the Alexandrians, a constellation of genius; the Elizabethans, not less; Sir Thomas More, Henry More, John Hales, John Smith, Lord Bacon, Jeremy Taylor, Ralph Cud worth, Sydenham, Thomas Taylor. Calvinism is in his Phaedro. Christianity is in it. Mahometanism draws all its philosophy, in its handbook of morals, the Akhlak-y-Jalaly, from him. Mysticism finds in Plato all its texts." We know not how much of the world's later poetry is due to the suggestion and nurture of the poet-philosopher. But in closing our studies of the poetry of reincarnation it may be of interest to group together the avowed Platonic poets.

Most illustrious of all the English disciples of this master, in the brilliant coterie of "Cambridge Platonists," was Dr. Henry More, whom Dr. Johnson esteemed "one of our greatest divines and philosophers and no mean poet." Hobbes said of him that if his own philosophy was not true he knew none that he should sooner adopt than Henry More's of Cambridge; and Hoadley styles him "one of the first men of this or any other country." Coleridge wrote that his philosophical works "contain more enlarged and elevated views of the Christian dispensation than I have met with in any other single volume; for More had both the philosophical and poetic genius supported by immense erudition." He was a devout student of Plato. In the heat of rebellion he was spared by the fanatics. They pardoned his refusal to take their covenant and left him to continue the philosophic occupations which had rendered him famous as a lovable and absorbed scholar. He wove together in many poems a quaint texture of Gothic fancy and Greek thought. His "Psychozoia" or "Life of the Soul," from which the following verses are taken, is a long Platonic poem tracing the course of the soul through ancient existences down into the earthly realm. Campbell said of this work that it "is like a curious grotto, whose labyrinths we might explore for its strange and mystic associations." Dr. More was an intimate friend of Addison and long a correspondent of Descartes.

From Henry More's "Philosophical Poems" ("Psychozoia").

I would sing the preexistency
  Of human souls and live once o'er again
By recollection and quick memory
  All that is passed since first we all began.
But all too shallow be my wits to scan
  So deep a point and mind too dull to climb
So dark a matter. But thou more than man
  Aread, thou sacred soul of Plotin dear,
Tell me what mortals are. Tell what of old they were.
A spark or ray of divinity
  Clouded with earthly fogs, and clad in clay,
A precious drop sunk from eternity
  Spilt on the ground, or rather slunk away.
For then we fell when we 'gan first t' essay
  By stealth of our own selves something to been

Uncentering ourselves from our one great stay,
    Which rupture we new liberty did ween,
And from that prank right jolly wits ourselves did deem.
Show fitly how the preexisting soul
    Enacts and enters bodies here below
And then entire unhurt can leave this moul,
    In which by sense and motion they may know
Better than we what things transacted be
    Upon the earth, and when they best may show
Themselves to friend or foe, their phantasmy
      Moulding their airy arc to gross consistency.

Milton imbibed from his college friend Henry More an early fondness for the study of Plato, whose philosophy nourished most of the fine spirits of that day, and he expresses the Greek sage's opinion of the soul in his "Comus":—

The soul grows clotted by oblivion,
Imbodies and embrutes till she quite lose
The divine property of her first being;
Such as those thick and gloomy shadows damp
Oft seen in charnel vaults and sepulchres
Lingering and setting by a new made grave
As loth to leave the body that it loved.

Milton's Platonic proclivities are also shown in his poem "On the Death of a Fair Infant":—

Wert thou that just maid, who once before
Forsook the hated earth, O tell me sooth,
And cam'st again to visit us once more?
Or wert thou that sweet smiling youth?
    Or any other of that heavenly brood
Let down in cloudy throne to do the world some good?
Or wert thou of the golden-winged host,
Who, having clad thyself in human weed,
To earth from thy prefixed seat didst post,
And after short abode fly back with speed

As if to show what creatures heaven doth breed;
  Thereby to set the hearts of men on fire,
To scorn the sordid world and unto heaven aspire.
  In the old library of poetry known as "Dodsley's Collection," is a Miltonic poem by an anonymous Platonist which is very interesting, and as it is difficult of access we quote the best part of it.

PREEXISTENCE
IN IMITATION OF MILTON

Now had th' archangel trumpet, raised sublime
Above the walls of heaven, begun to sound;
All aether took the blast and fell beneath
Shook with celestial noise; th' almighty host,
Hot with pursuit, and reeking with the blood
Of guilty cherubs smeared in sulphurous dust,
Pause at the known command of sounding gold.
At first they close the wide Tartarean gates,
Th' impenetrable folds on brazen hinge
Roll creaking horrible; the din beneath
O'ercomes the war of flames, and deafens hell.
Then through the solid gloom with nimble wing
They cut their shining traces up to light;
Returned upon the edge of heavenly day,
Where thinnest beams play round the vast obscure
And with eternal gleam drives back the night.
They find the troops less stubborn, less involved
In crime and ruin, barr'd the realms of peace,
Yet uncondemned to baleful beats of woe,
Doubtful and suppliant; all the plumes of light
Moult from their shuddering wings, and sickly fear
Shades every face with horror; conscious guilt
Rolls in the livid eyeball, and each breast
Shakes with the dread of future doom unknown.

'T is here the wide circumference of heaven
Opens in two vast gates, that inward turn
Voluminous, on jasper columns hung
By geometry divine: they ever glow
With living sculptures; they arise by turns
To imboss the shining leaves, by turns they set
To give succeeding argument their place;
In holy hieroglyphics on they move,
The gaze of journeying angels, as they pass
Oft looking back, and held in deep surprise.
Here stood the troops distinct; the cherub guard
Unbarred the splendid gates, and in they roll
Harmonious; for a vocal spirit sits
Within each hinge, and as they onward drive,
In just divisions breaks the numerous jars
With symphony melodious, such as spheres
Involved in tenfold wreaths are said to sound.
Out flows a blaze of glory: for on high
Towering advanced the moving throne of God.

- - - - - - - - - -

Above the throne, th'ideas heavenly bright
Of past, of present, and of coming time,
Fixed their immoved abode, and there present
An endless landscape of created things
To sight celestial, where angelic eyes
Are lost in prospect; for the shiny range
Boundless and various in its bosom bears
Millions of full proportioned worlds, beheld
With steadfast eyes, till more arise to view,
And further inward scenes start up unknown.

- - - - - - - - - -

A vocal thunder rolled the voice of God.
"Servants of God! and virtues great in arms,
We approve your faithful works, and you return

Blessed from the dire pursuits of rebel foes;
Resolved, obdurant, they have tried the force
Of this right hand, and known almighty power;
Transfixed with lightning, down they sunk and fell
Into the fiery gulf, and deep they plunge
Below the burning waves, to hide their heads.

— — — — — — — — — —

"For you, ye guilty throng that lately joined
In this sedition, since seduced from good,
And caught in trains of guile, by sprites malign
Superior in their order; you accept,
Trembling, my heavenly clemency and grace.
"When the long era once has filled its orb,
You shall emerge to light and humbly here
Again shall bow before his favoring throne,
If your own virtue second my decree:
But all must have their races first below.
See, where below in chaos wondrous deep
A speck of light dawns forth, and thence throughout
The shades, in many a wreath, my forming power
There swiftly turns the burning eddy round,
Absorbing all crude matter near its brink;
Which next, with subtle motions, takes the form
I please to stamp, the seed of embryo worlds
All now in embryo, but before long shall rise
Variously scattered in this vast expanse,
Involved in winding orbs, until the brims
Of outward circles brush the heavenly gates.
The middle point a globe of curling fire
Shall hold, which round it sheds its genial heat;
Where'er I kindle life the motion grows,
In all the endless orbs, from this machine;
And infinite vicissitudes that roll
About the restless centre; for I rear

In those meanders turned, a dusty ball,
Deformed all o'er with woods, whose shaggy tops
Inclose eternal mists, and deadly damps
Hover within their boughs, to cloak the light;
Impervious scenes of horror, till reformed
To fields and grassy dells and flowery meads
By your continual pains... Here Silence sits
In folds of wreathy mantling sunk obscure,
And in dark fumes bending his drowsy head;
An urn he holds, from whence a lake proceeds
Wide, flowing gently, smooth and Lethe named;
Hither compelled, each soul must drink long draughts
Of those forgetful streams, till forms within
And all the great ideas fade and die:
For if vast thought should play about a mind
Inclosed in flesh, and dragging cumbrous life,
Fluttering and beating in the mournful cage,
It soon would break its gates and wing away:
'Tis therefore my decree, the soul return
Naked from off this beach, and perfect blank
To visit the new world; and wait to feel
Itself in crude consistence closely shut,
The dreadful monument of just revenge;
Immured by heaven's own hand, and placed erect
On fleeting matter all imprisoned round
With walls of clay; the ethereal mould shall bear
The chain of members, deafened with an ear,
Blinded by eyes, and trammeled by hands.
Here anger, vast ambition and disdain,
And all the haughty movements rise and fall,
As storms of neighboring atoms tear the soul,
And hope and love and all the calmer turns
Of easy hours, in their gay gilded shapes,
With sudden run, skim o'er deluded minds,

As matter leads the dance; but one desire
Unsatisfied, shall mar ten thousand joys.
     "The rank of beings, that shall first advance,
Drink deep of human life, and long shall stay
On this great scene of cares. From all the rest,
That longer for the destined body wait,
Less penance I expect, and short abode
In those pale dreamy kingdoms will content;
Each has his lamentable lot. and all
On different rocks abide the pains of life.
     "The pensive spirit takes the lonely grove;
Nightly he visits all the sylvan scenes,
Where far remote, a melancholy moon
Raising her head, serene and shorn of beams,
Throws here and there her glimmerings through the trees.
The sage shall haunt this solitary ground
And view the dismal landscape limned within
In horrid shades, mixed with imperfect light.
Here Judgment, blinded by delusive sense,
Contracted through the cranny of an eye,
Shoots up faint languid beams to that dark seat,
Wherein the soul, bereaved of native fire,
Sets intricate, in misty clouds obscured.
"Hence far removed, a different being race
In cities full and frequent take their seat,
Where honor's crushed, and gratitude oppressed
With swelling hopes of gain, that raise within
A tempest, and driven onward by success,
Can find no bounds. For creatures of a day
Stretch their wide cares to ages; full increase
Starves their penurious soul, while empty sound
Fills the ambitious; *that* shall ever shrink,
Pining with endless cares, while *this* shall swell
To tympany enormous. Bright in arms

Here shines the hero, out he fiercely leads
A martial throng, his instruments of rage,
To fill the world with death, and thin mankind.

- - - - - - - - - -

"There savage nature in one common lies
And feels its share of hunger, care, and pain,
Cheated by flying prey; and now they tear
Their panting flesh; and deeply, darkly quaff
Of human woe, even when they rudely sip
The flowing stream, or draw the savory pulp
Of nature's freshest viands; fragrant fruits
Enjoyed with trembling, and in danger sought.
    "But where the appointed limits of a law
Fences the general safety of the world,
No greater quiet reigns: the blended loads
Of punishment and crime deform the world,
And give no rest to man; with pangs and throes
He enters on the stage; prophetic tears
And infant cries prelude his future woes;
And all is one continual scene of gulf
Till the sad sable curtain falls in death.

- - - - - - - - - -

    "Then the gay glories of the living world
Shall cast their empty varnish and retire
Out of his feeble views; the shapeless root
Of wild imagination dance and play
Before his eyes obscure; till all in death
Shall vanish, and the prisoner enlarged,
Regains the flaming borders of the sky."
    He ended. Peals of thunder rend the heavens,
And chaos, from the bottom turned, resounds.
The mighty clangor; all the heavenly host
Approve the high decree, and loud they sing
Eternal justice; while the guilty troops,

Sad with their doom, but sad without despair,
Fall fluttering down to Lethe's lake, and there
For penance, and the destined body wait.

Shelley's Platonic leanings are well known.* The favorite Greek conceit of preexistence in many earlier lives may frequently be found in his poems. The title over one of his songs of unrest, "The World's Wanderer," evidently alludes to himself, as do the lines in it

"Like the world's rejected guest."

The song of the spirits in "Prometheus Unbound" pictures vividly the human soul's descent into the gloom of the material world:—

To the deep, to the deep,
        Down, down!
Through the shade of sleep,
Through the cloudy strife
Of Death and of Life,
Through the veil and the bar
Of things which seem and are,
Even to the steps of the remotest throne,
        Down, down!
While the sound whirls around,
        Down, down!
As the fawn draws the hound,
As the lightning the vapor,
As a weak moth, the taper;
Death, despair; love, sorrow;
Time both; today, tomorrow;
As steel obeys the spirit of the stone,
        Down, down!
In the depth of the deep,
        Down, down!
Like the veiled lightning asleep,
Like the spark nursed in embers,

---

* See Dowden's *Life of Shelley*, from which a suggestive incident is quoted above, on page 92.

The last look Love remembers,
Like a diamond which shines
On the dark wealth of mines,
A spell is treasured but for thee alone,
Down, down!

The last stanza of "The Cloud" is Shelley's Platonic symbol of human life: —

I am the daughter of earth and water
  And the nursling of the sky,
I pass through the pores of the ocean and shores,
  I change, but I cannot die.
For after the rain when with never a stain
  The pavilion of heaven is bare,
  And the winds and sunbeams with their convex gleams
Build up the blue dome of air,
  I silently laugh at my own cenotaph,
And out of the caverns of rain,
  Like a child from the womb, like a ghost from the tomb,
I arise and unbuild it again.

Another poem, entitled "A Fragment," certainly refers to preexistence: —

Ye gentle visitants of calm thought,
  Moods like the memories of happier earth
  Which come arrayed in thoughts of little worth
Like stars in clouds by weak winds enwrought.

THE RETREAT
BY HENRY VAUGHAN

Happy those early days when
I Shined in my angel-infancy,
Before I understood this place
Appointed for my second race,
Or taught my soul to fancy aught

But a white celestial thought;
When yet I had not walked above
A mile or two from my first love,
And, looking back, at that short space,
Could see a glimpse of his bright face;
When on some gilded cloud or flower
My gazing soul would dwell an hour,
And in those weaker glories spy
Some shadows of eternity;
Before I taught my tongue to wound
My conscience with a sinful sound;
Or had the black art to dispense
A several sin to every sense,
But felt through all this flashy dress
Bright shoots of everlastingness.
Oh, how I long to travel back
And tread again that ancient track!
That I might once more reach that plain
Where first I left my glorious train;
From whence the enlightened spirit sees
That shady city of palm-trees.
But ah! my soul with too much stay
Is drunk and staggers in the way.
Some men a forward motion love,
But I by backward steps would move,
And when this dust falls to the urn,
In that state I came, return.

In Emerson, the Plato of the nineteenth century, the whole feeling of the Greek seems reflected in its most glorious development. Many of his poems clearly suggest the influence of his Greek teacher, as his "Threnody" upon the death of his young son, and "The Sphinx" in which these two stanzas appear:—

To vision profounder
  Man's spirit must dive;

His aye-rolling orb
  At no goal will arrive;
The heavens that now draw him
  With sweetness untold,
Once found for new heavens
  He spurneth the old.
Eterne alteration
  Now follows, now flies,
And under pain, pleasure —
  Under pleasure, pain lies.
Love works at the centre,
  Heart-heaving alway;
Forth speed the strong pulses
  To the borders of day.

Mrs. Elizabeth Rowe, the friend of Bishop Ken and of Dr. Isaac Watts, has left this allusion to preexistence in

A HYMN ON HEAVEN

Ye starry mansions, hail! my native skies!
Here in my happy, preexistent state
(A spotless mind) I led the life of Gods,
But passing, I salute you, and advance
To yonder brighter realms, allowed access.
Hail, splendid city of the almighty king,
Celestial salem, situate above, etc.

Some of the common church hymns glow with the enthusiasm of Platonic preexistence, and are fondly sung by Christians without any thought that, while their idea is of Biblical origin, it has been nourished and perpetuated by the Greek sage, and directly implies reincarnation. For instance: —

"I'm but a stranger, here, heaven is my home.
  Heaven is my fatherland, heaven is my home."
"My Ain Countrie."

"This world where grief and sin abideth,
  Is not the Christian's native clime."
"The home-land, blessed home-land."
"Jerusalem, my happy home."

Chapter VI
Reincarnation Among the Ancients

The ancient theologists and priests testify that the soul is conjoined to the body through a certain punishment, and that it is buried in this body as in a sepulchre.—PHILOLAUS, (a Pythagorean.)

Search thou the path of the soul, whence she came, or what way, after serving the body, by joining work with sacred speed, thou shalt raise her again to the same state whence she fell.—ZOROASTER.

Death has no power th'immortal soul to slay,
That, when its present body turns to clay,
Seeks a fresh home, and with unlessened might
Inspires another frame with life and light.
So I myself (well I the past recall),
When the fierce Greeks begirt Troy's holy wall,
Was brave Euphorbus: and in conflict drear
Poured forth my blood beneath Atrides' spear.
The shield this arm did bear I lately saw
In Juno's shrine, a trophy of that war.
PYTHAGORAS, in Dryden's Ovid.

He [Plato] spoke of Him
The lone, eternal One, who dwells above,
And of the soul's untraceable descent
From that high fount of spirit, through all the grades
Of intellectual being, till it mix
With atoms vague, corruptible and dark.
Nor yet ev'n thus, though sunk in earthly dross,
Corrupted all, nor its ethereal touch

Quite lost, but tasting of the fountain still
As some bright river, which has rolled along
Through meads of flowery light and mines of gold
When poured at length into the dusky deep
Disdains to take at once its briny taint,
But keeps unchanged awhile the lustrous tinge
Or balmy freshness of the scenes it left.

MOORE.

○ ○ ○ ○ ○ ○ ○ ○

The origin of the philosophy of reincarnation is prehistoric. It antedates the remotest antiquity all over the world, and appears to be cognate with mankind, springing up spontaneously as a necessary corollary of the immortality of the soul; for its undiminished sway has been well-nigh universal outside of Christendom. In the earliest dawn of Mother India it was firmly established. The infancy of Egypt found it dominant on the Nile. It was at home in Greece long before Pythagoras. The most ancient beginnings of Mexico and Peru knew it as the faith of their fathers.

■. In sketching the course of this thought among the men of old, the first attention belongs to India. Brahmanism, the most primitive form of this faith, has gone through vast changes during the four thousand years of history. The initial form of it, dating back into the remotest mists of antiquity and descending to the first chapters of authentic chronology, was an ideally simple nature-worship. The Rig-Veda and the oldest sacred hymns display the beauty of this adoration for every phase of nature, centering with especial fondness upon light as the supreme power, and upon the cow as the favorite animal. Professor Wilson's and Max Müller's translations have opened to the English race the charming thought of this primordial people, whose great child-souls found objects of reverence in all things. There were no distinct gods, but everything was divine, and through all they saw the flow of ever-changing life. Gradually an ecclesiastical system climbed up around this religion, clothing, stifling, and at last burying the vital organism, until Sakya Muni's reaction started Buddhism into vigorous growth as the beautiful protest against the disfigured and decayed form. About Buddhism, too, there has arisen a heavy weight of lifeless ritual, but every breath of life with which the slumbering mother and daughter continue their existence is perfumed with the rose-attar of reincarnation. How they have since continued to disseminate the idea of reincarnation is suggested in chapter IX, for the East of today is essentially a sculptured picture of what has been monotonously enduring for twenty centuries.

Of the ancient Indians we learn through Pliny, Strabo, Megasthenes, Plutarch, and Herodotus, who describe the Gymnosophists and Brahmans as ascetic philosophers who made a study of spiritual things, living singly or in celibate communities much like the later Pythagoreans. Porphyry says of them: "They live without either clothes, riches or wives. They are held in so great veneration by the rest of their countrymen that the king himself often visits them to ask their advice. Such are their views of death that with reluctance they endure life as a piece of necessary bondage to nature, and haste to set the soul at liberty from the body. Nay, often, when in good health, and no evil to disturb them, they depart life, advertising it beforehand. No man hinders them, but all reckon them happy, and send commissions along with them to their dead friends. So strong and firm is their belief of a future life for the soul, where they shall enjoy one another, after receiving all their commands, they deliver themselves to the fire, that they may separate the soul as pure as possible from the body, and expire singing hymns. Their old friends attend them to death with more ease than other men their fellow-citizens to a long journey. They deplore their own state for surviving them and deem them happy in their immortality." When Alexander the Great first penetrated their country he could not persuade them to appear before him, and had to gratify his curiosity about their life and philosophy by proxy, though he afterward witnessed them surrender themselves to the flames.

■■. Herodotus asserts that the doctrine of metempsychosis originated in Egypt. "The Egyptians are the first who propounded the theory that the human soul is imperishable, and that where the body of any one dies it enters into some other creature that may be ready to receive it, and that when it has gone the round of all created forms on land, in water and in air, then it once more enters a human body born for it; and that this cycle of existence for the soul takes place in three thousand years."* He continues, "Some of the Greeks adopted this opinion, some earlier, others later, as if it were their own."

The Egyptians held that the human race began after the pure gods and spirits had left earth, when the demons who were sinfully inclined had revolted and introduced guilt. The gods then created human bodies for these demons to inhabit, as a means of expiating their sin, and these fallen spirits are the present men and women, whose earthly life is a course of purification. All the Egyptian precepts and religious codes are to this end. The judgment after death decides whether the soul has attained purity or not. If not, the soul must return to earth in renewal of its expiation either in the body of a man, or animal or plant. As the spirit was believed to maintain its connection with the material form as long as this remained, the practice of embalming was designed to arrest the passage of the soul into other forms. The custom of embalming is also connected with their opinion that after three thousand years away from the body the soul would return to its former body provided it be preserved from destruction.† If it is not preserved, the soul would enter the most convenient habitation, which might be a wretched creature. They maintained, too, that the gods frequently inhabited the bodies of animals, and therefore they worshiped animals as incarnations of special divinities. The sacred bodies of these godly visitants were also embalmed as a mark of respect to their particular class of deities. For they placed certain gods in certain animals, the Egyptian Apollo choosing the hawk, Mercury the ibis, Mars the fish, Diana the cat, Bacchus the goat, Hercules the colt, Vulcan the ox, etc. This conceit was but a specialization of their general tenet of pantheism, insisting that all life is

* It will be noticed later that Plato reduced this term to one thousand years.
† Egyptologists disagree as to the real intent of embalming. We select the explanations best adapted to the theological doctrines of the Egyptians.

divine, that every living thing must be venerated, and that the highest creatures should be most devoutly worshiped.

The Egyptian conception of reincarnation as shaped by the priesthood is displayed in their classic, "Ritual of the Dead," which is one of their chief sacred books and describes the course of the soul after death. A copy of it was deposited in each mummy case. It opens with a sublime dialogue between the soul and the God of Hades, Osiris, to whose realm he asks admission. Finally Osiris says, "Fear nothing, but cross the threshold." As the soul enters he is dazzled with the glory of light. He sings a hymn to the sun and goes on taking the food of knowledge. After frightful dangers are passed, rest and refreshment come. Continuing his journey he reaches at last heaven's gate, where he is instructed in profound mysteries. Within the gate he is transformed into different animals and plants. After this the soul is reunited to the body for which careful embalming was so important. A critical examination tests his right to cross the subterranean river to Elysium. He is conducted by Anubis through a labyrinth to the judgment hall of Osiris, where forty-two judges question him upon his whole past life. If the decisive judgment approves him he enters heaven. If not, he is sentenced to pass through lower forms of existence according to his sins, or, if a reprobate, is given over to the powers of darkness for purgation. After three thousand years of this he is again consigned to a human probation.

■■■. Of the old Persian faith, it is difficult to obtain a trustworthy statement, except what is derived from its present form among the Parsees. The Magi, Zoroaster's followers, believed that the immortal soul descended from on high for a short period of lives in a mortal body to gain experience, and to then return again. When the soul is above it has several abodes, one luminous, another dark, and some filled with a mixture of light and darkness. Sometimes it sinks into the body from the luminous abode and after a virtuous life returns above; but if coming from the dark region, it passes an evil life and enters a worse place in proportion to her conduct until purified. The dualism of these fire-worshipers gave reincarnation a briefer period of operation than the other oriental religions.

IV. Pythagoras is mentioned by a Greek tradition as one of the Greeks who visited India before the age of Alexander. It is almost certain that he went to Egypt and received there the doctrine of transmigration which he taught in the Greek cities of lower Italy (b. c. 529). Jamblichus says: "He spent twelve years at Babylon, freely conversing with the Magi, was instructed in everything venerable among them, and learned the most perfect worship of the gods." He is said to have represented the human soul as an emanation of the world soul, partaking of the divine nature. At death it leaves one body to take another and so goes through the circle of appointed forms. Ovid's "Metamorphoses" contains a long description of the Pythagorean idea, from which these verses are taken, as translated by Dryden:—

> "Souls cannot die. They leave a former home,
> And in new bodies dwell, and from them roam.
> Nothing can perish, all things change below,
> For spirits through all forms may come and go.
> Good beasts shall rise to human forms, and men,
> If bad, shall backward turn to beasts again.
> Thus, through a thousand shapes, the soul shall go
> And thus fulfill its destiny below."

But it is very difficult to determine exactly what the views of Pythagoras were. Aristotle, Plato, and Diogenes Laertius say he taught that the soul when released by death must pass through a grand circle of living forms before reaching the human again. From Pythagoras himself we have only some aphorisms of practical wisdom and symbolic sentences; from his disciples a few fragments — all devoid of the grotesque hypothesis generally ascribed to him. Although his name is synonymous with the transmigration of human souls through animal bodies, the strong probabilities are that if this doctrine came from him it was entirely exoteric, concealing the inner truth of reincarnation. Some of his later disciples, especially the author of the work which is attributed to Timaeus the Locian, denied that he taught it in any literal sense, and said that by it he meant merely to emphasize the fact that men are assimilated in their vices to the beasts. (See Chapter XII.)

V. Plato is called by Emerson the synthesis of Europe and Asia, and a decidedly oriental element pervades his philosophy, giving it a sunrise color. He had traveled in Egypt and Asia Minor and among the Pythagoreans of Italy. As he died (b. c. 348) twenty years before Alexander's invasion of India he missed that opportunity of learning the Hindu ideas.

In the great "myth," or allegory, of Phaedrus, the classic description of the relation of the soul to the material world, what he says of the judgment upon mankind and their subsequent return to human or animal bodies coincides substantially with the Egyptian and Hindu religions. But his theory of preexistence and of absolute knowledge seems to be original. It grows out of his cardinal doctrine (and that of his master Socrates) concerning the reality and validity of truth, in opposition to the skepticism of contemporary sophists, who claimed that truth is mere subjective opinion—what each man troweth.

The Phaedrus myth is evidently suggested by the splendid religious procession which closed the Athenian festival. With gorgeous ceremony nearly the whole city's population participated in this crowning glory of their most sacred holiday. The procession wound through the finest streets of the city and then up the steep ascent of the Acropolis, whose precipitous incline kept the horses struggling for a foothold. That elevated site commanded a view of the busy city, the plains beyond, and the distant mountains and sea under the deep blue canopy of the Greek sky, presenting to the worshipers' sight a panorama of the changing aspects of human life and a type of heaven's repose. From this picture the poet-philosopher conjures up a sublimer procession marshalled by the king of gods and men, moving through the heavenly orbits of the soul's progress, until they ascend the celestial dome itself, whence the soul may gaze upon the unspeakable glories of spiritual Truth.*

The Socrates of the dialogue first likens the soul to "a winged team and their charioteer. In the case of the gods both horses and charioteer are all good and of good breed; those of the rest are mixed. And first of all, our charioteer drives a pair; in the next place, the one is

* See the article on "Preexistence," in the *Penn Monthly*, September, 1877.

good and noble in itself and by breed, while the other is the opposite in both regards. And so the management of the chariot must need be difficult and harassing. Just how the living being which is immortal is distinguished from that which is mortal, I must endeavor to tell you. All that is soul has the charge of that which is soulless, and traverses the whole heaven, appearing now in one form, now in another. When perfect and possessed of wings, she moves in mid air and controls the whole world *(kosmos)*. But if she loses her feathers, she is borne hither and thither until she lays hold of something that is fixed and solid, and there making her home, and taking to herself an earthly body, which seems to be self-moved by reason of the force she furnishes, soul and body are fastened together and come to be called mortal... But let us take up the reason of that stripping off the feathers by which the soul is brought to its fall. It is as follows: The power of the wing is designed to bear up that which is heavy through mid air, where the race of the gods dwells, and of all that is corporeal this has most in common with the divine; for the divine is the beautiful, the wise, the good, and everything of the sort, and by these the wing of the soul is nourished and grows especially. But by what is base and evil, and whatever else is the opposite of divine, it wastes away and is destroyed.

"Now Zeus, the great Leader in heaven, leads the van, driving a winged chariot, the marshal and guardian of all. And he is followed by the host of the gods and demons marshalled in eleven bands, for Hestia alone remains in the house of the gods, and those of the rest who belong to the number of The Twelve [Great Gods] lead on as captains of their companies, each in the order to which he has been assigned. Now there are within heaven many and blessed views and ways of passage in which the race of the happy gods pass to and fro, each of them doing his own work, and whoever can and will follow, for envy stands aloof from the choir of the gods.

"But whenever they go to banquet and to feast, then they proceed all together up towards the lofty vault of heaven. Now the chariots of the gods, being well balanced and obedient to the rein, proceed easily, but the rest with difficulty. For the horse that partakes of evil slips

downward, sinking and gravitating towards the earth, if he has not
been properly broken in by the charioteer. Then it is that toil and most
extreme conflict press hard upon the soul. But those souls which are
called immortal, when they reach the summit, go forth and stand upon
the back [the convex] of the heaven, and as they stand the revolution
[of the sphere] carries them around with it, and they behold the things
which are outside of the heaven.

"Now the place which is above the heaven no earthly poet has ever
praised as it deserves, nor ever will: but it is thus. For I must dare to
tell the truth, especially when I am talking about Truth. The colorless,
formless, and intangible Being which *is* Being, is visible only to the
Reason *(nous)*, which is the governor of the soul. Round about this [pure
Being] is located the true sort of knowledge. Since then the intelligence
of God — like that of every soul in so far as it is to receive what best
befits it — is nourished on Reason and pure Knowledge, in beholding
at last the Being it loves it, and in contemplating the Truth is nourished and gladdened, until the revolution [of the sphere] brings it round
again to its starting-place. And in this circuit it beholds Righteousness
itself, beholds Temperance itself, beholds Knowledge — not that which
has origin, nor that which differs in the different things to which we
ascribe existence, but Knowledge which has a real being in that which
is Being indeed. And other equally real existences she beholds and is
feasted upon, and then reentering the heaven she returns homeward.
And when she has come thither, the charioteer, staying his horses at
their stall, fodders them with ambrosia, and waters them with nectar.
And this is the life of the gods.

"But as to the other souls, that which best follows God and is most
like Him lifts up the head of the charioteer to the place outside the
heaven, and is carried around the revolution with Him, disturbed indeed by the horses, and beholding the things which have true being
with difficulty. Another lifts up the head at times, at others draws it
in because compelled by the horses, and therefore beholds some and
not others; the rest one and all desire and follow that which is above,
but not being able to reach it, they are carried around submerged be-

neath the heaven, they tread and fall upon each other, each trying to get precedence of the other. Noise, and rivalry, and sweat to the last degree ensue, whereupon many are maimed in their wings by the fault of their charioteers. And all of them, after long toil, depart uninitiated into the vision of Being, and when they have gone are fed on the food of opinion. Whence then that great desire of theirs to behold the plain of Truth? Is it not because the pasturage which befits what is best in the soul happens to grow in that meadow, and the growth of the wing by which the soul soars is nourished with this?

"And this is this law of Adrastea [or Nemesis, the inevitable Order]: whatsoever soul has shared with God, in beholding any of those things that are true and real, is unharmed until the next period, and if she is always able to do this, is always unhurt. But should it happen that she cannot follow on to know, and by any mischance grows heavy through being filled with forgetfulness and faultiness, and through that heaviness loses her feathers and falls to the earth, then the law is that this soul shall not take upon her the nature of any beast in the first generation [or birth], but the soul that has seen most shall come to the birth of a man who is to be a philosopher, or an artist, or of some musician and lover; and the second, [to the birth] of a lawful king, or warrior and ruler; the third, of a statesman, or of some financier, or man of affairs; the fourth, of a toil-loving gymnast, or of some one who is to be a physician; the fifth, the life of a soothsayer, or some hierophantic function; to the sixth, the life of a poet, or of some other sort of mimic, will be suitable; to the seventh, that of an artisan or a husbandman; to the eighth, that of a sophist or a demagogue; to the ninth, that of a tyrant. And whoever in any of these positions conducts himself rightly receives a better lot; but whoever behaves otherwise, a worse.

"No soul arrives at that place from whence it came for ten thousand years, except it be that one who is honestly a philosopher, or a lover who has a share of philosophy. These in the third period of a thousand years, if thrice successively they have chosen this manner of life, and have thus received their wings, depart thither in the three thousandth year. But the rest, when they have finished the first life assigned them, undergo a judgment. And after the judgment, some of them proceed to the prison-house under the earth and receive punishment; and the others, having been raised by the judgment to a place in the heaven, pass their time in a manner worthy of the life they lived in human form.

"And when, in the thousandth year, they come to a casting of lots and a choice of their second life, each chooses whichever she wishes. And thereupon a human soul comes to the life of a beast; and one that has been a man becomes from a beast a man again.

"But that soul which has never beheld the Truth will never come into this [human] form; the understanding of general truth collected from many perceptions into unity by rational thought is an essential of humanity. And this is the recollection of those things which our soul has once seen when accompanying God, and disdaining those things which we now speak of as being, and lifting up our heads to behold true Being. Wherefore it is just that the intelligence of the philosopher alone receives wings; for he is ever with all his might busied with the recollections of these things, occupation with which makes God what he is. And only the man who makes right use of such recollections, and thus continually attains initiation into perfect mysteries, becomes truly perfect; and for giving up human pursuits and becoming en wrapt in the divine, he is esteemed by the many as beside himself, for they fail to see that he is God-possessed.

... "As has been said, every human soul is by nature a beholder of Being, else she would not have entered into this form of life. But it is not easy for every soul to awaken those recollections which she brought from thence, or they may then have had but scant vision of what was there, or since they have fallen thence they may have had the mischance to be diverted by bad associations to that which is unjust, and to fall into forgetfulness of the holy things which they then beheld. A few are left, who retain enough of the recollection; but whenever they behold any resemblance of what is there, they are struck with astonishment, and are no longer masters of themselves; but they know not why they are thus affected, because they have no adequate perception. But there is no brilliancy in those earthly likenesses of justice and temperance, and whatever else is precious to the soul; for through obscure instruments, it is given with difficulty and to but few to draw near to those images and behold what manner of thing it is that they represent. But then it was permitted to behold Beauty in all its splendor, when along with the blessed chorus, we [philosophers] following Zeus, others some other of the gods, we shared in the beatific vision and contemplation, and were initiated into mysteries which it is just to call the most perfect of all, and whose rapturous feast we kept in innocence, and while still inexpert of those evils which were awaiting us in a time still future. And we beheld visions innocent and simple and peaceful and happy, as if spectators at the mysteries, in pure array, ourselves pure, and without a sign upon us of this which we now carry about with us and call a body, and are bound thereto like an oyster to his shell. Let us indulge in these memories, whereby we are led to speak the longer from desire of the things which we then saw."*

We penetrate into the inmost secret of Plato's thought in the super-celestial plain, the dwelling-place of substantial ideas, the essential Truth, the absolute knowledge, in which the pure Being holds the supreme place which we assign to God, the Hindu to Brahma, and the Egyptian to Osiris, but which the polytheist could not ascribe to his gods. Plato, like the initiated priests of India and Egypt, to whom the highest deity was nameless, knew the objects of common worship were but exalted men, above whom was One whose nature was undisclosed to men, and of whom it was audacious childishness to assert human attributes. The Highest was the centre of those Realities dimly shadowed in earthly appearance, and Plato's pictorial representation of his thought is only a parable cloaking the essential principle that during the eternal past we have strayed from the real Truth through repeated lives into the present.

Of Plato's philosophy of preexistence, Professor W. A. Butler says in his masterly lectures on Ancient Philosophy: "It is certain that with Plato the conviction was associated with a vast and pervading principle, which extended through every department of nature and thought. This principle was the priority of mind to body, both in order of dignity and

* From Jowett's translation.

in order of time; a principle which with him was not satisfied by the single admission of a *divine* preexistence, but extended through every instance in which these natures could be compared. A very striking example of the manner in which he thus generalized the principle of priority of mind to body is to be found in the well-known passage in the tenth book of his 'Laws,' in which he proves the existence of divine energy. The argument employed really applies to every case of motion and equally proves that every separate corporeal system is but a mechanism moved by a spiritual essence anterior to itself. The universe is full of gods, and the human soul is, as it were, the god or demon of the human body."

VI. The Jews had the best parallel of Plato's Phaedrus in the third chapter of Genesis, describing the fall of Adam and Eve. The theological comments upon that popular summary of the origin of sin have always groped after reincarnation, by making all Adam's descendants responsible in him for that act. Many Jewish scholars undertook to fuse Greek philosophy with their national religion. The Septuagint translation, made in the third century before Christ, gives evidence of such a purpose in suppressing the strong anthropomorphic terms by which the Old Testament mentioned God. Aristobulus, a Jewish-Greek poet of the second century, writes of Hebrew ideas in Platonic phrases. Similar passages are found in Aristeas and in the second book of the Maccabees. Pythagoreanism was blended with Judaism in the beliefs and practices of the Jewish Therapeutse of Egypt, and their brethren the Essenes of Palestine.

Of the Essenes, Josephus writes: "The opinion obtains among them that bodies indeed are corrupted, and the matter of them not permanent, but that souls continue exempt from death forever; and that emanating from the most subtle ether they are unfolded in bodies as prisons to which they are drawn by some natural spell. But when loosed from the bonds of flesh, as if released from a long captivity, they rejoice and are borne upward."

The most prominent Jewish writer upon this subject is Philo of Alexandria, who lived in the time of Christ, and adapted a popular version of Platonic ideas to the religion of his own people. He turned the Hebrew stories into remarkably deft Platonic allegories. His theory of preexistence and rebirths is practically that of his master Plato, as is shown in this extract: "The company of disembodied souls is distributed in various orders. The law of some of them is to enter mortal bodies and after certain prescribed periods be again set free. But those possessed of a diviner structure are absolved from all local bonds of earth. Some of these souls choose confinement in mortal bodies because they are earthly and corporeally inclined. Others depart, being released again according to supernaturally determined times and seasons. Therefore, all such as are wise, like Moses, are living abroad from home. For the souls of such formerly chose this expatriation from heaven, and through curiosity and the desire of acquiring knowledge they came to dwell abroad in earthly nature, and while they dwell in the body they look down on things visible and mortal around them, and urge their way thitherward again whence they came originally: and call that heavenly region in which they live their citizenship, fatherland, but this earthly in which they live, foreign." In choosing between the Mosaic and the Platonic account of the Fall, as to which best expressed the essential truth, although a Jew, he decided for Plato. He considers men as fallen spirits attracted by material desires and thus brought into the body's prison, yet of kin to God and the ideal world. The philosophic life is the means of escape, with the aid of the divine Logos, or Spirit, to the blessed fellowship from which they have fallen. Regeneration is a purification from matter. Philo renounced the creed of his fathers in order to reform it, and his influence was profoundly felt for centuries. The origin of the Jewish Cabala is involved in endless dispute. Jewish scholars claim that it is prehistoric. Although a portion of it is held to have been composed in the Middle Ages, it is certain that its teachings had been handed down by tradition from very early times, and that some parts come from the Jewish philosophers of Alexandria and others from the later Neo-Platonists and Gnostics. Preexistence and reincarnation appear here, not in Philo's speculative form of it, but in a much simpler and more matter-of-fact character—affirming that human spirits are again and again born into the world, after long intervals, and in entire forgetfulness of their previous experiences. This is not a curse, as in Plato's religions, but a blessing, being the process of purification by repeated probations. "All the souls," says the Zohar, or Book of Light, "are subject to the trials of transmigration; and men do not know which are the ways of the Most High in their regard. They do not know how many transformations and mysterious trials they must undergo; how many souls and spirits come to this world without returning to the palace of the divine king. The souls must reenter the absolute substance whence they have emerged. But to accomplish this end they must develop all the perfections, the germ of which is planted in them; and if they have not fulfilled this condition during one life, they must commence another, a third, and so forth, until they have acquired the condition which fits them for reunion with God."

Chapter VII
Reincarnation in the Bible

Out from the heart of nature rolled
The burdens of the Bible old.—EMERSON.

The more diligently the student works this mine (the Bible), the richer and
more abundant he finds the ore ; new light continually beams from this source
of heavenly knowledge to direct and illustrate the work of God and the ways
of men.— SIR WALTER SCOTT.

The divine oracles are not so silent in this matter as is imagined. But truly
I have so tender a sense of the sacred authority of that holy volume that I
dare not be so bold with it as to force it to speak what I think it intends not.
Wherefore I would not willingly urge Scripture as a proof of anything, but
what I am sure by the whole tenor of it Is therein contained. Would I take
the liberty to fetch in everything for a Scripture evidence that with a little
industry a man might make serviceable to his design, I doubt not but I should
be able to fill my margent with quotations which should be as much- to pur-
pose as have been cited in general Catechisms and Confessions of Faith...
And yet I must needs say that there is very fair probability for Preexistence
in the written word of God, as there is in that which is engraved upon our
rational natures.— GLANVIL, in *Lux Orientalis.*

○ ○ ○ ○ ○ ○ ○ ○

The vitality of the doctrine of Reincarnation does not in the least depend upon a scriptural endorsement of it, but the fact that it is surprisingly conspicuous here is certainly interesting and confirmatory. Every
candid Christian student must acknowledge that the revelation of truth
is no more confined to the central book of Christendom than sunshine

is limited to the Orient. There must be great principles of philosophy, like that of evolution, outside of the Bible; and yet the most skeptical thinker has to concede that this volume is the richest treasury of wisdom — the best of which is still unlearned.

Although most Christians are unaware of it, reincarnation is strongly present in the Bible, chiefly in the form of pre existence. It is not inculcated as a doctrine essential to redemption. Neither is immortality. But it is taken for granted, cropping out here and there as a fundamental rock. Some scholars consider it an unimportant oriental speculation which is accidentally entangled into the texture. But the uniform strength and beauty of its hold seem to rank it with the other essential threads of the warp upon which is woven the noblest fabric of religious thought.

A sufficient evidence of the Biblical support of preexistence, and of the consequent wide-spread belief in it among the Jews, is found in Solomon's long reference to it among his Proverbs. The wise king wrote of himself: "The Lord possessed me in the beginning of his way before the works of old. I was set up from everlasting, from the beginning, or ever the earth was. When there were no depths, I was brought forth; when there were no foundations abounding with water. Before the mountains were settled, before the hills was I brought forth: while as yet he had not made the earth, nor the fields, nor the highest part of the dust of the world. When he prepared the heavens I was there: when he set a compass upon the face of the depth: when he established the clouds above: when he strengthened the foundations of the deep: when he gave to the sea his decree, that the waters should not pass his commandment: when he appointed the foundations of the earth: then I was by him, as one brought up with him: and I was daily his delight, rejoicing always before him; rejoicing in the habitable part of the earth; and my delights were with the sons of men."* This passage disposes of the theory of Delitzseh that preexistence in the Bible means simply an existence in the foreknowledge of the creator. Such a mere foreknowledge would not place him previous to the parts of creation which preceded his earthly appearance. And the last two clauses

* Proverbs VIII. 22-31.

clearly express a prior physical life. The prophets, too, are assured of their prenatal antiquity. Jeremiah hears Jehovah tell him, "Before I formed thee in the belly I knew thee; and before thou earnest forth out of the womb I sanctified thee."*

Skipping passages of disputed interpretation in Job and the Psalms which suggest this idea, there is good evidence for it all through the Old Testament, which is universally conceded by commentators, and was always claimed by the Jewish rabbis. The translators have distinguished the revealed form of Deity, as successively recorded in the Hebrew Scriptures, by the word LORD, in capitals, separating this use of the word from other forms, as the preexistent Christ. "The angel of the Lord" and "the angel of Jehovah" are other expressions for the same manifestation of the Highest, which modern theology regards as the second person of the Trinity. Wherever God is said to have appeared as man, to Abraham at Mamre, to Jacob at Peniel, to Joshua at Gilgal, to the three captives in the Babylonian furnace as "a fourth, like to the Son of God," etc., Christian scholarship has maintained this to be the same person who afterward became the son of Mary. The Jews also consider these various appearances to be their promised Christ. After the captivity they held the same view concerning all persons. The apocryphal "Wisdom of Solomon" teaches unmistakably the preexistence of human souls in Platonic form, although it probably is older than Philo, as when it says (IX. 15), "I was an ingenuous child, and received a good soul; nay, more, being good, I came into a body undefiled;" and "the corruptible body presseth down the soul, and the earthly tabernacle weigheth down the mind that museth upon many things." Glimpses of it appear also in "Ecclesiasticus."

The assertion of Josephus that this idea was common among the Pharisees is proven in the Gospels, where members of the Sanhedrin cast the retort at Jesus, "Thou wast altogether born in sins."† The prevalence of this feeling in the judgments of daily life is seen in the question put to Jesus by his disciples, "Which did sin, this man or his parents, that

* Jeremiah I. 5.
† John IX. 34.

he was born blind?"* referring to the two contending popular theories, that of Moses, who taught that the sins of the fathers would descend on the children to the third and fourth generation, and that of reincarnation, subsequently adopted, by which a man's discomforts resulted from his former misconduct. Jesus' reply, "Neither," is no denial of the truth of reincarnation, for in other passages he definitely affirms it of himself, but merely an indication that he thought this truth had better not be given those listeners then, just as he withheld other verities until the ripe time for utterance. This very expression of preexistence used by the disciples he employs toward the man whom he healed at Bethesda's pool after thirty-eight years of paralysis: "Sin no more, lest a worse thing come unto thee."† Repeatedly he confirms the popular impression that John the Baptist was a reincarnation of Elijah. To the throng around him he said: "Among them that are born of women there hath not risen a greater than John the Baptist." "If ye will receive it, this is Elias, which was for to come."‡ That John the Baptist denied his former personality as Elijah is not strange, for no one remembers distinctly his earlier life. Often Jesus refers to his descent from heaven, as when he says, "I came down from heaven, not to do mine own will, but the will of him that sent me;"§ and what he means by heaven is shown by his words to Nicodemus, "No man hath ascended up to heaven but he that came down from heaven, even the Son of man *which is in heaven*"¶ The inference is that the heaven in which he formerly lived was similar to the heaven of that moment, namely earth. Again, Jesus asked his disciples, "Whom say men that I am?" And his disciples state the popular thought in answering, "Some say Elijah, others Jeremiah, and others one of the old prophets." "But whom say ye that I am?" Peter, the spokesman, replies, "Thou art the Christ, the Son of God," and so

* John IX. 2.
† John V. 14.
‡ Matt. XI. 14; also, Matt. XVII. 12, 13. See Professor Bowen's remarks upon these texts, page 114.
§ John VI. 38.
¶ John III. 13.

expresses another phase of the same prevailing idea, for the Christ was also an Old Testament personage. And Jesus approves this response. After Herod had decapitated John the Baptist, the appearance of Jesus, also preaching and baptizing, roused in him the apprehension that the prophet he killed had come again in a second life.

Preexistence, the premise necessarily leading to reincarnation, is the keynote of the most spiritual of the Gospels. The initial sentence sounds it, the body of the book often repeats it, and the final climax is strengthened by it. From the proem, "In the beginning was the word, and the word was with God," all through the story occur frequent allusions to it: "The word was made flesh" (John I. 14); "I am the living bread which came down from Heaven" (VI. 51); "Ye shall see the Son of man ascend up where he was before" (VI. 62); "Before Abraham was, I am" (VIII. 58); and finally, "Glorify thou me with the glory which I had with thee before the world was" (XVII. 5); "For thou lovedst me before the foundation of the world" (XVII. 24). It is always phrased in such a form as might be asserted by any one, though the speaker says it only of himself.

What the fourth Gospel dwells upon so fondly, and what is echoed in other New Testament books — as in Philippians II. 7, "He took on him the form of a servant," in 2 Cor. VIII. 9, "Though he was rich, yet for your sakes he became poor," and in 1 John I. 2, "That eternal Life which was with the Father, and was manifested unto us," — is a thought not limited to the Christ. Precisely the same occurs in the mention of the prophet-baptizer John: "There was a man sent from God" (John I. 6). The obvious sense of this verse to the Christians nearest its publication appears in the comments upon it by Origen, who says that it implies the existence of John the Baptist's soul previous to his terrestrial body, and hints at the universal belief in preexistence by adding, "And if the *Catholic opinion* hold good concerning the soul, as not propagated with the body, but existing previously and for various reasons clothed in flesh and blood, this expression, 'sent from God,' will no longer seem extraordinary as applied to John." No words could more exactly suit the aspirations of an oriental believer in reincarnation than these in the

Apocalypse: "Him that overcometh will I make a pillar in the temple of my God, *and he shall go no more out*" (Pev. III. 12).

More important than any separate quotations is the general tone of the Scriptures, which points directly toward reincarnation. They represent the earthly life as a pilgrimage to the heavenly country of spiritual union with God. It is our conceit and ignorance alone which deems a single earthly life sufficient to accomplish that purpose. They teach the sinful nature of all men and their responsibility for their sin, which certainly demands previous lives for the acquisition of that condition, as shown well by Chevalier Ramsay. (See pages 83-87.) St. Paul's idea of the Fall and of God are precisely those of Philo and Origen. The Bible also treats Paradise as the ancient abode of man and his future home, which requires a series of reincarnations as the connecting chain.

Chapter VIII
Reincarnation in Early Christendom

Our soul having lost its heavenly mansion came down into the earthly body as a strange place — PHILO.

The soul leaving the body becomes that power which it has most developed. Let us fly, then, from here below, and rise to the intellectual world, that we may not fall into a purely sensible life, by allowing ourselves to follow sensible images; or into a vegetative life, by abandoning ourselves to the pleasures of physical love and gluttony: let us rise, I say, to the intellectual world, to intelligence, to God himself. — PLOTINUS.

The order of things is regulated by the providential government of the whole world; some powers falling down from a loftier position, others gradually sinking to earth: some falling voluntarily, others being cast down against their will: some undertaking of their own accord the service of stretching out the hand to those who fall, others being compelled to persevere for a long time in the duty which they have undertaken. — JEROME.

All that flesh doth cover
Souls by source sublime
Are but slaves sold over
To the master Time,
To work out their ransom
For the ancient crime.

○ ○ ○ ○ ○ ○ ○ ○

The first centuries of Christianity found reincarnation still the prevailing creed, as in all the previous ages, but with various shades of interpretation. What these different phases of the same central thought were may be gathered from Jerome's catalogue, after the strife between Eastern and Western ideas had been working for some centuries and the present tendency of Europe had asserted itself. Jerome writes: "As to the origin of the soul, I remember the question of the whole church: whether it be fallen from heaven, as Pythagoras and the Platonists and Origen believe; or be of the proper substance of God, as the Stoics, Manichæans and Priscillian heretics of Spain believe; or whether they are kept in a repository formerly built by God, as some ecclesiastics foolishly believe; or whether they are daily made by God and sent into bodies according to that which is written in the Gospel: 'My Father worketh hitherto and I work;' or whether by traduction, as Tertullian, Apollinarius, and the greater part of the Westerns believe, *i. e.*, that as body from body so the soul is derived from the soul, subsisting by the same condition with animals."

In the form of Gnosticism it so strongly pervaded the early church that the fourth Gospel was specially directed against it; but this Gospel according to John attacked it only by advocating a broader rendering of the same faith. We have seen that Origen refers to pre existence as the general opinion. Clemens Alexandrinus (Origen's master) taught it as a divine tradition authorized by St. Paul himself in Romans V. 12, 14, 19. Rurfinus in his letter to Anastasius says that "This opinion was common among the primitive fathers." Later, Jerome relates that the doctrine of transmigration was taught as an esoteric one communicated to only a select few. But Nemesius emphatically declared that all the Greeks who believed in immortality believed also in metempsychosis. Delitzsch says, "It had its advocates as well in the synagogues as in the church."

The Gnostics and Manichæans received it, with much else, from Zoroastrian predecessors. The Neo-Platonists derived it chiefly from a blending of Plato and the Orient. The Church Fathers drew it not only from these sources, but from the Jews and the pioneers of Christianity. Several of them condemn the Persian and Platonic philosophies and yet hold to reincarnation in other guises. Aside from all authority, the doctrine seems to have been rooted among the inaugurators of our era in its adaptation to their mental needs, as the best explanation of the ways of God and the nature of men.

■. The Gnostics were a school of eclectics which became conspicuous amid the chaotic vortex of all religions in Alexandria, during the first century. They sought to furnish the young Christian church with a philosophic creed, and ranked themselves as the only initiates into a mystical system of Christian truth which was too exalted for the masses. Their thought was an elaborate structure of Greek ideas built upon Parsee Dualism, maintaining that the world was created by some fallen spirit or principle, and that the spirits of men were enticed from a preexistent higher stage by the Creator into the slavery of material bodies. The evils and sins of life belong only to the degraded prison-house of the spirit. The world is only an object of contempt. Virtue consists in severest asceticism. To combat their theory that Jesus was one of a vast number of beings between man and God, the fourth Gospel was written. They spread widely through the first and second centuries in many branches of belief. But most of their strength was absorbed into Manichæism, which was a more logical union of Persian with Christian and Greek ideas. In this simple faith the world is a creation not of a fallen spirit, but of the primary evil principle, while the spirit of man is the creation of God, and the conflict between flesh and spirit is that between the powers of light and darkness. The Gnostic and Manichæan notions of preexistence perpetuated themselves in many of the medieval sects, especially the Bogomiles, Paulicians, and Priscillians. Seven adherents of the Priscillian heresy were put to death in Spain a. d. 385, as the first instance of the death penalty visited by a Christian magistrate for erroneous belief. The Italian Cathari were another sect holding this form of reincarnation, against whom the Albigensian Crusade of the elder De Montfort was sent, and the inquisition devised by St. Dominic. Still they thrived in secret and possessed a disguised hierarchy which long survived their violent persecution. Similar sects descended from them still exist among the Russian dissenters.

■■. Contemporary with the Alexandrian Gnostics arose the philosophical school of the Neo-Platonists which gathered into one the doctrines of Pythagoras, Plato, and Buddhism,* and constructed a theology which might make headway against Christianity by satisfying in a rational way the longings which the new religion addressed. They too disclosed the reality and nearness of a spiritual world, a reconciliation with God, and the pathway for returning to Him. The distinguishing principle of Neo-Platonism is *emanation*, which took the place of creation. From the eternal Intelligence proceeds the multiplicity of souls which comprise the intelligible world, and of which the world-soul is the highest and all-embracing source. They insisted upon the distinct individuality of each soul, and earnestly combated the charge of Pantheism. Souls who have descended into the delusion of matter did so from pride and a desire of false independence. They now forget their former estate and the Father whom they have deserted. The mission of men, in the dying words of Plotinus, is "to bring the divine within them into harmony with that which is divine in the universe." The Neo-Platonists fought Gnosticism as fiercely as Christianity. Plotinus, by far the best of their writers, as well as the oldest whose works are preserved, devotes a whole book of his Enneads to the refutation of the doctrines of Valentinus, the brightest of the Gnostics. Contrary to the latter's thought, that men are fallen into the miry pit of matter which is wholly bad, Plotinus claims that the world of matter, although the least divine part of the universe because remotest from the One, is still good and the best place for man's development. From its former life he insists the soul has not fallen and cannot, but has descended into the lower stage of existence through innate weakness of intellect in order to be prepared for a higher exaltation.

The most important of this group of thinkers were Ammonius Saccas, Plotinus, and Porphyry in the third century, Jamblichus in the fourth, Hierocles and Proclus in the fifth, and Damascius in the sixth. It flourished with energy for over three hundred years, and as its ideas were largely appropriated by Christian theologians and philosophers, beginning with Origen, it has never ceased to be felt through Chris tendom.

* The close parallelism between Buddhism and Platonism peculiarly facilitated this.

Giordano Bruno, the martyr of the Italian reformation, popularized it, and handed it over to later philosophers. The philosophy of Emerson is substantially a revival of Plotinus. Coleridge is also strongly influenced by him.

As Plotinus is in some respects the most interesting of all the older writers, and taught reincarnation in a form thoroughly rational and supremely helpful, meeting Western needs in this regard more directly than any other philosopher, we quote at some length from his scarce essay on "The Descent of the Soul."

"When any particular soul acts in discord from the One, flying from the whole and apostazing from thence by a certain disagreement, no longer beholding an intelligible nature, from its partial blindness, in this ease it becomes deserted and solitary, impotent and distracted with care; for it now directs its mental eye to a part, and by a separation from that which is universal, attaches itself as a slave to one particular nature. It thus degenerates from the whole and governs particulars with anxiety and fatigue, assiduously cultivating externals and becoming not only present with body, but profoundly entering into its dark abodes. Hence, too, by such conduct the wings of the soul are said to suffer a defluxion and she becomes fettered with the bonds of body, after deserting the safe and innoxious habit of governing a better nature which flourishes with universal soul. The soul, therefore, falling from on high, suffers captivity, is loaded with fetters, and employs the energies of sense; because in this case her intellectual longing is impeded from the first. She is reported also to be buried and to be concealed in a cave; but when she converts herself to intelligence she then breaks her fetters and ascends on high, receiving first of all from reminiscence the ability of contemplating real beings; at the same time possessing something supereminent and ever abiding in the intelligible world. Souls therefore are necessarily of an amphibious nature, and alternately experience a superior and inferior condition of being; such as are able to enjoy a more intimate converse with Intellect abiding for a longer period in the higher world, and such to whom the contrary happens, either through nature or fortune, continuing longer connected with these inferior concerns....

"Thus, the soul, though of divine origin, and proceeding from the regions on high, becomes merged in the dark receptacle of the body, and being naturally a posterior god, it descends hither through a certain voluntary inclination, for the sake of power and of adorning inferior concerns. By this means it receives a knowledge of its latent powers, and exhibits a variety of operations peculiar to its nature, which by perpetually abiding in an incorporeal habit, and never proceeding into energy, would have been bestowed in vain. Besides the soul would have been ignorant of what she possessed, her powers always remaining dormant and concealed: since energy everywhere exhibits capacity, which would otherwise be entirely occult and obscure, and without existence, because not endued with one substantial and true. But now indeed every one admires the intellectual powers of the soul, through the variety of her external effects...

"Through an abundance of desire the soul becomes profoundly merged into matter, and no longer totally abides with the universal soul. Yet our souls are able alternately to rise from hence carrying back with them an experience of what they have known and suffered in their fallen state; from whence they will learn how blessed it is to abide in the intelligible world, and by a comparison, as it were, of contraries, will more plainly perceive the excellence of a superior state. For the experience of evil produces a clearer knowledge of good. This is accomplished in our souls according to the circulations of time, in which a conversion takes place from subordinate to more exalted natures.

"Indeed, if it were proper to speak clearly what appears to me to be the truth, contrary to the opinions of others, the whole of our soul also does not enter into the body, but something belonging to it always abides in the intelligible, and something different from this in the sensible world: and that which abides in the sensible world, if it conquers, or rather if it is vanquished and disturbed, does not permit us to perceive that which the supreme part of the soul contemplates; for that which is understood then arrives at our nature when it descends within the limits of sensible inspection. For every soul possesses something which inclines downwards to body, and something which tends upwards toward intellect; and the soul, indeed, which is universal and of the universe, by its part which is inclined towards body, governs the whole without labor and fatigue, transcending that which it governs.

"But souls which are particular and of a part are too much occupied by sense, and by a perception of many things happening contrary to nature are surrounded by a multitude of foreign concerns. It is likewise subject to a variety of affections, and is ensnared by the allurements of pleasure. But the superior part of the soul is never influenced by fraudulent delights, and lives a life always uniform and divine."

███. Many of the orthodox Church Fathers welcomed reincarnation as a ready explanation of the fall of man and the mystery of life, and distinctly preached it as the only means of reconciling the existence of suffering with a merciful God. It was an essential part of the church philosophy for many centuries in the rank and file of Christian thought, being stamped with the authority of the leading thinkers of Christendom, and then gradually was frowned upon as the Western influences predominated, until it became heresy and at length survived only in a few scattered sects.

Justin Martyr expressly speaks of the soul inhabiting more than once the human body, and denies that on taking a second time the embodied form it can remember previous experiences. Afterwards, he says, souls which have become unworthy to see God in human guise, are joined to the bodies of wild beasts. Thus he openly defends the grosser phase of metempsychosis.

Clemens Alexandrinus is declared by a contemporary to have written "wonderful stories about metempsychosis and many worlds before Adam."

Arnobius, also, is known to have frankly avowed this doctrine.

Noblest of all the church advocates of this opinion was Origen. He regarded the earthly history of the human race as one epoch in an historical series of changeful decay and restoration, extending backward and forward into aeons; and our temporal human body as the place of purification for our spirits exiled from a happier existence on account of sin. He taught that souls were all originally created by God *minds* of the same kind and condition, that is of the same essence as the infinite Mind, and that they exercised their freedom of will, some wisely and well, others with abuse in different degrees, producing the divergences now apparent in mankind. From that old experience some souls have retained more than others of the pristine condition. The lapsed souls God clothed with bodies and sent into this world, both to expiate their temerity and to prepare themselves for a better future. The variety of their offenses caused the diversity of their terrestrial conditions. In these bodies, each enjoys that lot which most exactly suited his previous habits. On these the whole earthly circumstances of man, internal and external, even his whole life from birth, depend. In this way alone he thought the justice of God could be defended. But when men keep themselves free from contagion in bodily existence and restrain the turbulent movements of sense and imagination, being gradually purified from the body they ascend on high and are at last changed into *minds*, of which the earthly souls are corruptions. In his own words, "Here is the cause of the diversing among rational creatures, not in the will or decision of the creature, but in the freedom of individual liberty. For God justly disposing of his creatures according to their desert united the diversities of minds in one congruous world, that he might, as it were, adorn his mansion (in which ought to be not only vases of gold and silver, but of wood also and clay, and some to honor and some to dishonor) with these diverse vases, minds, or souls. To these causes the world owes its diversity, while Divine Providence disposes each according to his tendency, mind, and disposition.

"If from unknown reasons the soul be already not exactly worthy of being born in an irrational body, nor yet exactly in one purely rational, it is furnished with a monstrous body, so that reason cannot be fully developed by one thus born, the nature of the body being fashioned either of a higher or lower body according to the scope of the reason.

"I think this is a question how it happens that the human mind is influenced now by the good now by the evil. The causes of this I suspect to be more ancient than this corporeal birth.

"If our course be not marked out according to our works before this life, how is it true that it is not unjust in God that the elder should serve the younger and be hated, before he had done things deserving of servitude and of hatred.

"By the fall and by the cooling from a life of the Spirit came that which is now the soul, which is also capable of a return to her original condition, of which I think the prophet speaks in this: 'Return unto thy rest, O my soul.' So that the whole is this — how the mind becomes a soul and how the soul rectified becomes a mind."

Concerning preexistence in the Bible, Origen writes, in his "De Principiis": "The Holy Scriptures have called the creation of the world by a new and peculiar name, terming it καταβολή which has been very improperly translated into Latin by 'constitutio'; for in Greek καταβολή signifies rather 'dejicere,' *i.e.*, to cast downwards — a word which has been improperly translated into Latin by the phrase 'constitutio mundi,' as where the Saviour says, 'And there will be tribulation in those days, such as was not since the beginning of the world;'* in which passage καταβολή is rendered by beginning (constitutio). The Apostle also has employed the language, saying, 'Who hath chosen us before the foundation of the world;'† and this foundation he calls καταβολή to be understood in the same sense as before. It seems worthwhile, then, to inquire what is meant by this new term; and I am, indeed, of the opinion that as the end and consummation of the saints will be in those (ages) which are not seen, and are eternal, we must conclude that rational creatures had also a similar beginning. And if they had a beginning such as the end for which they hope, they existed undoubtedly from the very beginning in those (ages) which are not seen, and are eternal. And if this is so, then there has been a descent from a higher to a lower condition, on the part not only of those souls who have deserved the change by the variety of their movements, but also on that of those who, in order to serve the whole world, were brought down from those higher and invisible spheres to these lower and visible ones, although against their will. From this it follows that by the use of the word καταβολή a

* Matt. XXIV. 21.
† Ephesians I. 4.

descent from a higher to a lower condition, shared by all in common, would seem to be pointed out. The hope of freedom is entertained by the whole of creation — of being liberated from the corruption of slavery — when the sons of God, who either fell away or were scattered abroad, shall be gathered into one, and when they shall have fulfilled their duties in this world."

Many contemporaneous and subsequent writers censured Origen for this opinion, but his doctrine was maintained by a large number of strong followers and independent thinkers.

Even in Jerome and Augustine certain passages indicate that they held this theory in part. In his Epistle to Avitus, Jerome agrees with Origen as to the interpretation of the passage above mentioned by Origen, "Who hath chosen us before the foundation of the world." He says "a divine habitation, and a true rest above, I think, is to be understood, where rational creatures dwelt, and where, before their descent to a lower position, and removal from invisible to visible (worlds), and fall to earth, and need of gross bodies, they enjoyed a former blessedness. Whence God the Creator made for them bodies suitable to their humble position, and created this visible world and sent into the world ministers for their salvation."

The Latin Fathers Nemesius, Synesius, and Hilarius boldly defend preexistence, though taking exception to Origen's form of it. Of Synesius, most familiar to English readers as the convent patriarch in "Hypatia," it is known that when the citizens of Ptolemais invited him to their bishopric, he declined that dignity for the reason that he cherished certain opinions which they might not approve, as after mature reflection they had struck deep roots in his mind. Foremost among these he mentioned the doctrine of preexistence. Vestiges of this belief are discerned in his writings; for example, in the Greek hymn paraphrased as follows:—

> Eternal Mind, thy seedling spark
> Through this thin vase of clay
> Athwart the waves of chaos dark
> Emits a timorous ray!
> This mind-enfolding soul is sown

Incarnate germ in earth.
In pity, blessed Lord, then own
    What claims in Thee its birth.
Far forth from Thee, Thou central fire,
    To earth's sad bondage cast,
Let not the trembling spark expire,
    Absorb Thine own at last.

Another of this group, Prudentius, entertained nearly the same idea as that of Origen concerning the soul's descent from higher seats to earth, as appears in one of his hymns:—

O Saviour, bid my soul, thy trembling spouse,
    Return at last to Thee believing.
Bind, bind anew those all unearthly vows
    She broke on high and wandered grieving.

Although Origen's teaching was condemned by the Council of Constantinople in 551, it permanently colored the stream of Christian theology, not only in many scholastics and medieval heterodoxies, but through all the later course of religious thought, in many isolated individuals and groups.

Chapter IX
Reincarnation in the East Today

A man may travel from one end of the kingdom to the other without money, feeding and lodging as well as the people.— A MISSIONARY IN BURMAH. *Buddhism has not deceived, and it has not persecuted. In this respect it can teach Christians a lesson. The unconditioned command, "Thou shalt not kill," which applies to all living creatures, has had great influence in softening the manners of the Monguls. This command is connected with the doctrine of transmigration of souls, which is one of the essential doctrines of this system as well as of Brahmanism. Buddhism also inculcates a positive humanity consisting of good actions.*— JAMES FREEMAN CLARKE.

> *He lived musing the woes of man,*
> *The ways of fate, the doctrines of the books,*
> *The secrets of the silence whence all come,*
> *The secrets of the gloom whereto all go,*
> *The life that lies between like that arch flung*
> *From cloud to cloud across the sky, which hath*
> *Mists for its masonry and vapory piers.*
> THE LIGHT OF ASIA.

○ ○ ○ ○ ○ ○ ○ ○

The religious philosophy of the Orient, like everything else there, remains now substantially the same as in ancient times. History cannot say when Brahmanism did not flourish among the multitudes of India. Buddhism, the later Protestant phase of the old faith, which abolished its abuses of priesthood and caste and spread its reformation broadcast through Asia, did not alter the original teaching of rebirth, but rather confirmed and popularized the truth that has lain at the heart of India from remotest ages. Reincarnation is the sap-root of eastern religion and permeates the Veda scriptures.

While it is claimed by the West that the religion of Sakya Muni is below that of Jesus, as inspiring an exalted selfishness in distinction to the generous sacrifice taught by Christianity; while it is true that the best Buddhists lead a passive, submissive life which made them easy spoil for conquering races and has not accomplished any result in civilization since the first ancient subjugation; while Buddhism with its mortification and self-centred goodness is even more distasteful to the western race than the meditative dreamy asceticism of Brahmanism: it is equally certain that these eastern religions are far more really lived by their followers than Christianity is with us; it must be admitted that a spiritual selfishness, which is so thoroughly practiced as to bear all the fruits of generous love, is preferable to a noble sacrifice, which is so largely precept as to appear to the naked eye a civilized barbarism; and it is worth considering whether Christendom may not gain as much by learning the secret of Eastern superiority to materialism, as the Orient is gaining by the infusion of Western activity. Travelers agree that in many parts of inner China, Tibet, Central India, and Ceylon the daily life of Buddhism is so like the realization of Christianity, as to give strong support to the theory of the Indian origin of our religion. There is a practical demonstration of what reincarnation will do for a race, and a hint of the grander result which would accrue from grafting that principle into the real life of the stronger Saxon, Teutonic, and Celtic stock. Knowing the indestructibility of the soul, the evanescence of the body, and the permanence of spiritual traits as formed by thought, word, and deed, the whole energy of life is focused upon purity of self and charity to others. To love one's enemies, to abstain from even defensive warfare, to govern the soul, to obey one's superiors, to venerate age, to provide food and shelter, to tolerate all differences of opinion and religion, are guiding maxims of actual life. They are as vitally and generally translated into flesh and blood as in primitive Christianity or in Count Tolstoi's flock. Honesty, modesty, and simplicity prevail in these sections. Women are held in the same esteem as in the ancient

Sanskrit epoch, and children are treated more beautifully than in many Christian homes. A lady traveler, known to the writer, who witnessed this, said that if her lot were that of a friendless woman, she knew no place on earth where she would labor and dwell more happily than in Ceylon. As the peasantry receive reincarnation in the simplest and most extreme form of human rebirths in animal bodies, every living creature is regarded by them as a possible relative. Gentleness to the animal creation abounds as nowhere else in the world. It is a sin to kill any beast. It is a virtue to offer one's life for a distressed animal, as the popular tradition holds that Buddha did in one life by throwing himself to a famished tigress. Death is no object of dread, but a welcome benefactor, transferring, them forward in their progress to the goal of rest. To die for any good purpose, as under the sacred Brahman car of Juggernaut, or in some one's behalf, is the common aspiration; so much so that it is difficult for the missionaries to gain any feeling for the death on the cross, as they think any one would easily suffer that.

The Brahmans have for ages studied the problems of ontology and the soul's future, by severest introspection and acutest thought, to build their system, which is a vast elaboration of religious metaphysics, upon a theistic basis. Reincarnation is the cornerstone of this structure. Many of the higher Brahmans are believed to have penetrated the veils concealing past existences. It is related, for instance, that when Apollonius of Tyana visited India, the Brahman Iarchus told him that "the truth concerning the soul is as Pythagoras taught you and as we taught the Egyptians," and mentioned that he (Apollonius) in a previous incarnation was an Egyptian steersman, and had refused the inducements offered him by pirates to guide his vessel into their hands. The common people of India are sure that certain of the Brahmans and Buddhists are still able to verify by their finer senses the reality of reincarnation. And many educated natives and resident foreigners in India have witnessed evidences of this keen power of insight associated with other extraordinary qualities which compelled them to believe in it.

Brahmanism and Buddhism are practically agreed upon the philosophy of reincarnation, as the great Buddhist revolt against priestcraft only emphasized this doctrine. Every branch of these systems aims at the means of winning escape from the necessity of repeated births. The ardent and final desire of all is expressed by the words of the sage Bharata:—

"And may the purple self-existent god (Siva),
Whose vital energy pervades all space,
From future transmigrations save my soul."

There are, however, great differences in these two faiths as to the means and the result. Both contend that all forms are the penance of nature. They regard personal existence as an empty delusion and the exemption from it as true salvation. The Brahman seeks Nirvana, which is absorption in Brahm, as the reality at the heart of things; the Buddhist considers this also unreal, and finds no reality but in the silence and peace attained beyond Nirvana. In the Brahman's paradise, one is so free from desire that no need remains for perpetuating his individual existence. But after that comes Pan-Nirvana, which is utter inaction and disappearance, a condition so difficult for a Western mind to comprehend that it persists in falsely calling it and Nirvana alike — annihilation. The Buddhist's one duty of life and the means of attaining his goal is mortification, the extinction of affection and desire. But the Brahman's work is contemplation, illumination, communion with Brahm, religious study, and asceticism. The creed of Buddhism is universal; that of Brahmanism is exclusive. The Buddhist saint may come from any class, for the *raison d'être* of his faith is the abolition of caste. But only the wearer of the sacred Brahman thread can aspire to direct union with Brahm; the lower castes must undergo painful fakir penances until they attain the Brahman estate.

Northern Buddhism has been defined as almost identical with Gnosticism. It has spun a dense fabric of legend and speculation about this central thought of the soul's gradual evolution from the natural to the spiritual. The Hindus believe that human souls emanated from the Supreme Being, and became gradually immersed in matter, forgetting their divine origin, and straying in bewildered condition back to him through many lives, after a protracted round of births in partial reparation. Having become contaminated with sin, we must work out our release through earthly lives in the delusive arena of sense until the reality of spiritual existence is attained. So long as the soul is not pure enough for re-mergence into Brahm, we must be born again repeatedly, and the degree of our impurity determines what these births shall be. So closely is the account of the soul's misdeeds kept that it may pass through thousands of years in one or another of the heavens in reward for good deeds, and yet be obliged later to descend to earth for certain ancient sins. The Laws of Manu give a standard by which the moral consequences of various human actions are measured with great detail.* A more general doctrine is based on the assumption of three Cosmic qualities — goodness, passion, and darkness — in the human soul. On this ground Manu and other writers built an intricate theory, providing that souls of the first quality become deities, those of the second, men, and those of the third, beasts.

The Hindu conception of reincarnation embraces all existence — gods, men, animals, plants, minerals. It is believed that everything migrates, from Buddha down to inert matter. Hardy tells us that Buddha himself was born an ascetic eighty-three times, a monarch fifty-eight times, as the soul of a tree forty-three times, and many other times as ape, deer, lion, snipe, chicken, eagle, serpent, pig, frog, etc., amounting to four hundred times in all. A Chinese authority represents Buddha as saying, "The number of my births and deaths can only be compared to those of all the plants in the universe." Birth is the gate which opens into every state, and merit determines into which it shall open. Earth and human life are an intermediary stage, resulting from many previous places and forms and introducing many more. There are multitudes of inhabited worlds upon which the same person is successively born according to his attractions. To the earthly life he may return again and again, dropping the memory of past experiences, and carrying, like an embryonic germ, the concisest summary of former lives into each coming one. Every act bears upon the resultant which shall steer the soul into its next habitation, not only on earth, but in the more exalted or debased regions of

* See page 273.

"Heaven" and "Hell." Thus "the chain of the law" binds all existences, and the only escape is by the final absorption into Brahm.

While the Hindus generally hold that the same soul appears at different births, the heretical Southern Buddhists teach that the succession of existences is a succession of souls, bred from one another, like the sprouting of new generations from plants and animals, and like the new light kindled from an old lamp, the result, but not the identity of the former. Another curious aspect of these Indian speculations is the view of certain Northern Buddhists, who divide eternity into gigantic cycles which shall at length bring around again a precise repetition of earlier events. This is similar to the grand periodic year of the Stoics and of the Epicurean Atomists, and to the continual metempsychosis of Pythagoras, which provided that the identical Plato would again and again, at certain tremendous intervals staggering any one but a Greek or Hindu metaphysician, appear at the same Academy and deliver the same lectures, etc.

Zoroastrians and Sufi Mohammedans, with their usual antipathy to Indian thought, limit their conceptions of reincarnation to a few repeated lives on earth, which some of the Persian and Arabian nasties stretch out to a larger number, but soon disappearing either back into the original source or into darker scenes.

Chapter X
Eastern Poets upon Reincarnation

Here shalt thou pluck from the most ancient shells The whitest pearls of wisdom's treasury.— EDWIN ARNOLD.

Young and enterprising is the West,
Old and meditative is the East.
Turn, O youth! with intellectual zest
Where the sage invites thee to his feast.
Eastward roll the orbs of heaven,
Westward tend the thoughts of men.
Let the poet, nature-driven,
Wander eastward now and then.
MILNES.

○ ○ ○ ○ ○ ○ ○ ○

All Eastern poetry finds a favorite theme in metempsychosis, and the literature of India is thoroughly saturated with it. The fervent passion, the subtle thought, the luxuriant imagery which permeate Asiatic life are centred upon this common philosophy. But the best portion of this enormous wealth of fantasy is withheld from us simply because of its revelry in this very thought which is generally unattractive to the West. What oriental poetry enters our language is chiefly erotic or epic, and the most characteristic of all is left for the few educated natives to enjoy. We can therefore only select a few representative gems from this unworked mine, illustrating the Muses of India, Persia, and Arabia. Among the ancient Sanskrit epics are discovered beautiful renderings of the thought of many births. The delicacy and tenderness of Persian poetry furnish charming expressions of the Zoroastrian aspirations for release from earthly bondage to reascend homeward. The Arabian mysticism of the Sufis directs their intense subjectivity into ecstatic phrasing of the same idea.

In the wonderful ancient Sanskrit drama "Sakoontala" by Kalidesa, translated by Monier Williams, occur these passages:—

> This peerless maid is like a fragrant flower
> Whose perfumed breath has never been diffused.
> A gem of priceless water, just released
> Pure and unblemished from its glittering bed.
> Or rather is she like the mellowed fruit
> Of virtuous actions in some former birth
> Now brought to full perfection.
> That song has filled me with a most peculiar sweetness.
> I seem to yearn after some long forgotten love.
> Not seldom in our happy hours of ease'
> When thought is still, the sight of some fair form,
> Or mournful fall of music breathing low
> Will stir strange fancies thrilling all the soul
> With a mysterious sadness and a sense
> Of vague yet earnest longing. Can it be
> That the dim memory of events long passed,
> Or friendships formed in other states of being
> Flits like a passing shadow o'er the spirit?

The Sanskrit "Katha Upanishad," in Edwin Arnold's rendering as "The Secret of Death," contains a full explanation of the Eastern doctrine.

For his noble sacrifice Yama (Death) grants to Nachiketas the privilege of asking three boons. After naming and receiving the first two Nachiketas says:—

"Thou dost give peace—is that peace nothingness?
Some say that after death the soul still lives,
Personal, conscious; some say, nay, it ends:
Fain would I know which of these twain be true,
By the enlightened. Be my third boon this."
Then Yama answered, "This was asked of old,

Even by the gods! This is a subtle thing,
Not to be told, hard to be understood:
Ask me some other boon: I may not grant."
Nachiketas insists upon this, and will not accept the wealths, powers,
and pleasures which Death offers as a substitute.

        Then Yama yielded, granting the great boon,
        And spake: "Know, first of all, that what is Good
        And what is Pleasant—these be separate!
        By many ways, in diverse instances
        Pleasure and Good lay hold upon each man!
        Blessed is he who, choosing high, lets go
        Pleasure for Good. The Pleasure-seekers lose
        Life's end, so lived. The Pleasant and the Good
        Solicit men: the sage, distinguishing
        By understanding, followeth the Good,
        Being more excellent. The foolish man
        Cleaveth to Pleasure, seeking still to have,
        To keep, enjoy. The foolish ones who live
        In ignorance, holding themselves as wise
        And well instructed, tread the round of change
        With erring steps, deluded, like the blind
        Led by the blind. The necessary road
        Which brings to life unchanging is not seen
        By such: wealth dazzles heedless hearts: deceived
        With shows of sense, they deem their world is real
        And the unseen is naught; so, constantly,
        Fall they beneath my stroke. To reach to Being
        Beyond all seeming Being, to know true life—
        This is not gained by many; seeing that few
        So much as hear of it, and of those few
        The more part understandeth not.

          "The uttermost true soul is ill-perceived
        By him who, unenlightened, sayeth: I
        Am I: thou, thou; and the life divided:

He That knoweth life undifferenced, declares
The spirit, what it is, One with the
All. And this is Truth. But nowise shall the truth
Be compassed, if thou speak of small and great.
    "Excellent youth! the knowledge thou didst crave
Comes not with speech: words are the false world's signs.
By insight surely comes it if one hears.
Lo! thou hast loved the Truth, and striven for it.
I would that others, Nachiketas, strove!
    "Only the wise who patiently do sever
Their thought from shows and fix it upon truths,
See HIM, the Perfect and Unspeakable,
Hard to be seen, retreating, ever hid
Deeper and deeper in the uttermost;
Whose house was never entered, who abides
Now and before and always; and so seeing
Are freed from griefs and pleasures."
    "Make it known to me," he saith,
"Who is He? what? whom thou hast knowledge of."
                                  Then Yama spake:
"The answer whereunto all vedas lead;
The answer whereunto as penance strives;
The answer whereunto those strive that live
As seekers after God—hear this from me.
Who knoweth the word Om (which meaneth God)
With all its purports; what his heart would have
His heart possesseth. This of spoken speech
Is wisest, deepest, best, supremest. He
That speaketh it, and wotteth what he speaks
Is worshiped in the place of Brahm, with Brahm!
Also, the soul which knoweth thus itself
It is not born. It doth not die. It sprang
From none, and it begetteth none. Unmade,
Immortal, changeless, primal. I can break

The body, but that soul I cannot harm."
  "If he that slayeth thinks 'I slay'; if he
Whom he doth slay thinks 'I am slain,' then both
Know not aright. That which was life in each
Cannot be slain nor slay. The untouched soul,
Greater than all the worlds (because the worlds
By it subsist); smaller than subtleties
Of things minutest; last of ultimates,
Sits in the hollow heart of all that lives!
Whoso hath laid aside desire and fear,
His senses mastered and his spirit still,
Sees in the quiet light of verity
Eternal, safe, majestical — his soul:
Resting it ranges everywhere: asleep
It roams the world, unsleeping: who, save I,
Know that divinest spirit as it is,
Glad beyond joy, existing outside life?
Beholding it in bodies bodiless,
Amid impermanency permanent,
Embracing all things, yet in the midst of all
The mind enlightened casts its grief away:
It is not to be known by knowledge: man
Wotteth it not by wisdom: learning vast
Halts short of it: only by soul itself
Is soul perceived — when the Soul wills it so
There shines no lisrht save its own lioht to show
Itself unto itself: none compasseth
Its joy who is not wholly ceased from sin,
Who dwells not self-controlled, self-centred, calm,
Lord of himself. It is not gotten else.
Brahm hath it not to give.
  "The man unwise, unmindful, evil-lived
Comes not to that fixed place of peace; he falls
Back to the region of sense life again.

The wise and mindful one, heart purified,
Attaineth to the changeless Place, wherefrom
Never again shall births renew for him.
Then hath he freedom over all worlds
And, if it wills the region of the Past,
The fathers and the mothers of the Past
Come to receive it; and that soul is glad:
And if it wills the regions of the Homes,
The Brothers and the Sisters of the Homes
Come to receive it; and that soul is glad:
And if it wills the region of the Friends,
The well-beloved come to welcome it
With love undying; and that soul is glad.
And if it wills a world of grace and peace
Where garlands are and perfumes and delights
Of delicate meats and drinks, music and song,
Lo! fragrances and blossoms and delights
Of dainty banquets and the streams of song
Come to it; and that soul is glad.
Whoso once perceiveth Him that is
Without a name, Unseen, Impalpable, Bodiless,
Timeless, such an one is saved,
Death hath not power upon him."

Although not an Asiatic poem in the ordinary sense, we do not hesitate to place in this cluster Edwin Arnold's "Light of Asia." After the festival scene in which the prince distributed prizes to the maiden victors in the sports, and his love had centred upon Yasodhara, the last of the contestants, follow these lines:—

Long after, when enlightenment was full,
Lord Buddha, being prayed why thus his heart
Took fire at first glance of the Sakya girl,
Answered: "We were not strangers as to us
And all it seemed; in ages long gone by
A hunter's son, playing with forest girls

By Yamun's springs, where Nandadevi stands
Sate umpire while they raced beneath the firs
Like hares at eve that run their playful rings;
One with flower-like stars crowned he, one with long plumes,
Plucked from the pheasant and the jungle cock,
One with fir apples; but who ran the last
Came first for him, and unto her the boy
Gave a tame fawn and his heart's love beside.
And in the wood they lived many glad years,
And in the wood they undivided died.
Lo! as hid seed shoots after rainless years,
So good and evil, pains and pleasures, hates
And loves, and all dead deeds come forth again
Bearing bright leaves or dark, sweet fruit or sour.
Thus was I he and she Yasodhara;
And while the wheel of birth and death turns round
That which hath been must be between us two."

In other passages of the same poem Buddha tells how his athletic triumph over the suitors for Yasodhara, in which she wore a black and gold veil, was but a new version of an ancient forest battle, when as a tiger he conquered all the rival claimants for the black and gold-striped tigress Yasbdhara; how ages before in time of famine, when he was a Brahman, he compassionately threw himself to a starving tigress; and how his final salvation of Yasodhara by the en-lightened doctrine repeated a transaction centuries old, when he was a pearl merchant and sacrificed the priceless gem containing all his fortune to rescue this same wife Yasodhara from hunger.

A typical expression of the Zoroastrian phase of reincarnation is found in this poem:—

FROM THE PERSIAN
BY ARCHBISHOP R. C. TRENCH.

Happy are you, starry brethren, who from heaven do not roam,

In the eternal Father's mansion from the first have dwelt at home.
Round the Father's throne forever standing in his countenance,
Sunning you, you see the seven circling heavens around you dance.
Me he has cast out to exile in a distant land to learn
How I should love Him the Father, how for that true country yearn.
I lie here, a star of heaven, fallen upon this gloomy place,
Scarce remembering what bright courses I was once allowed to trace.
Still in dreams it comes upon me, that I once on wings did soar;
But or e'er my flight commences this my dream must all be o'er.
When the lark is climbing upward in the sunbeam, then I feel
Even as though my spirit also hidden pinions could reveal.
I a rosebud to this lower soil of earth am fastly bound,
And with heavenly dew besprinkled still am rooted to the ground.
Yet the life is struggling upward, stirring still with all their might,
Yearning buds that cry to open to the warmth and heavenly light.
From its stalk released, my flower soars not yet a butterfly,
But meanwhile my fragrant incense evermore I breathe on high.
By my Gardener to his garden I shall once transplanted be,
There where I have been already written from eternity.
Oh, my brothers blooming yonder, unto Him the ancient—pray
That the hour of my transplanting He will not for long delay.

Hafiz, the prince of Persian poets, figures the soul as the phoenix alighting on Tuba, the Tree of Life:—

> My phoenix long ago secured
> His nest in the sky-vault's cope;
> In the body's cage immured
> He was weary of life's hope.
> Round and round this heap of ashes
> Now flies the bird amain,
> But in that odorous niche of heaven
> Nestles the bird again.
> Once flies he upward he will perch
> On Tuba's golden bough;
> His home is on that fruited arch

Which cools the blest below.
If over this sad world of ours
His wings my phoenix spread,
How gracious falls on land and sea
The soul-refreshing shade!
Either world inhabits he,
Sees oft below him planets roll;
His body is all of air compact,
Of Allah's love, his soul.

The following Sufi poem will illustrate the passionate phase of reincarnation which appears in the spiritual absorption of the Mohammedan mystics. It is not surprising that the intensity of their rapturous piety has drawn among their ranks of meditative devotees the most distinguished religionists, philosophers, and poets of the whole Persian and Arabian Orient:

THE SUCCESSFUL SEARCH

I was before a name had been named upon earth —
Ere one trace yet existed of aught that has birth —
When the locks of the Loved One streamed forth for a sign,
And being was none save the Presence Divine 1
Ere the veil of the flesh for Messiah was wrought
To the Godhead I bowed in prostration of thought.
I measured intensely, I pondered with heed
(But ah! fruitless my labor) the Cross and its creed.
To the Pagod I rushed, and the Magian's shrine,
But my eye caught no glimpse of a glory divine:
The reins of research to the Caaba I bent,
Whither hopefully thronging the old and young went;
Candasai and Herat searched I wistfully through,
Nor above nor beneath came the Loved One to view!
I toiled to the summit, wild, pathless and lone,
Of the globe-girding Kaf, but the Phoenix had flown.

The seventh earth I traversed, the seventh heaven explored,
But in neither discerned I the Court of the Lord.
I questioned the Pen and the Tablet of Fate,
But they whispered not where He pavilions his state.
My vision I strained, but my God-scanning eye
No trace that to Godhead belongs could descry.
But when I my glance turned within my own breast,
Lo! the vainly sought Loved One, the Godhead confessed.
In the whirl of its transport my spirit was tossed
Till each atom of separate being I lost:
And the bright sun of Tanniz a madder than me
Or a wilder, hath never yet seen, nor shall see.

Chapter XI
Esoteric Oriental Reincarnation

Life's thirst quenches itself
With draughts which double thirst, but who is wise
Tears from his soul this Trishna, feeds his sense
No longer on false shows, files his mind
To seek not, strive not, wrong not; bearing meek
All ills which flow from foregone wrongfulness,
And so constraining passions that they die.
Thus grows he sinless: either never more
Needing to find a body and a place,
Or so informing what freer frame it takes
In new existence that the new toils prove
Lighter and lighter not to be at all,
Thus "finishing the path"; free from earth's cheats;
Released from all the skandhas of the flesh;
Broken from ties—from Upadan—saved
From whirling on the wheel; aroused and sane
As is a man wakened from hateful dreams.
Till aching craze to live ends, and life glides
Lifeless—to nameless quiet, nameless joy,
Blessed Nirvana—sinless, stirless rest—
That change which never changes.

THE LIGHT OF ASIA.

o o o o o o o o

Throughout the East today, as in all past time, the higher priesthood controls a spiritual science which has been accumulated by long ages of severest study, and is concealed from the vulgar world. This is no mere elaboration of fanciful philosophy, as is much of eastern metaphysics, patiently spun from secluded speculation like the mediaeval scholasticism of Europe. It is a purely rational development of psychology by the aid of scientific inquiry. Through protracted investigation and crucial tests repeatedly applied to actual experience and through retrospective and prophetic insight they have probed many of the secrets of the soul. The falsity of materialism and the all-commanding power of spirit are proven beyond a cavil. How the soul is independent of the physical body, sometimes leaving and returning to it, and moulding it to suit its needs; how all nature is but a vast family embodied in physical clothing and inextricably interlaced in living brotherhood, from lowest atom to sublimest archangel; how the gradual evolution of all races proceeds through revolving cycles in a constantly ascending order of things;—these and many other stupendous spiritual facts are to them familiarly known. These masters of human mystery hold themselves apart from the populace and seldom appear to any but their special disciples, but they are universally believed in by the natives of India, as the miraculous evidences of their penetration into nature's heart have been seen of many. Moreover, ocular demonstration of the existence and phenomenal capacities of these Mahatmas has frequently been given to well-known officials and reputable foreigners, whose testimony is on record.

Although these highest adepts keep most of their discoveries secret, preferring to enlighten mankind indirectly and by a wholesome gradual uplifting, occasional expressions have been given of the occult philosophy derived from their funds of science, and from these we abridge what they are said to teach concerning reincarnation. Even in the books containing their doctrine, as "Man," "Esoteric Buddhism," "Light on the Path," and "Through the Gates of Gold,"* we surmise that portions relating to specific details are more or less arbitrary and exoteric. Therefore we confine our attention to a synopsis of their central principles of the subject.

These masters tell us that man is composed of seven principles intri-

---

* Beside these recent English books the Appendix gives many older ones.

cately interwoven so as to constitute a unit and yet capable of partial separation. This septenary division is only a finer analysis of the common triple distinctions, body, soul, and spirit, and runs through the entire universe. The development of man is in the order of these divisions, from body to spirit and from spirit to body, in a continual round of incarnations. The progress may be best illustrated by a seven-coiled spiral which sweeps with a wider curve at every ascent. The spiral is not a steady upward incline, but at one side sags down into materiality and at the other side rises into spirituality—the material portion of each ring being the lowest side of its curve, but always higher than the corresponding previous descent. Furthermore, each ring of the spiral is itself a seven-fold spiral, and each of these again is a seven-fold spiral, and so on to an indefinite number of subdivisions.

The evolutionary process requires for its complete unfoldment a number of planets* corresponding to the seven principles. On each of these planets a long series of lives is necessary before one can advance to the next. After a full circuit is made the course must be repeated again on a higher plane, until many successive series of the planetary rotations, each involving hundreds of separate lives, has developed the individual into the perfect fullness of experience. Some of these planets are unknown to astronomy, being of too fine a materiality for our present perceptions, and on them man is very unlike his terrestrial appearance.

Since the first human souls began their career through these cycles they have moved along the entire planetary chain three times, and now, for the fourth time, we have reached the fourth planet—Earth.

* In the explicit phrasing from which this section is derived, there are mentioned *seven* planets, through each of which the soul makes *seven* rounds, each round including *seven* races, and each race *seven* sub-races, and these again containing *seven* branches, multiplying the whole number of lives into a compound of seven. Everywhere the sacred number appears, but contrary to the strict interpretation of many students of oriental thought, we are certain that these figures are only symbols. Just as the spectrum might be split into only three essential components, or into a much larger number than seven, so the dissection of these courses of the soul into any one number seems to be an arbitrary mathematical representation of the fact that each division must include such components as will fit together in one indissoluble entirety.

We are therefore, roughly speaking, about half developed, physically. During the previous series of earthly inhabitations we were exceedingly different from our present form, and during the later ones we shall enter upon still more marvelous stages. With each grand series (or round) a dimension is added to man's conception of space. The fourth dimension will be a common fact of consciousness before we complete the present set of earthly lives. Before reaching the perfection attainable here at each round every soul must pass through many minor circuits. We are said to be in the middle of the fifth circuit (or race) of our fourth round, and the evolution of this fifth race began about a million years ago. Each race is subdivided, and each of these divisions again dissected, making the total number of lives allotted to each round very large. No human being can escape the earth's attraction until these are accomplished, with only rare exceptions among those who by special merit have outstripped the others : for although all began alike, the contrasted uses of the universal opportunities have produced all the variations now existing in the human race. The geometrical progression of characteristics selected by each soul has resulted in vast divergences.

Long before the twilight of our birth into the present life we passed through an era of immense duration on this planet as spiritual beings, gradually descending into matter to enter the bodies which were developed up from the highest animal type for our reception. Our evolution therefore is a double one — on the spiritual side from ethereal races of infinite pedigree, and on the physical side from the lower animals.

In the first earthly circuit of the last great series (or round) we passed through seven ethereal sub-races.

Each of these developed one astral sense, until the seventh sub-race had seven senses. What the sixth and seventh were we cannot imagine, but in time we shall know, as we are at present tracing over again that path more perfectly, and have reached only the fifth of the seven stages on this circuit. The first of these seven sub-races slowly acquired the sense of physical sight. All the other parts of the sensuous nature were in shadowy latency. They had no notion of distance, solidity, sound, or smell. Even colors were hidden from the earliest men, all being white at first. Each incarnation in this race developed more of the prismatic hues in their rainbow order, beginning with red. But the one sense of sight was so spiritual that it amounted to clairvoyance. The second sub-race inherited sight and developed newly touch. Through the repeated lives in this rank the sense of feeling became wonderfully delicate and acute, possessing the psychometric quality and revealing the inner as well as the outer nature of the things to which it was applied. The third sub-race attained hearing, and its spiritual development of this sense was so keen that the most subtle sounds, as the budding leaf and the motion of the heavenly bodies, was clearly perceived. The fourth sub-race added smell to the other three senses, and the fifth entered into taste. The sixth and seventh unfolded the remaining senses, which are beyond our present ken.

In the second circuit (or race) the soul began once more with a single sense and passed through another course of sub-races, rehearsing the scale of the senses with a larger control of them, though less spiritual. But even in the third circuit the repeated unfoldment of the senses toward their physical destiny had still retained a large degree of spiritual quality, as the men themselves were still ethereal.

Our first terrestrial appearance in the present circuit (the fifth race) was in spiritual form, having only astral bodies. This primitive ethereal race occupied the earth long before it was geologically prepared for the historical human races. The development of the physical senses in their present form marks the stages of our reincarnation in the present race, which is called the descent into matter. Each turn in this circuit has carried forward the evolution of the senses in a fixed order, until now we have a firmer hold than ever before upon those five which indicate the extent of our progress in the present stage. Our repeated rebirths have obscured the long vista of the ages through which we have traveled to this point, running through the seven-toned gamut over and over again, first in broad rough outline, then finishing the details more carefully at each iteration. Their early spiritual forms have gradually given way to the modern physical forms, but some persons still retain a portion of those old guises that once were universal, in certain peculiarly delicate senses known as second sight, psychometry, clairaudence, tasting through the fingers, and smelling like a hound. In our present era the sense of taste has become the last and most fully developed and the characteristic sense. At first the body did not require food; then becoming grosser it inhaled it with the air, and as the condition approached which now prevails, man became an eating animal and is grown to an epicure. When we shall have completed the full number of rounds on this earth we shall have not only the other two senses, but shall govern all seven in a triple form as physical, astral, and spiritual.

The most important fact in our evolution, and the cause of the present phase of existence, with its blinding encasements of matter and evil, is the growth of a personal will. This is the forbidden fruit of the Bible Paradise. It originated many cycles back and gradually flourished, until its impress was stamped upon all our fellow-creatures. At first starting as selfish desires, then urging motives for rivalry, it resulted in fierce contest between man and man. The concentration of the soul in selfish energy clouded the inner spiritual nature, destroyed the trace of ethereal descent, and buried us deep in the material world. But this "fall into matter" is really but a necessary curve of the spiral, and is the dawn of a brighter day such as humanity has never seen.

Death marks the origin of the turn which human evolution is at present describing. The earlier races had no sense of age and did not die. Like Enoch, they "walked with God" into the next period of their life. At present when a man dies his *ego* holds the impetus of his earthly desires until they are purged away from that higher self, which then passes into a spiritual state, where all the psychic and spiritual forces it has generated during the earthly life are unfolded. It progresses on these planes until the dormant physical impulses assert themselves and curve the soul around to another incarnation, whose form is the resultant of the earlier lives.

The successive appearances of the soul upon one or many earths are a series of personalities which are the various masks assumed by one individuality, the numerous parts played by one actor. In each birth the personality differs from the prior and later existence, but the one line of individual continuity runs unbroken through all the countless forms; and as the soul enters into its highest development it gradually comprehends the whole course of forgotten paths which have led to the summit.

The time spent by each soul in physical life is only a small fraction of the whole period elapsing before the next incarnation. The larger part of the time is passed in the spiritual existence following death, in which the physical desires and spiritual qualities derived from the earthly life determine the condition of being, until the impetus of unconscious character brings the individual into another earthly life.

Chapter XII
Transmigration Through Animals

All things are but altered, nothing dies,
And here and there th' unbodied spirit flies
By time and force or sickness dispossessed
And lodges where it lights in man or beast.

PYTHAGORAS, in Dryden's Ovid

What is the opinion of Pythagoras concerning wild-fowl?
That the soul of our grandam might haply inhabit a bird.
What thinkest thou of his opinion?
I think nobly of the soul, and no way approve of his opinion.

SHAKESPEARE.

Whoever leaves off being virtuous ceases to be human; and since he cannot attain to a divine nature he is turned into a beast.—BOETHIUS.

Be not under any brutal metempsychosis while thou livest and walkest about erectly under the form of man. Leave it not disputed at last how thou hast predominantly passed thy days.—SIR THOMAS BROWNE.

That which has saved India and Egypt through so many misfortunes and preserved their fertility is neither the Nile nor the Ganges; it is the respect for animal life by the mild and gentle heart of man.—MICHELET.

Oh! the beautiful time will, must come when the beast-loving Brahmin shall dwell in the cold north and make it warm, when man who now honors humanity shall also begin to spare and finally to protect the animated ascending and descending scale of living creatures.—RICHTER.

As many hairs as grow on the beast, so many similar deaths shall the man who slays that beast for his own satisfaction in this world pass through in the next from birth to birth. — LAWS OF MANU.

○ ○ ○ ○ ○ ○ ○ ○

The idea of reincarnation is so intimately connected and so generally identified with the notion that human souls sometimes descend into lower animals, that it is necessary for us to thoroughly understand the exoteric and gross nature of this grotesque phrasing of a solemn and beautiful truth.

All the philosophies and religions teaching reincarnation seem to teach also the wandering of human souls through brute forms. It was the common belief in Egypt and still is in Asia. All animals were sacred to the Egyptians as the masks of fallen gods, and therefore worshiped. The same reverence for all creatures still reigns in the East. The Hindu regards everything in the vast tropical jungle of illusion as a human soul in disguise. The Laws of Manu state: "For sinful acts mostly corporeal, a man shall assume after death a vegetable or mineral form; for such acts mostly verbal, the form of a bird or beast; for acts mostly mental, the lowest of human conditions."

"A priest who has drunk spirituous liquors shall migrate into the form of a smaller or larger worm or insect, of a moth or some ravenous animal.

"If a man steal grain in the husk he shall be born a rat; if a yellow-mixed metal, a gander; if water, a plava or diver; if honey, a great sting-ing gnat; if milk, a crow; if expressed juice, a dog; if clarified butter, an ichneumon weasel.

"A Brahman killer enters the body of a dog, a bear, an ass, a tiger, or a serpent."

Not only does this conception permeate the domains of Brahmanism and Buddhism; it prevailed in Persia before the time of Zoroaster as since. Pythagoras is said to have obtained it in Babylon from the Magi, and through him it scattered widely through Greece and Italy. More closely than with any other teacher, this false doctrine is associated with the sage of Crotona, who is said to have recognized the voice of a deceased friend in the howling of a beaten dog. Plato seems to endorse it also. Plotinus says: "Those who have exercised human faculties are born again men. Those who have used only their senses go into the bodies of brutes, and especially into those of ferocious beasts, if they have yielded to bursts of anger; so that even in this case, the difference between the bodies that they animate conforms to the difference of their propensities. Those who have sought only to gratify their lust and appetite pass into the bodies of lascivious and gluttonous animals. Finally, those who have degraded their senses by disuse are compelled to vegetate in the plants. Those who have loved music to excess and yet have lived pure lives, go into the bodies of melodious birds. Those who have ruled tyrannically become eagles. Those who have spoken lightly of heavenly things, keeping their eyes always turned toward heaven, are changed into birds which always fly toward the upper air. He who has acquired civic virtues becomes a man: if he has not these virtues he is transformed into a domestic animal, like the bee."

Some of the church fathers also believed it. Proclus and Syrianus argued that the brute kept its own soul, but that the human soul which passed into the brute body was bound within the animal soul. Nearly all mythology contains this view of transmigration in some form. In the old Norse and German religions the soul is poetically represented as entering certain lower forms, as a rose, a pigeon, etc., for a short period before assuming the divine abode. The Druids of old Gaul also taught it. The Welsh bards tell us that the souls of men transmigrate into the bodies of those animals whose habits and characters they most resemble, till, after a circuit of such penitential miseries, they are purified for the celestial presence. They mention three circles of existence: the circle of the all-inclosing circle which holds nothing alive or dead but God; the second circle, that of felicity, in which men travel after they have meritoriously passed through their terrestrial changes; the circle of evil, in which human nature passes through the varying stages of existence which it must undergo before it is qualified to inhabit the circle of felicity, and this includes the three infelicities of necessity, oblivion, and death, with frequent trials of the lower animal lives.* " Sir Paul Rycant gives us an account of several well-disposed Mohammedans that purchase the freedom of any little bird they see confined to a cage, and think they merit as much by it as we should do here by ransoming any of our countrymen from their captivity at Algiers. The reason is because they consider every animal as a brother or sister in disguise, and therefore think themselves obliged to extend their charity to them, though under such mean circumstances. They tell you that the soul of a man, when he dies, immediately passes into the body of another man, or some brute which he resembled in his humor, or his fortune, when he was one of us."† Pythagorean transmigration is apparent also in the natives of Mexico, who think that the souls of persons of rank after death inhabit the bodies of beautiful, sweet singing birds and the nobler quadrupeds, while the souls of inferior persons pass into weasels, beetles, and other low creatures. Among 'the Negroes, the Sandwich Islanders, the Tasmanians, in short, among nearly all the world outside of Christendom, this faith rules unquestioned.

The lowest forms of this belief are found among the tribes of Africa and America, which think that the soul immediately after death must seek out a new tenement, and, if need be, enter the body of an animal. Some of the Africans assume that the soul will choose the body of a person of similar rank to its former one, and therefore bury the dead near the houses of their relatives, enabling the unbodied souls to occupy their newborn children. Sometimes holes are dug in the grave to facilitate the soul's egress,, and the house-doors are left open for its admission. The Druses hold firmly to the theory of transmigration. The folklore of all nations has various ways of telling how the soul of a man can inhabit an animal's body, in stories of wehr-wolves, swanmaidens, mermaids, etc.

In many parts of Europe the belief in the man-wolf still flourishes in

* From Addison's *Spectator*.

† This corresponds to the Hindu triple existence mentioned in the Laws of Mann: "Souls endued with goodness attain always the state of deities; those filled with ambitious passions, the condition of men; and those immersed in darkness, the nature of beasts. This is the threefold order of transmigration."

connection with a crazy person, or a monomaniac, who is said to be transformed into the brute nature. Northern Europe receives this superstition as the man-bear. In India it is the man-tiger; in Abyssinia, the man-hyena; in South Africa, the man-lion; each country associating the depraved human nature, which sometimes runs riot as an epidemic mania, with the animal most dreaded.

But it is all a coarse symbol caricaturing the inner vital truth of reincarnation, and springing from the striking resemblance between men and animals, in feature and disposition, in voice and mien. The intelligence and kindness of the beasts approaching near to human character, and the brutality of some men, would seem to indicate that both races were closely enough related to exchange souls. As an English writer says: "A judicious critic or observant reader will scarce allow that more than four or five in the long catalogue of Roman emperors had any humanity; and although they might perhaps have a just claim to be styled Lords of the Earth, they had no right to the title of Man. There is an excellent dissertation in Erasmus on the princely qualities of the eagle and the lion; wherein that great author has demonstrated that emperors and kings are very justly represented by those animals, or that there must be a similarity in their souls, as all their actions are similar and correspondent."* Emerson has a paragraph upon this in his essay on Demonology: "Animals have been called 'the dreams of nature.' Perhaps for a conception of their consciousness we may go to our own dreams. In a dream we have the instinctive obedience, the same torpidity of the highest power, the same unsurprised assent to the monstrous, as these metamorphosed men exhibit. Our thoughts in a stable or in a menagerie, on the other hand, may well remind us of our dreams. What comparison do these imprisoning forms awaken! You may catch the glance of a dog sometimes which lays a kind of claim to sympathy and brotherhood. What! somewhat of me down there? Does he know it? Can he, too, as I, go out of himself, see himself, per-

* Dr. William King, in the *Dreamer*, a series of satirical dreams, which humorously illustrate the alleged doctrine of Pythagoras and Plato, as well as the abuses of religion, etc.

ceive relations? We fear lest the poor brute should gain one dreadful glimpse of his condition. It was in this glance that Ovid got the hint of his metamorphoses; Calidasa, of his transmigration of souls. For these fables are our own thoughts carried out. What keeps these wild tales in circulation for thousands of years? What but the wild fact to which they suggest some approximation of theory? Nor is the fact quite solitary, for in varieties of our own species where organization seems to predominate over the genius of man, in Kalmuck or Malay or Flathead Indian, we are sometimes pained by the same feeling; and sometimes, too, the sharp-witted prosperous white man awakens it. In a mixed assembly we have chanced to see not only a glance of Abdiel, so grand and keen, but also in other faces the features of the mink, of the bull, of the rat, and the barn-door fowl. You think, could the man overlook his own condition, he could not be restrained from suicide."

The remarkable mental cleverness of the highest animals, the cunning of the fox, the tiger's fierceness, the serpent's meanness, the dog's fidelity, seem to be human traits in other forms, and the animal qualities are striking enough in many men for them to be fitly described as a fox, a hog, a snake, etc. The characteristics of animals are accurately termed in expressions first applied to mankind, and the community of disposition between the erect and the debased animal creation has furnished words for human qualities from the lower orders of life — as leonine, canine, vulpine, etc. Briefly, "the rare humanity of some animals and the notorious animality of some men" first suggested the idea of interchanging their souls among the primitive peoples, and has nourished it ever since among the oldest portion of the race as a vulgar illustration of a vital reality.

As the fruits of this idea are beneficial, it was firmly held by the priests and philosophers as a moral fable, through which they popularly taught not only reincarnation, but respect for virtue and for life. It wrought a poetic love of nature in the masses such as has never been seen under any other influence — and which Christianity has strangely failed to establish. Lecky candidly says in his "European Morals": "In the inculcation of humanity to animals on a wide scale the Mohammedans and the Brahmins have considerably surpassed the Christians."

To the eastern mind life is a stream flowing through endless transformations, and everything containing it is divine, from the commonest onion to the crowned king; and as all living things are the possible
casements of human souls, it is the height of impiety to abuse anything.
The kindness of the Orient toward the brute creation is a beautiful com-
ment upon the genuineness of this faith. The mercy due from man to
his friends the lower animals is a noble bequest which has there been
treasured for the world. As the wholesome lesson of transmigration,
Asia has thoroughly learned that

> He prayeth best who loveth best
> All things both great and small,
> For the dear Lord who loveth us
> He made and loveth all.

But the intelligent leaders of oriental thought were far from believing
transmigration literally. The occult theory of the priests of Isis, like that
of the Brahmans, Buddhists, and Chaldeans, never really held that human souls inhabit animals, or that animal souls occupy men, although
many orientalists have not penetrated beyond this outer court of eastern doctrine. It was simply an allegorical gospel for the masses with a
double purpose — to picture the inner truth which acute thinkers would
reach and which the crowds need not know, and to instill respect for
all life. The Egyptian priesthood adopted three styles of teaching all
doctrine. The vulgar religion of the populace was a crude shaping of
the priestly thought. The priests of the outer temple received the half-
veiled tenets of initiates. But only the hierophants of the inner temple,
after final initiation, were allowed to know the pure truth. The same
triple shaping of the central thought, adapted to the audience, was followed by Pythagoras, Plato, and all the great masters. Although the
name of Pythagoras is synonymous with the idea of soul-wandering
through animals, a careful perusal of the fragments of his writings, and
of his disciples' books, shows that he tremendously realized the fact that
souls must always, by all the forces of the universe, find an adequate
expression of their strongest nature, and that it would be as impossible

for a gallon to be contained in a pint measure, as for a human spirit to inhabit an animal body. That the teaching of Pythagoras on this point was purely allegorical is proven by the abridgment of his philosophy given by his disciple Hierocles: "The man who has separated himself from a brutal life by the right use of reason, purified himself as much as is possible from excess of passions, and by this become a man from a wild beast, shall become a God from a man, as far as it is possible for a man to become a God...We can only cure our tendency downwards by the power that leads upwards, by a ready submission to God, by a total conversion to the divine law. The end of the Pythagorean doctrine is to be all wings for the reception of divine good, that when the time of death comes we may leave behind us upon earth the mortal body, and be ready girt for our heavenly journey. Then we are restored to our primitive state. This is the most beautiful end."

Hierocles also comments on the Golden Verses of Pythagoras: "If through a shameful ignorance of the immortality annexed to our soul, a man should persuade himself that his soul dies with his body, he expects what can never happen; in like manner he who expects that after his death he shall put on the body of a beast, and become an animal without reason, because of his vices, or a plant because of his dullness and stupidity—such a man, I say, acting quite contrary to those who transform the essence of man into one of the superior beings, is infinitely deceived, and absolutely ignorant of the essential form of the soul, which can never change; for being and continuing always man, it is only said to become God or beast by virtue or vice, though it cannot be either the one or the other."* The early Neo-Platonists of Alexandria limited the range of human metempsychosis to human bodies and denied that the souls of men ever passed downwards into brutal states. Even the apparent endorsement of that conceit by Plotinus, quoted above, was merely a simile. Porphyry, Jamblichus, and Hierocles forcibly emphasized this distinction. Wilkinson shows that the initiated priests taught that " dis-

* From Dacier's *Life of Pythagoras, with his Symbols and Golden Verses, together with the Life of Hierocles, and his Commentaries upon the Verses*, p. 335. London, 1721.

solution is only the cause of reproduction. Nothing perishes which has once existed. Things which appear to be destroyed only change their natures and pass into another form." But Ebers demonstrates that the inner circle of the temple held this truth in a form wholly above the system of embalming, animal worship, and transmigration ingeniously devised by them for the people. Like the ruling priestcraft in all times and countries, they considered it necessary to disguise their sacred secrets for the crowd. The symbols of reincarnation which everywhere have typi-fied the same doctrine — in Egyptian architecture by the flying globe, in Chinese pagodas and Indian temples by the intricate unfoldment of germinant designs ascending through successive stories to culminate in a gilded ball, in the Grecian friezes of religious processions, in the Druidical cromlechs and cairns of Wales and the circular stone heaps of Britain — all expressed a threefold significance, telling the masses of their transition through all living conditions, reminding the common priesthood of an exalted series of transformations, and picturing for the initiates the hidden principles of immortal progress. For all alike these emblems reiterated the solemn and vital reality of universal brother-hood throughout Nature; but the keenest students, who guided the bulk of religious thought, read in them simply the eternal law of cause and effect divinely ruling the soul through incessant changes. It would be as unjust to construe literally the poetic statements of the human soul wandering through animals, etc., by which metaphor the noblest leaders of western thought convey the idea of spiritual evolution (see chapter V.), as to call this lowest phase of the philosophy the real belief of those who shaped it.

And yet there is a sense in which the most intelligent orientals ad-here to this, and in which western science endorses it — namely in the axiomatic truth that human atoms and emanations traverse the entire round of lower natures. When the Laws of Manu speak of the trans-migration of men through all animal stages, these eastern authorities say that they mean not souls, but men's physical selves. When the Laws assert that "a Brahman killer enters the body of a dog, bear, ass, etc.," they do not mean that the murderer of a priest becomes a dog, bear, ass,

etc. The inner meaning of the Law is that he who kills and extinguish-
es the Brahman or divine nature, condemns his soul to lower human
circumstances, and the downward affinity of his passions carries every
particle of his body by magnetic relations into more degraded ranks
of existence. The Brahmans have distorted the inward purpose of this
Law in their own interest by insisting upon its outward meaning. So the
various accounts of the descent of human into animal or vegetative nature, whether given by Hindu, Pythagorean, Platonist, Egyptian, Norse,
or Barbarian, are actual facts as far as the migration of the composing
atoms and emanations of the outer individual are concerned. For these
atoms obey the directing impulses of degrading passion or ascending
principle. The imponderable force of these atomic changes is proven by
the psychometric evidence of sensitives, who perceive the various un-
expressed moods of a person by the kinds of lambent particles flowing
from him, and trace the permanent course of these particles after they
have lodged on objects widely separated from him. The tell-tale characteristics of these scattered atoms remain a long while as stamped by
their source, and guide them to what is most congenial. This scientific
fact, confirmed by many experiments,* but generally ignored, shaped
the old atomic hypotheses in which Pythagoras, Epicurus, Zeno, and
all the old philosophers down to Plato found delight, and Plato himself
simply spiritualized it into a more enduring form.

The attitude of the dominant disciples of reincarnation upon this
point may be gathered from the following statement of a Brahman to
the writer: "The whole question of rebirths rests upon the right understanding of what it is that is born again. Obviously not the body, nor is
it the ego, which is the same whether in a man or in a worm. The ego is
colorless of all attributes of which we have any knowledge in practice.
The only thing that can be said to be reborn is the character of a being,
through spiritual blindness confounded with the ego, in the same way
as light is commonly confounded with the objects illuminated and said
to be red, blue, or any other color. The essential characteristic of human-

* See the psychometric recorded investigations in Professor Deuton's book *The
Soul of Things*.

ity cannot possibly exist in an animal form, for otherwise it cannot be essential to humanity. Whenever in a human being the ego is identified in the above manner with what is essentially human, birth in an animal form is as certain as any relative truth can be not to take place.

"Atoms enter into organic combinations according to their affinities, and when released from one individual system they retain a tendency to be attracted by other systems, not necessarily human, with similar characteristics. The assimilation of atoms by organisms takes place in accordance with the law of affinities. It may be hastily contended that the relation between the mental characteristics of an individual and the atoms of his body ceases when the atoms no longer constitute the body. But the fact that certain atoms are drawn into a man's body shows that there was some affinity between the atoms and the body before they were so drawn together. Consequently there is no reason to suppose that the affinity ceases at parting. And it is well known that psychometers can detect the antecedent life history of any substance by being brought into contact with it. It must be insisted that the true human ego in no sense migrates from a human body to an animal body, although those principles which lie below the plane of self-consciousness may do so. And in this sense alone is transmigration accepted by Esoteric Science."

Chapter XIII
What then of Death, Heaven, and Hell?

When we die, we shall find that we have not lost our dreams; but that we have only lost our sleep.—RICHTER.

Life is a kind of sleep. Old men sleep longest. They never begin to wake but when they are to die.—DE LA BRUYERE.

There is no death: what seems so is transition.
This life of mortal breath Is but a suburb of the life Elysian,
Whose portal we call Death.
                                    LONGFELLOW.

We can hardly do otherwise than assume that the future being must be so involved in our present constitution as to be therein discernible.—ISAAC TAYLOR.

When I leave this rabble rout and defilement of the world, I leave it as an inn, and not as a place of abode. For nature has given us our bodies as an inn, and not to dwell in.—CATO.

He that soweth to the flesh shall of the flesh reap corruption; but he that soweth to the spirit shall of the spirit reap life everlasting.—ST. PAUL.

But all lost things are in the angels' keeping, Love. No past is dead for us, but only sleeping, Love. The years of heaven will all earth's little pain make good. Together there we can begin again in babyhood.—HELEN HUNT.

REINCARNATION · A STUDY OF FORGOTTEN TRUTH

Death is another life. We bow our heads At going out, we think, and en-
ter straight Another chamber of the king's, Larger than this we leave and
lovelier.— BAILEY.

The deep conviction of the indestructibleness of our nature through
death, which everyone carries at the bottom of his heart, depends alto-
gether upon the consciousness of the original and eternal nature of our be-
ing.— SCHOPENHAUER.

○ ○ ○ ○ ○ ○ ○ ○

The latest developments of science agree with the occultists and poets that there is no death, and that nothing is dead. What seems to
be extinction is only a change of existence. What appears to have no
vitality has only a lower order of the life principle. Everything is pulsing with energy, stones and dirt as well as animals and trees. The same
force which animates the human body, the beasts, birds, and reptiles in
their brief periods, also vitalizes the oaks and vines in a smaller degree
with longer lives, and individualizes the mineral world into crystals on
a still lower plane but with lifetimes reckoned by thousands of years.
And below crystal-life, in the constituent atoms of shapeless matter, is
a tremendous thrill of undiminished activity. Life, the occultists say, is
the eternal uncreated energy. The physicists grasp at the same tiling in
their Law of Continuity, and modern science concedes that " energy has
as much claim to be regarded as an objective reality as matter itself."*
This life is the one essential energy acting under protean forms. It always
inheres in every particle of matter, and makes no distinction between
organic and inorganic, except one of grade, the former containing life-
energy actively and the latter in dormant form. Because the scientist
is unable to awaken into activity the latent life of inorganic matter, he
insists, by the law of biogenesis, that life can only come from life. But
that only marks the limit of his knowledge. The world's development
has bridged all the gaps now yawning between the different kingdoms

* Stewart and Tait, in *The Unseen Universe.*

224 · Reincarnation · A Study of Forgotten Truth   E.D. Walker

of nature, though nothing remains now to show how it was done, and science has to confess its ignorance. There is nothing to contradict and much to enforce the occult axiom that the same life animates man, plant, and rock simply in different states of the one indestructible force — the Universal Soul — making all nature what Goethe terms "the living visible garment of God."

It is impossible for a person to cease to exist. When the tenant of the body moves out, the forces binding together the dwelling scatter to the nearest uses awaiting them. The positivists would have it that the individual soul also dissolves into an impersonal fund of being — a sort of immediate chilling Nirvana, out-freezing any eastern conception of remotest destiny. This melancholy result of western materialism is boldly confronted by reincarnation with a proven hypothesis, which illuminates the mystery of death and the future, and shows the unimpeachable reality of immortality. Reincarnation demonstrates that the personal ego, which permanently maintains its identity amid the constant changes of the bodily casement and the mental consciousness, must continue its individuality. In addition to the evidences already adduced for the genuineness of this truth, there stands the honest reliable testimony of spiritualism (a small core of veritable fact around which is gathered an enormous concretion of deceptions, mischievously intentional or pathetically unconscious), and the actual experience of some orientals whose intense devotion to pure invisible realities has pushed them into the perception of ultra-mortal things.

It is the strong attachment to physical existence which makes death the king of terrors. Those who have learned the lesson of life find him the blessed angel who ushers them through the golden gates. There shall at length come to every ascending soul the experience of those whose departure from this life cannot be called death, as Jesus, Elijah, or Enoch, who "walked with God and he was not, for God took him." They became so buoyed with spiritual forces that a slight touch shifted the equipoise and translated them into the invisible. The clarified spirit greets death with a welcome, and sings his praise as did Paul Hamilton Hayne in his dying song: —

Sad mortal! couldst thou but know
  What truly it means to die,
The wings of thy soul would glow,
  And the hopes of thy heart beat high;
Thou wouldst turn from the Pyrrhonist schools,
  And laugh their jargon to scorn,
As the babbling of midnight fools
  Ere the morning of Truth be born:
But I, earth's madness above,
  In a kingdom of stormless breath—
I gaze on the glory of love
  In the unveiled face of Death.
I tell thee his face is fair
  As the moon-bow's amber rings,
And the gleam in his unbound hair
  Like the flash of a thousand springs;
His smile is the fathomless beam
  Of the star-shine's sacred light,
When the summers of Southland dream
  In the lap of the holy Night:
For I, earth's blindness above,
  In a kingdom of halcyon breath—
I gaze on the marvel of love
  In the unveiled face of Death.

When death severs the soul from its mortal shell, the ruling tendencies of the soul carry it to its strongest affinities. If these still dwell on earth, the soul hovers affectionately among the old scenes and insensibly mingles with its heart-friends, ministering and being ministered to, with no essential difference from the former condition.* Many veritable experiences, apart from all possibility of delusion, confirm this, although the darkness of matter blinds most of us to the psychic life. At length, as shifting time unties the bonds of earth, the soul moves on with its strongest allies to the realms of its choice. There the soul lives out an

* See *The Gates Between*, by Elizabeth Stuart Phelps.

era of its true life, an expression of its deepest nature, as much more full and more real than the late physical life, as the waking state exceeds the dreaming. For the escape from material confinement allows the freest activity, in which the dominant desires, unconsciously nourished in the spirit, have the mastery. This liberty rouses the spirit from the earthly lethargy into its permanent individuality. The startling bound of the spirit into its own sphere must transfer the self-consciousness from its terrestrial form to a far higher vividness; but, as the wakefulness of day includes the somnambulence of night and knows itself superior to that dumb life, so the burst of unconstrained spiritual existence does not annul, but transcends the material phase.

The condition of the period intervening between death and birth, like all other epochs, is framed by the individual. The inner character makes a Paradise, a Purgatory, or an Inferno of any place. As Jesus said he was in heaven while talking with his followers, as Dante found all the material for hell in what his eyes witnessed, so in the environments beyond death, where the subjective states of the soul are supreme, the appearance of the universe and the feelings of self are created, well or ill, by the central individual. There must be as many heavens and hells as there are good and bad beings. All the attempts to describe the future are inadequate and erroneous, and must necessarily be so. Plato, in the last book of the Republic, quotes the narrative of the Pamphylian Er, who had been killed in battle but came to life again on his funeral pyre, and declared that he was returned to earth to disclose the nature of the coming life. He found things about as Plato's allegory pictures them: the good and the wicked who had just died being assigned their places in heaven or under the earth. A number of souls whose thousand years of one or the other experience had expired were made to cast lots for a choice out of a large number of human and animal lives, and to drink of the River of Indifference, and to traverse the Plain of Forgetfulness before entering the world again. As with all the visions of after-death, this simply reflected the opinions of the Platonic thinker. St. John's Revelation paints the scene by colors obtained from his Jewish training, on the canvas of his Patmos imprisonment. Bunyan's description shows a simple imagination saturated with the Apocalypse. Protestant visionaries always discover a Protestant heaven and hell. Catholic ecstatics always add purgatory. Swedenborg found the gardens of heaven laid out in the Dutch fashion of his time. English clairvoyants and mediums are properly orthodox and evangelical. American spirits talk broad theology with ridiculous details. The divergence in all these alleged liftings of the veil betrays their subjectiveness.

It is impossible in the nature of things that one should permanently leave the physical condition until the business of that existence is accomplished in transferring the affections from material to spiritual things. While the ruling attraction to a soul remains in this world, all the forces of the universe conspire to continue the association of the two in repeated lives. On the other hand, a person dominated by spiritual proclivities finds infinite magnetisms drawing him away from temporal surroundings to the inscrutable glories of the eternal. In Swedenborg's phrase, "a man's loves make his home." The residual impulses coming from the momentums of past lives determine what and when shall be the next embodiment. The time and manner of reincarnation vary with each individual according to the impetus engendered by his lives. Between these lives the spiritual effect of the earth-life is absorbed from the personal soul manifested on earth into the immortal and unmanifested ego. This process may require days, years, centuries, or millenniums, depending upon the intensity of the mundane aspirations which draw the spirit to earth and hinder its liberation into pure spiritual life. But as in dreams a whole life's history is sometimes condensed into a few seconds, time has no existence to the disembodied spirit. Whether the interval be long or short, the entire spiritual effect of the last life must be assimilated and shaped into a form that will spring up in coming lives. The instances of alternate consciousness indicate that some such marked difference from the previous incarnation appears in each earthly life, losing all remembrance of the previous chapter, and working out the tendencies which embodied that particular life in a career that will achieve redemption or condemnation.

At the first thought reincarnation carries the unwelcome inference that death and rebirths separate us from the dearest present ties and introduce us as strangers into new phases of activity where everything — friends, knowledge, and occupations — must be found afresh. This is a mistake. The unnoticed habits of thought and action derived from the alliance of cherished comrades strengthen into ungovernable steeds whose course directs the soul on every journey toward those favorite companions. Among the thousands of acquaintances made in a lifetime, the rare friends whose intimacy strikes down into the inmost depths of the soul must continue as irresistible attractions in the next life. Orpheus could not fail to discover Eurydice in the spirit realm. In this earthly existence, which is the Heaven, or Purgatory, or Hell of the last one, we go straying among unfamiliar forms, frequently mistaking them for true friends, until suddenly we meet a soul with which there conies so intense and permanent an affection that every other person is forgotten. Such a fusion of spirits must hail from the shores of long distant loves, and its new unrecognized mastery develops a mightier union than would be possible in one uninterrupted flow. The poets like to symbolize this as the blending of two hemispheres long since separated into their original perfect whole. The most probable explanation of such intimacies rests in the idea that they are repetitions of previous attachments. A sense of ancient familiarity grows upon these closest ties, notwithstanding the absence of memory's confirmation. The powerful attractions residing in families and kinships may well be the result of ancestral affinities which have bound together in many earlier combinations, like a turning kaleidoscope, the same individuals.

Chapter XIV
Karma, the Companion Truth of Reincarnation

We are our own children.—Pythagoras.

Nothing can work me damage but myself.—St. Bernard.

Our acts our angels are, or good or ill Our fatal shadows that walk with us still.—Beaumont & Fletcher.

The kingdom of heaven is within you.—Jesus.

We make our fortunes and we call them fate.—B. Disraeli

Men must reap the things they sow. Force from force must ever flow.—Shelley.

The soul contains in itself the event that shall presently befall it, or the event is only the actualizing of its thoughts.—Emerson.

> Seldom went such grotesqueness with such pain;
> I never saw a brute I hated so.
> He must be wicked to deserve such pain.
>   Browning.

Not from birth does one become a slave; not from birth does one become a saint; but by conduct alone.—Gautama.

We sleep, but the loom of life never stops; and the pattern which was weaving when the sun went down is weaving when it comes up tomorrow.—Beecher.

Then spake he of that answer all must give
For all things done amiss or wrongfully,
Alone, each for himself, reckoning with that
The fixed arithmetic of the universe,
Which meteth good for good, ill for ill,
Measure for measure unto deeds, words, thoughts,
Making all futures fruits of all the pasts.

THE LIGHT OF ASIA.

○ ○ ○ ○ ○ ○ ○ ○

Karma is the eastern word for what the West knows as the Law of Causation, applied to personal experience. In Christendom the full recognition of this great principle, like that of its mate, reincarnation, lies dormant; but it is merely an extension into the spiritual domain of the fundamental premise of all science, the substratum of common sense, the cardinal axiom of every philosophy — that each effect has an adequate cause, and each cause works infinite consequences. Briefly, the doctrine of karma is that we have made ourselves what we are by former actions, and are building our future eternity by present actions. There is no destiny but what we ourselves determine. There is no salvation or condemnation except what we ourselves bring about. God places all the powers of the universe at our disposal, and the handle by which we use them to construct our fate has been and is and always shall be our own individual will. Action (karma) of the spirit, whether in the inner consciousness alone, or by vocal expression, or in outward act, is the secret force which directs our journeys through infinity, driving us down into the gloomy regions of evil, of matter, and of selfishness, or up toward the luminous fields of good, of spirit, and of love.

The most adamantine of facts is that of an infinite all-comprehending power of which nature is the pulsing body, an eternal reality shaping the shadowy appearances of time, and variously named Force, Fate, Justice, Righteousness, Love, Mind, The Over-Soul, God. The most essential attribute of this unfathomable Being is that of Almighty Equity.

Confronting this fact is the puzzling fact of our spiritual personality enveloped in matter. The thought always associated with this, never practically forsaken, though sometimes theoretically denied, is individual responsibility. "Two things fill me with wonder," said Kant, "the starry heavens and the sense of moral responsibility in man." When Daniel Webster was asked what was the greatest thought that ever stirred his soul, he replied, "The thought of my personal accountability to God." Every balanced mind agrees with these intellectual giants on this point. The inevitable outcome of grouping these two actualities (God and responsibility) is the conception that the Universal Sustainer is giving every creature the best thing for it, and that each soul is in some way accountable for its condition. Single observations seem to contradict this idea, but the long trend of life's experience verifies it. Because it offers no shelter for culpable actions and necessitates a sterling manliness, it is less welcome to weak natures than the easy religious tenets of vicarious atonement, intercession, forgiveness, and death-bed conversions. But it rings through the inner soul-world as the fundamental harmonic tone, setting the key for all wholesome poetry, philosophy, religion, and art, and inspiring the magnificent sweep of progress which is rationalizing modern Christendom. For it is identical with the essence of Bible truth, as these representative sentences will suggest:—

"Keep thy heart with all diligence, for out of it are the issues of life." (Solomon.)

"Sin no more, lest a worse thing come upon thee." (Jesus.)

"Work out your own salvation. Whatsoever a man soweth, that shall he also reap." (St. Paul.)

The embryos of all animals are at the earliest stage indistinguishable from one another. The biologist who has lost his labels cannot tell which would become a fish, which a cat, and which a man; but nature knows the past records and therefore the future possibility of each. So within souls apparently similar there hide unsuspected germs of vast difference, resulting from the forgotten pasts, which may develop into corresponding divergent futures. The ancient behaviors of every soul have accumulated a grand heritage of influences from which our present bequest is derived. Using another figure, as each piece of "new" soil contains through all its depth a multitude of various seeds sown in past ages, which patiently bide their time to be brought to light and bear fruit, so the kernels of remote conducts shall eventually all have their unfoldment in the revolution of our lives, until at last, if we refuse weeds and harbor only worthy germs, we shall bear a continual harvest of good.

The "bonds of action" include the whole range of material for character — not only the recognized habits of the soul, but, of more consequence still, the unconscious inner thought whence the outward manifestations spring. Whatever impulses are secretly cherished, these feed the acts of life, and mould all our environments to fit them. The nurtured thought of killing produces a thousand unseen murders and must continue wreaking crimes in immensely larger degree than hangable horrors. Our favorite inclinations show what we have been doing in ancient ages. Within the germ of today's conduct are coiled interminable consequences of good and evil.

The relentless hand which metes out our fortunes with the stern justice most vividly portrayed by the Greek dramatists in their Nemesis, Fates, and Furies, takes from our own savings the gifts bestowed on us. "Alas! we sow what we reap; the hand that smites us is our own." In the domain of eternal justice, the offense and the punishment are inseparably connected as the same event, because there is no real distinction between the action and its outcome. He who injures another in fact only wrongs himself. To adopt Schopenhauer's figure, he is a wild beast who fastens his fangs in his own flesh. But linked with the awful fact of our undivided responsibility for what we now are, goes the inspiring assurance that we have in our control the remedy of evil and the increase of good. We can, and we alone can, extricate ourselves from the existing limitations, by the all-curing powers of purity, love, spirituality. In eastern phraseology, the purpose of life is to work out our bad karma (action) and to stow away good karma. As surely as the harvest of today grows from the seed-time of yesterday, so shall every kernel of thought and feeling, speech and performance, bring its crop of reward or rebuke. The inherent result of every quiver of the human will continually tolls the Day of Judgment, and affords immeasurable opportunities for amelioration.

The worthy soul straitened with misfortune is shifting off the chains of old wrong-doing. The vicious soul enjoying comforts is reaping the benefits of old virtues. So intricately are all situations connected with untraceable lineages that only the Omniscient can penetrate below appearances in the real natures of men. The world is like a garden in which is newly planted a huge assortment of unknown plants. To the common observer the fresh sprouts are only deceptive, for the most promising stalk may prove to be a weak, fragile thing, and the uninviting leaflets may introduce a sturdy growth. But the all-wise Gardener knows each seed, and that it will ultimately show its ancestry. The stupendous issues of conduct endure through all changes. After one has climbed to high summits of character the surprising reappearance of some forgotten sin may stay his progress and require all his forces to conquer the viper whose *egg* he long ago nested in his bosom. The man plunged into the abyss of degradation may be a saint much farther advanced than those exalted persons who despise him.

It is karma, or our old acts, that draws us back into earthly life. The spirit's abode changes according to its karma, and this karma forbids any long continuance in one condition, because *it* is always changing. So long as action is governed by material and selfish motives, just so long must the effect of that action be manifested in physical rebirths. Only the perfectly selfless man can elude the gravitation of material life. Few have attained this; but it is the goal of mankind. Some have reached it and have voluntarily returned as saviors of the race.

An illustrious explanation of karma appears at the close of "The Light of Asia":

> KARMA—all that total of a soul
> Which is the things it did, the thoughts it had,
> The "self" it wove with woof of viewless time
> Crossed on the warp invisible of acts.
> What hath been bringeth what shall be, and is,

Worse — better — last for first and first for last
The angels in the heavens of gladness reap
Fruits of a holy past.
The devils in the underworlds wear out
Deeds that were wicked in an age gone by.
Nothing endures: fair virtues waste with time,
Foul sins grow purged thereby.
Who toiled a slave may come anew a prince
For gentle worthiness and merit won;
Who ruled a king may wander earth in rags
For things done and undone.
Before beginning, and without an end,
As space eternal and as surety sure,
Is fixed a Power divine which moves to good,
Only its laws endure.
It will not be contemned of any one:
Who thwarts it loses, and who serves it gains;
The hidden good it pays with peace and bliss,
The hidden ill with pains.
It seeth everywhere and marketh all:
Do right — it recompenseth! do one wrong —
The equal retribution must be made,
Though DHARMA* tarry long.
It knows not wrath nor pardon; utter-true
Its measures mete, its faultless balance weighs;
Times are as naught, tomorrow it will judge,
Or after many days.
By this the slayer's knife did stab himself;
The unjust judge hath lost his own defender;
The false tongue dooms its lie; the creeping thief
And spoiler rob, to render.
Such is the law which moves to righteousness,
Which none at last can turn aside or stay;

* Perfect Justice.

The heart of it is love, the end of it
Is peace and consummation sweet. Obey!
- - - - - - - - - -

The books say well, my brothers! each man's life
The outcome of his former living is;
The bygone wrongs bring forth sorrows and woes,
The bygone right breeds bliss.
That which ye sow ye reap. See yonder fields!
The sesamum was sesamum, the corn
Was corn. The silence and the darkness knew;
So is a man's fate born.
He cometh, reaper of the things he sowed,
Sesamum, corn, so much cast in past birth;
And so much weed and poison-stuff, which mar
Him and the aching earth.
If he shall labor rightly, rooting these,
And planting wholesome seedlings where they grew
Fruitful and fair and clean the ground shall be,
And rich the harvest due.
If he who liveth, learning whence woe springs,
Endureth patiently, striving to pay
His utmost debt for ancient evils done
In love and truth alway;
If making none to lack, he throughly purge
The lie and lust of self forth from his blood;
Suffering all meekly, rendering for offence
Nothing but grace and good:
If he shall day by day dwell merciful,
Holy and just and kind and true; and rend
Desire from where it clings with bleeding roots,
Till love of life have end:
He—dying—leaveth as the sum of him
A life-count closed, whose ills are dead and quit,
Whose good is quick and mighty, far and near,

So that fruits follow it.
No need hath such to live as ye name life;
That which began in him when he began
Is finished: he hath wrought the purpose through
Of what did make him man.
Never shall yearnings torture him, nor sins
Stain him, nor ache of earthly joys and woes
Invade his safe eternal peace; nor deaths
And lives recur. He goes
Unto NIRVANA. He is one with Life Yet lives not.
He is blest, ceasing to be.
OM, MANI PADME, OM! the dewdrop slips
Into the shining sea!

- - - - - - - - - -

This is the doctrine of the KARMA. Learn!
Only when all the dross of sin is quit,
Only when life dies like a white flame spent.
Death dies along with it.

Conclusion

The glories of the Possible are ours.—BAYARD TAYLOR.

The majesty and beauty of the world are latent in any iota of the world.
—WALT WHITMAN.

There is no life of a man, but is a heroic poem of its sort, rhymed or un-rhymed. –Would'st thou plant for eternity: then plant into the deep infinite faculties of man.—CARLYLE.

Life is a mission. Every other definition of life is false, and leads all who accept it astray. Religion, Science, Philosophy, though still at variance upon many points, all agree in this, that every existence is an aim.—MAZZINI.

> *A sacred burden is this life ye bear.*
> *Look on it, lift it, bear it solemnly;*
> *Stand up and walk beneath it steadfastly;*
> *Fail not for sorrow, falter not for sin;*
> *But onward, upward, till the goal ye win.*
>   FRANCES A. KEMBLE.

Know that this world is one stage of eternity. For those who are journey-ing in the right way, it is the road of religion. It is a market opened in the wilderness where those who are travelling on their way to God may collect and prepare provisions for their journey.—AL GAZZALI.

> *Life is but a means unto an end—that end,*
> *Beginning, mean, and end of all things—God.*
> *We live in deeds, not years; in thoughts, not breaths;*
> *In feelings, not in figures on a dial.*

We should count time by heart throbs. He most lives
Who thinks most, feels the noblest, acts the best.

BAILEY.

Heaven is not reached at a single bound,
But we build the ladder by which we rise
From the lowly earth to the vaulted skies,
And we mount to its summit round by round.

J. G. HOLLAND.

○ ○ ○ ○ ○ ○ ○ ○

We are lotus-eaters, so engrossed with the ignoble attractions around us as to have forgotten the places through which we have long strayed away from home, and to heed not the necessity of many more perilous journeys before we can reach our glorious destination. It is only by rousing ourselves to the important fact of the past pilgrimage by which we have traveled hither, and to the still more vital reality of the incalculable sequences of our present route, that we can attain the best progress. Our repugnance to the idea of a cycle of lives, with myriad meanderings through varied forms, is the cry of Tennyson's Lotus-Eaters:

> While all things else have rest from weariness,
> All things have rest, why should we toil alone?
> - - - - - - - - - -
> Nor ever fold our wings
> And cease our wanderings.
> Why should we only toil, the roof and crown of things?

This is virtually the longing for Nirvana, and the cause of the irrational belief in an eternal Heaven immediately following this life. But it is neither wise nor religious to ignore the necessity of continuing our ascent at the present pace, until we have journeyed all the way to that distant goal. The restlessness of our nature comes from the established habit of straying about in temporal realms, and has developed a love of adventure in which the occidental world finds profounder delight than in the oriental yearning for inactivity, and which shall have abundant exercise before it disappears. The only path to that perfect satisfaction which is found in complete oneness with the Supreme winds through the ascending planes of material embodiment.

> Still must I climb if I would rest:
> The bird soars upward to his nest;
> The young leaf on the tree-top high
> Cradles itself within the sky.
> I cannot in the valley stay;
> The great horizons stretch away!
> The very cliffs that wall me round
> Are ladders into higher ground.
> And heaven draws near as I ascend;
> The breeze invites,the stars befriend.
> All things are beckoning to the Best;
> I climb to Thee, my God, for rest!*

In which one of its various guises we shall receive reincarnation depends upon the individual. Whether it shall be in the crude form of transmigration through animals as received by most of the world; or in the Persian and Sufi faith as the unjust banishment from our proper home by the powers of evil; or, following Egypt, Pythagoras, Plato, Origen, and the Druids, as a purgatorial punishment for prenatal sins; or, in the form of some Christian teaching, as a probationary stage testing our right to higher existence and ushering us into a permanent spiritual condition; or, as maintained alike by the acutest Eastern philosophy and the soundest Western thought, as a wholesome development of germinal soul-forces;—through all these phrasings the same central truth abides, furnishing what Henry More called "the golden key" for the problem of life, and explaining the plot of this "drama whose prologue

* From Lucy Larcom.

and catastrophe are both alike wanting." But the broadest intelligence leads us directly into the evolutionary aspect of reincarnation, and finds the others inadequate to the full measure of human nature. In this view the present life is one grade of a stupendous school, in which we are being educated for a destiny so far beyond our comprehension that some call it a kind of deity. The experiences through which we have come were needful for our strengthening. Even though we have descended below former altitudes, the only path to the absolute lies through the sensuous earthly vale. Sin itself, after we have escaped it, will lead to a mightier result than would be possible without it, or it would not be permitted. The richest trees of all the forest world spring from the unclean miasmic fens. The severest present disciplines, coming from our earlier errors, are training us for a loftier growth than we ever knew. Our physical schooling, through all the grades necessary to our best unfoldment, will build a character as much sublimer than our primitive condition as virtue overtowers innocence, and when the race finally emerges from the jangling turmoil of self-will into complete harmony with the Perfect One, as it must at last, the multitudes of our lives will not seem too enormous a course of experience for the establishment of that consummation. The victorious march of Evolution through all the provinces of thought will at length be followed by the triumphal procession of Reincarnation.

> There is a spirit in all things that live
>   Which hints of patient change from kind to kind;
> And yet no words its mystic sense can give,
>   Strange as a dream of radiance to the blind.
> And as in time unspeakably remote
>   Vague frenzies in inferior brains set free
> Presaged a power no language could denote,
>   So dreams the mortal of the God to be.*

The Father's purpose with us seems to be to educate us as His children

* From A. E. Lancaster.

so that we shall be in complete sympathy with the divine mind. The only method of accomplishing this glorious result is for us to enter with Him into all the phases of His being. Our long series of physical lives will finally give us a thorough knowledge of the grosser nature with which He cloaks Himself. We penetrate the animal existence in human form more successfully than would be possible if we transmigrated into all the species of zoology; for here we carry sufficient intelligence, along with the material condition, to comprehend these creatures around us which cannot understand themselves. We cannot expect to permanently leave this department of God's house until we have essentially grasped the secret of all earthly life. The highest individuals of mankind, the saviors of the race, the true prophets and poets, attain this intimate communion with nature, this mastery over the lower creation, which demonstrates their fitness for introduction to a higher stage.

It is difficult to account for the great geniuses except by the consideration that they are the result of many noble lives. Emerson arrives at this conclusion in his essay on Swedenborg. "In common parlance, what one man is said to learn by experience, a man of extraordinary sagacity is said, without experience, to divine. The Arabians say that Abul Khain, the mystic, and Abu Ali Scena, the philosopher, conferred together; and on parting the philosopher said, 'All that he sees, I know;' and the mystic said, 'All that he knows, I see.' If one should ask the reason of this intuition, the solution would lead us into that property which Plato denoted as reminiscence, and which is implied by the Brahmans in the tenet of transmigration. The soul having been often born, or, as the Hindus say, 'traveling the path of existence through thousands of births,' having beheld the things which are here, those which are in heaven, and those which are beneath, there is nothing of which she has not gained the knowledge: no wonder that she is able to recollect, in regard to one thing, what formerly she knew. For all things in nature being linked and related, and the soul having heretofore known all, nothing hinders but that any man who has recalled to mind, or, according to the common phrase, has learned one thing only, should of himself recover all his ancient knowledge, and find out again all the rest, if he have but courage, and faint not in the midst of his researches. For inquiry and learning is reminiscence all. How much more, if he that inquires be a holy, god-like soul! For by being assimilated to the original soul, by whom, and after whom, all things subsist, the soul of man does then easily flow into all things, and all things flow into it: they mix; and he is present and sympathetic with their structure and law."

A recent instance of the glaring facts inexplicable by any other theory than reincarnation appears in the little musical prodigy Josef Hofmann, whose phenomenal genius holds complete mastery of the piano, and charms vast audiences with his exquisite rendering of most difficult concertos, and particularly with his marvelous improvisations upon themes suggested at a moment's notice. He presents the uncanny phenomenon of a child of ten who has little more to learn in the most difficult of arts. The natural explanation occurring to any candid mind is thus suggested by the *Boston Herald* in its report of a Hofmann concert: "It almost seems as if the spirit of some great composer had been put into this boy by nature, waiting to be developed in accordance with our modern art to shine forth again in all its glory in his work." What if he actually were the reappearance of Mozart hastening to fill out the life that was cut sadly short? There may be means of verifying such a presumption by the character of his later compositions, when he gets the full expression of his natural bent. An art so independent of time and place, as music, might fairly be traced through two historic individuals, when literature and painting would not permit it. At any rate it is significant that the young prodigies in any particular kind of skill do not come until that skill has been well established on the earth. Guido followed generations of great painters. Pascal was preceded by a long course of mathematicians. Pope "lisped in numbers" after a vast procession of poets. And Mozart waited until the new era of musical harmony had been well inaugurated. The colossal characters who stand out from the race, with no predecessors equal to them, like Homer, Plato, Jesus, Raphael, Shakespeare, Beethoven, all reach their maturity later than other prodigies, after infancy and youth have fastened the Lethean gates upon the prehistoric scenes from which they seem to hail. But the unfathomable vagaries of the soul, as it works out successively its dominant impulses, easily disguise the individual in different personalities, so long as the physical realm is most attractive to it. Yet it is noticeable that the great minds of history come together in galaxies, when the fullness of time for their capacities draws them together. Witness the Sanskrit sages, the Greek poets and philosophers, the Augustan writers and generals, the Italian artists of the Renaissance, the German masters of music, the Elizabethan authors, the nineteenth-century scientists. The traits of the commonest child, however, as much as the miracles of a genius, have no satisfactory explanation outside of the philosophy of rebirths.

Evolution of the physical nature and of material strength attaches our future to body and matter. But the attachment hastens toward a release by at length proving these to be low steps in the ascent of life. As in the geological programme of animal development each era carried its type to gigantic dimensions and then was surmounted by a higher order of creatures, which in turn grew monstrous as tyrants of their age and then succumbed to a still higher rank: so the soul's progress from the earthly domain lies through the mastery of physical things to mental, thence to psychic, and at last to spiritual. And the passion for material achievement animating our side of the planet should not be underestimated, since it governs an important epoch in the world's growth. But the danger lies in esteeming it a finality. It is chiefly valuable as the foundation upon which we may build skyward, in an evolution of character. When the structure is made high enough, the buoyancy of the upper stories will conquer the weight of the base and float away our abode to ethereal climes. Only the education of the spiritual in us, of sacrifice, nobility, and divinity, can divorce us from these uneasy earthly affinities to the permanent rest of union with God. While we must not abandon the glories of physical beauty, power and pleasure, we must not forget that the true business of life is to wean our affections from the visible to the invisible, to transfer the preponderance of our magnetisms from shadows to substances. For we bridge the two kingdoms of matter and spirit, and we have the choice between them more freely than we know.

The mechanical transmigration which was fancifully told in Grecian mythology, gathered and beautifully rendered by Ovid, which was taught in the Egyptian and Pythagorean dogmas and still floats broadcast throughout the vast realms of Brahmanism, Buddhism, and barbarism, which fascinates the thought of our poets, and which is daily enacted by a myriad object-lessons in nature, is merely the objective expression of a subjective truth, discerned by all the mystics, seers, and philosophers, and most elaborately stated by Swedenborg. It means that the infinite progress of the soul conveys it through countless epochs, moving in perfect succession by the dynamic laws of its own being. During this development, the universe arranges itself peculiarly to each individual according to his thought and character. We shape the outer world by our inner nature, and we say just how long our stay shall be among dust and mortality.

The true and wholesome aspect of the earthly life, under the religious philosophy of reincarnation, transforms the spectacle from a trivial show, or a gloomy arena of despair, to a majestic stage in the ascending series of human sojournings on the way to the Absolute. In the words of the old martyr-philosopher Giordano Bruno, the father of Descartes, Spinoza, and Leibnitz, the cherisher of that thought, "being present in the body, is yet, as by an indissoluble oath, bound and united to divine things, so that he is not sensible either of love or hatred for mortal things, knowing he is greater than these, and that he must not be the slave of his body, which is to be regarded as no other than the prison of his liberty, a snare for his wings, a chain upon his limbs, and a veil impeding his sight." His life flows beauteously in aspiration for the invisible kingdom of permanence, as this same Bruno, the Nolan, phrased it in verse: —

> While that the sun upon his round doth burn
> And to their source the roving planets flee,
> Things of the earth do to the earth return
> And parted waters hasten to the sea:
> So shall my spirit to the high gods turn
> And heaven-born thought to Heaven shall carry me.

Instead of being a cold pagan philosophy as it is frequently considered, reincarnation throbs with the most vital spirit of Christianity. It is no more Buddhism, than kindliness is Christianity. It is the hidden core of the gospel of Jesus as of all other great religions and philosophies. This is what has preserved them in spite of their degrading excrescences. It is "the religion of all sensible men" who refuse the weak sentiment and bigoted dogmas that obscure the light of Christianity in the churches: for it clearly unfolds what they unconsciously believe, in the laws of cause and effect. It spurns the despairing doctrine of total depravity, but shows the cause of partial depravity. It teaches salvation as Jesus did, not by heaping our sins upon him, but by recognizing the Fatherhood of the Supreme, entering the new birth into spiritual life, and watchfully growing Godward. It revolts against the thought of everlasting punishment for brief errors, but provides infinite opportunities for restoration and advancement, while emphasizing most vigorously the unescapable results of all action" It is therefore a corrective of modern Christianity holding fast to the strength and beauty of what the Nazarene taught and lived, but including those very principles which breed religious skepticism in the extreme advocates of science and evolution. It enlarges Christianity to a grander capacity than it has hitherto known, and so furnishes at once an inspiring religion for the loftiest spiritual aspiration, a most satisfactory philosophy for the intellect, and the strongest basis for practical nobility of conduct. There is no reason why reincarnation and Christianity should not grasp hands and magnificently advance together, each keeping the other steadfastly true. Only in this union can Christianity escape its present downward sag. Since western religion fails to spiritually sustain us and has largely gone over to the enemy—materialism, it is time for another oriental tide to sweep over the West. Having already a partial possession here, reincarnation promises to flow in freely to revitalize Christianity, to spiritualize science. As Christianity has degenerated in the West, so has reincarnation in the East, and the hope of the race lies in an exalted marriage of them. They need each other, as husband and wife, allied in purest devotion, supplementing the defects and strengths of each other, and regenerating their lower unassociated tendencies. The religion of Jesus tends to sink into an irrational sentimentality which is commonly relegated to women and effeminate men. The spiritual philosophy of India declines into passionless fatalism or an ungenerous self-absorption. Superstition darkens both alike. But reincarnation keeps Christianity thoroughly rational, and Christianity will sustain reincarnation in vigorous unselfishness. This alliance of the best truths of both hemispheres will teach a reverential submission to the divine will without its sequel of stagnation, a heroic self-reliance without its danger of atheism, a regenerative communion with the Highest without the sacrilegious folly of selfish prayer.

Reincarnation unites all the family of man into a universal brotherhood more effectively than the prevailing humanity. It promotes the solidarity of mankind by destroying the barriers that conceit and circumstances have raised between individuals, groups, nations, and races. All are alike favored with perfect poetic justice. The children of God are not ordained some to honor and others to abasement. There are no special gifts. Physical blessings, mental talents, and moral successes are the laborious result of long merit. Sorrows, defects, and failures proceed from negligence. The upward road to the glories of spiritual perfection is always at our feet, with perpetual invitations and aids to travel higher. The downward way into sensual wreckage is but the other direction of the same way. We cannot despise those who are tending down, for who knows but we have journeyed that way ourselves? It is impossible for us to scramble up alone, for our destiny is included in that of humanity, and only by helping others along can we ascend ourselves. The despondent sadness of the world which dims the lustre of every joy, chanting the minor key of nature, haunting us in unaccountable ways, cropping out in all literature and art, making the grandest of poetry tragic and the sublimest music sombre, is the unconscious voice of mankind, humming its keynote of life. While we continue to dwell in the murky realm of sense, that must prevail. But the bright rifts illuminating the advance guard herald the approach of day, and assure us that the trend of restless human gyrations is away from that condition.

Contrary to the common opinion of eastern thought, reincarnation is optimistic. The law of causation is not a blind meting of eye for eye and tooth for tooth. It opens out into a scheme of beneficent progress. Science recognizes this in the *vis medicalrix remedia naturce*, the healing power of nature. What was once denied in the creed of the alchemists concerning the ascending impulse of all things is now preached by science, which declares in Tyndall's words that "matter contains within it the promise and potency of all life." All minerals have the rudimentary possibility of plants and animals. Crystals strive after a higher life by assuming arborescent and mossy shapes. Plants display the embryonic qualities of low animals. No naturalist can mark infallibly the boundaries of the three kingdoms, so closely are they interlinked. A zoologist does not doubt the possibility of minerals becoming plants and these mounting into animals. The movement of vital energy is manward, and the cry of mankind is "excelsior," towards God. Poetry cherishes the same conviction that somehow good Shall be the final goal of ill, For pangs of nature, sins of will, Defects of doubt and taints of blood;

> That nothing walks with aimless feet;
> That not one life shall be destroyed
> Or cast as useless to the void
> When God shall make this pile complete.
> Behold! we know not anything.
> We can but trust that good shall fall
> At last, far off, at last, to all,
> And every winter turn to spring.

And Tennyson's uncertain faith is an undoubted verity in the Orient, thus phrased by Edwin Arnold:—

> Ye are not bound! the soul of things is sweet,
>   The heart of being is celestial rest;
> Stronger than woe is will: that which was good
>   Doth pass to better—best.

Acknowledging that the forces of evil are terrific and multiply themselves prodigiously, there can be no question that the predominant powers are infinitely good. And the supremacy of good in the universe diminishes the full force of evil, makes the higher attractions outlive the lower, and hastens the final disappearance of darkness. This insures the amelioration of all life by the benign process of rebirth; for

> The Heart of all is a boundless Love
>   Pulsing through every part
> In streams that thrill the hosts above
>   And make the atoms dart.

The strongest objection to reincarnation, our ignorance of past lives, is met by the fact permeating all nature and experience, that progress depends upon forgetfulness. Every great stage of advancement is accompanied by the mental loss of earlier epochs. One of Montaigne's best essays shows the blessedness of defective memory. All deep philosophy agrees that after an experience is absorbed into the soul, its purpose is accomplished, and the only chance of improvement consists in "forgetting those things which are behind and reaching forth unto those things which are before." It would be intellectually impossible for the memory to grasp anything new, if it clung to all it had known. One of the grandest discourses of that greatest English preacher of the last generation, Frederick W. Robertson, is upon the theme of "Christian Progress by Oblivion of the Past." The experience of the race affords no sufficient endorsement of the continuation of our mortal memories. It is impossible to escape the liberal scientific teaching that the mind is only an instrument of the soul, and when it decays with the body, the soul retains of its earthly possessions only what has sunk down into the character. The logician of the Scriptures expresses this in saying, "Whether there be knowledge it shall vanish away." But the everlastingness of character insures the permanence of our identity and of our dearest ties. And as the scale of being on earth shows a gradual development of memory from the lowest protozoon to man, so in man the unconscious memory shall become more and more conspicuous, until it reveals the course of our complete career.

The glorious unfoldment of our dormant powers in repeated lives presents a spectacle magnificent beyond appreciation, and approaches more grandly than any other conception to the sublimity of human development. Addison wrote: "There is not, in my opinion, a more pleasing consideration than that of the perpetual progress which the soul makes towards the perfection of its nature, without ever arriving at a period in it. To look upon the soul as going on from strength to strength, to consider that she is to shine forever with new accessions of glory and brighten to all eternity; that she will be still adding virtue to virtue and knowledge to knowledge, carries in it something wonderfully agreeable to that ambition which is natural to the mind of man. Nay, it must be a prospect pleasing to God himself, to see his creatures forever beautifying in his eyes, and drawing nearer to Him by greater degrees of resemblance." Reincarnation shows the programme by which this stupendous scheme is being worked out, step by step, in the gradual method of all God's doings, and glorifies the present cycle as a specimen of eternity which shall ever grow brighter until the full brilliancy of the Highest shall radiate from every life.

The practical application of this truth not only dispels the haunting enigmas of life, but incites us to the strongest habits of virtuous conduct in ourselves, and of generous helpfulness toward others. It inspires us to nurture all the means of developing noble traits, since the promise of all good, and the only highway out of the bogs of physical life into the mountain heights of spirituality, is character. It reminds us most forcibly that

> Every thought of purity,
>   Every deed of right,
> Conquers sin's obscurity,
>   Speeds the reign of light;
> Moves with might supernal
>   Toward rest and home,

Leads to life eternal,
Prays, "Thy kingdom come."

It is not strange, therefore, that one of the leading writers of Great Britain says of reincarnation: "The ethical leverage of the doctrine is immense. Its motive power is great. It reveals as magnificent a background to the present life, with its contradictions and disasters, as the prospect of immortality opens up an illimitable foreground, lengthening out the horizon of hope. It binds together the past and the present and the future in one ethical series of causes and effects, the inner thread of which is both personal to the individual and impersonal, connecting him with two eternities, one behind and the other before. With peculiar emphasis it proclaims the survival of moral individuality and personal identity along with the final adjustment of external conditions to the internal state of the agent."*

Alongside of the Scotch professor's words we place these sentences from an eastern teacher, that the wisdom of the antipodes may grasp hands in one common brotherhood for the instruction of the world:—

"There is in each incarnation but one birth, one life, one death. It is folly to duplicate these by persistent regrets for the past, by present cowardice, or fear of the future. There is no Time. It is Eternity's now that man mistakes for past, present, and future.

"The forging of earthly chains is the occupation of the indifferent; the awful duty of unloosing them through the sorrows of the heart is also their occupation.

"Liberate thyself from evil actions by good actions."†

Emerson, who unites in one personality the sublimest intuitions of the Orient with the broadest observations of the West, may well represent a noble harmony of these distant kinships when he says: "We must infer our destiny from the preparation. We are driven by instinct to hive innumerable experiences which are of no visible value, and we may revolve through many lives before we shall assimilate or exhaust

* Professor William Knight.
† An adept of India.

them. Now there is nothing in nature capricious, or whimsical, or accidental, or unsupported. Nature never moves by jumps, but always in steady and supported advances. ... If there is the desire to live, and in larger sphere, with more knowledge and power, it is because life and knowledge and power are good for us, and we are the natural depositaries of these gifts. The love of life is out of all proportion to the value set on a single day, and seems to indicate a conviction of immense resources and possibilities proper to us, on which we have never drawn. All the comfort I have found teaches me to confide that I shall not have less in times and places than I do not yet know."

We conclude, therefore, with the conviction that all the best teachers of mankind — religion, philosophy, science, and poetry — urge the soul to

> Be worthy of death ; and so learn to live
> That every incarnation of thy soul
> In varied realms, and worlds, and firmaments
> Shall be more pure and high.

Discovery Publisher is a multimedia publisher whose mission is to inspire and support personal transformation, spiritual growth and awakening. We strive with every title to preserve the essential wisdom of the author, spiritual teacher, thinker, healer, and visionary artist.

www.ingramcontent.com/pod-product-compliance
Lightning Source LLC
Chambersburg PA
CBHW031106260626
47172CB00001B/245